8

847 cm 2:

no trim

THE

SPEECHES

OF THE

RIGHT HONOURABLE

GEORGE CANNING.

WITH A

MEMOIR OF HIS LIFE.

BY R. THERRY, ESQ.

OF GRAY'S INN, BARRISTER AT LAW.

IN SIX VOLUMES.

VOL. III.

THIRD EDITION.

"He had ambition to prevail in great things. He had, likewise, honour, which hath three things in it: the vantage ground to do good,—the approach to kings and principal persons,—and the raising of a man's own fortune."

BACON.

LONDON:
JAMES RIDGWAY & SONS, 169, PICCADILLY.

MDCCCXXXVI.

LONDON:
PRINTED BY T. BRETTELL, RUPERT STREET, HAYMARKET.

CONTENTS

OF THE

THIRD VOLUME.

---

* The reader is requested to notice, that the speech on the Change in the Administration should have been inserted before the speech on the Catholic Claims. Mr. Canning spoke on two occasions on the subject of Ministerial changes at this period. One of his speeches is not inserted here, as the principal passage of it will be found introduced as a quotation in the summary that is given of Mr. Peel's speech on Mr. Canning's appointment to the Premiership, in the sixth volume of this work.—Ed.

SPEECHES,

&c. &c.

VOTE OF CREDIT BILL.

JUNE 15th, 1810.

THE CHANCELLOR OF THE EXCHEQUER moved the order of the day for the third reading of the Vote of Credit Bill. The amount of the vote of credit was £3,000,000. On the question being put—

MR. WHITBREAD took an extensive review of our internal and foreign relations, and dissented from so large a vote of credit, at the same time that he declined dividing the House upon the question. The principal points in his speech are brought so clearly into view in the following very eloquent speech of Mr. Canning, as to supersede the necessity of introducing here a summary of his arguments. The Chancellor of the Exchequer and Mr. Canning rose at the same time. The Chancellor of the Exchequer gave way.

MR. CANNING then spoke to the following effect :—I should hesitate, Sir, to avail myself of the courtesy of my right honourable friend, especially as there are some topics in the speech of the honourable gentleman (Mr. Whitbread), to which a person in my right honourable friend's situation, as one of His Majesty's Ministers, can alone be competent to afford a satisfactory answer, were it not that the honourable gentleman has done me the honour to address himself, in many parts of his speech, personally to me, and in a manner which naturally makes me anxious to reply to him. I trust, therefore, that I shall meet the indulgence of the House, while I state distinctly, but as shortly as I can, the reasons which induce me to give my most cordial assent to the measure which the honourable gentleman opposes.

As to the grounds which the honourable gentleman has laid for this opposition in the character which he ascribes to the present administration, and the distrust which he professes to feel in them, it is not my intention to follow the honourable gentleman through that part of his speech. I leave these topics to those who may hereafter take part in the debate. It is sufficient for me to say, that whatever might be my general opinion of any administration, yet, if they continued in office at the end of a session of Parliament, I know nothing that would justify me in leaving them, during the recess, unarmed with the means usually placed at the disposal of all administrations, to provide for unforeseen contingencies, and to take advantage of any fortunate, though unexpected change in the situation of Europe.

A Government does exist, to which His Majesty has entrusted the administration of public affairs, and from which the confidence of Parliament has not been withdrawn. If the determination of the honourable gentleman be to withhold from this Government such means as have never been hitherto refused to any other, far from approving of the candour which he has shown in putting off his opposition to the last stage of the bill now under discussion, I should have thought that he had acted more consistently with that determination on his part, if he had made some distinct motion for placing the administration of affairs in other hands. To tie up the hands of those who are still left in the conduct of the Government, appears to me to be neither a wise mode of marking distrust, nor a happy expedient for remedying imbecility.

If, then; the present Government be entitled to the usual confidence given to every administration, by a vote of credit at the close of a session, there remains only the question as to the amount of that vote—a question of degree, which would equally apply to any government, even to one in which the honourable gentleman could place the most unlimited confidence. That a vote to some amount ought to be granted, is a proposition which, I apprehend, will not be denied, if the functions of the Government are to be discharged at all, and the affairs of the nation to be at all administered. But the amount of such a vote is undoubtedly matter fit for discussion, and is to be decided by the view which the House may take of actual and probable circumstances in the situation of the country.

The view which the honourable gentleman would induce the House to take of those circumstances is such as would justify, in his mind, the withholding of any vote of credit, or, at least, of the vote proposed; though he has not stated exactly in what degree he would desire that vote to be diminished. He foresees no use, at least no advantageous use, that can be made of it. To whatever points he directs his view, all prospect of good seems closed upon him; he looks for nothing from continued exertion but renewed disappointment, and ultimate despair.

The honourable gentleman, I perceive, (and not without some degree of surprise) has not concluded his speech this night in the same manner as his former annual exhibitions at the close of the session, by a declaration of the necessity of peace, and an avowal of his conviction that the attainment of peace is practicable. If to terminate a contest, into which this country has been forced, and in which it is compelled to continue by the violence and injustice of the enemy, the honourable gentleman could have contended that a safe and honourable peace might be obtained, and had recommended the immediate opening of negociations for the purpose of obtaining it; however I might be disposed to disagree with the honourable gentleman in that opinion, I should yet be compelled to admit that he had laid some parliamentary ground for the course which he is taking. He might argue, that, if a secure and honourable peace, the only legitimate end of all war, could be procured, this House ought not to grant to the Government the means of meeting the contingencies of unnecessarily protracted warfare. But as the honourable gentleman appears to have abandoned the opinion which he entertained respecting peace—("I have not abandoned it," said Mr. Whitbread across the table, "I omitted to state it")—well then, the honourable member has not abandoned his opinion, but he has omitted to state it: if the omission was voluntary, that honourable gentleman's sentiments have clearly undergone a considerable change; if inadvertent, it at least shews that he does not feel quite so confidently upon the subject as heretofore; for no man forgets the main article of his creed while his faith continues unshaken. In either case, therefore, it is obvious that, according to the honourable gentleman's own present views we are to look to, and ought to provide for, a state of indefinite, not to say interminable, war.

The observations made by the honourable gentleman respecting the rapid and unexpected changes which have of late years taken place in Europe, appear to me to suggest a reply to much of his general reasoning; because the more frequent these sudden changes, the greater is the chance that some one may be favourable; and the more necessary is it for this House to furnish to the Government the means of taking advantage of such a change. Let the honourable gentleman retrace the awful and extraordinary events of the last year, and then say whether it appears even to him prudent to shut our eyes to the variations of the still shifting scene, and wantonly to put it out of our power to profit of any possible opening, not to say of any probable contingency, in our favour? The honourable gentleman admits that he felt sanguinely in the cause of Spain at the outset; but had he anticipated that glorious struggle? Did he foresee or foretell that sudden ebullition of the heroic spirit of Spain, that simultaneous and universal effort against the formidable French force, which, at the time, occupied every advantageous position in that country? The honourable gentleman augured unfavourably, and expected little, from the result of the war in which Austria embarked last year. He told us so (to do him justice) at the moment when that war broke out. But while he indulged these forebodings, had he any notion that, within the space of one month from the date of his prophecy, such a turn of affairs would have arrived as not only arrested the victorious career of the enemy, but rendered the issue of the campaign doubtful, and, by poising equally for one critical month the chances of the war, opened to the nations of Europe a cheering, though alas! a short lived prospect of deliverance? Was either of these chances foreseen? Was either of them not worth seizing as it arose? Argue then from the past to the future, and let the honourable gentleman say whether, in the unsettled and anomalous situation of the continent, it is not now equally impossible to foresee what events may burst upon us, in the course of a few months, with as little previous notice as those to which I have referred?

But although events are not exhausted, the honourable gentleman's hopes are so. Is Parliament then not to make provision for any possible case but such a one as may have in it demonstrable certainty of success? Or is there in the present state of the Spanish cause, to which the honourable gentleman's expressions of despondency particularly apply, such utter hopelessness, such irrecoverable exhaustion and decay, that nothing can henceforth be rationally attempted on its behalf; and that on that ground alone, therefore, to prevent a wasteful application of the resources of this country, to an absurd and unattainable object, Government ought to be left without any discretionary power of applying them?

If the honourable gentleman is resolved to despair of Spain, I cannot hinder him. But I think I can prove to him that he has no right to despair, on the same principles on which he has despaired so often during the last fourteen years, (and so often, I am grieved to add, has been justified by the event) respecting the other states of Europe.

What has been the nature of those former contests—and what the character of the states which have been successively subdued by France? What that of France as compared with them? I speak, Sir, of the earlier stages of the French Revolution, and refer to the language then held by the honourable gentleman and his friends. France was then a nascent Republic—the neighbouring nations were governed by old and feeble despotisms—military despotisms, it is true, but feeble from the inherent vices of their constitution. In France, a liberal and enlightened philosophy had brought forth a spirit of revolutionary freedom—had reared this new and formidable birth to a sudden maturity of strength and vigour—had

> "Torn from his tender limbs the bands away
> And bade the infant giant run and play."

He did so, and the effete and tottering monarchies

of the continent, military despotisms though they were, fell before the first touch of this regenerating conqueror.

But now the spirit, at least, if not the strength, has changed sides. France—as if, according to the doctrines of barbarian superstition, the soul of the slain had transmigrated into the slayer—France is herself become a military despotism. She is opposed in that character to the new-born independence of Spain; and, if victory had been faithful to the precepts of the honourable gentleman and his friends, victory ought no longer to declare in favour of arms which are no longer wielded in the cause of freedom, but in that of tyranny and oppression.

Victory, indeed, the Spaniards have not to boast. The military power of France has unfortunately outlived the causes which produced it; and in spite of theory, flourishes not only unsupported by freedom, but opposed to it. But yet the theory is not wholly shamed. And, if France has not at once lost her good fortune because she is enslaved, there is yet sufficient distinction between the degrees of resistance opposed to her by Spain and that of any other country, to justify the generous belief, that a truly national spirit is not to be subdued.

In other instances, when once the French armies had overcome the regular and disciplined armies of the continent, the conquered power fell without further effort, and submitted to the will of the conqueror. But is that the case in Spain? Has the enemy, with all his military superiority, and with all the advantage of having taken the Spaniards unprepared—of having occupied in peace the strong holds, which he afterwards turned to the purposes of war—has he yet succeeded in establishing his will as the law of Spain? Whatever faults the honourable gentleman may find with the Spaniards, I am sure he cannot accuse them of tame submission, or of a want of persevering exertions in the glorious contest, into which they have been driven and betrayed. We have seen their armies beaten down, their towns taken and razed; yet have not those calamities broken their spirits. From the ashes of their slaughtered countrymen, and from the smoking ruins of their cities and their hamlets, has burst forth a renovated flame, kindling anew that ardour and enthusiasm, which misfortune may for a time smother and overwhelm, but has not power to extinguish. A people so animated and so resolute may be exterminated, but they cannot be subdued; from each disaster that befalls them they derive new energies as they do fresh motives of resistance. Immediate and decisive success was not to be expected in such a contest; but surely to have so long protracted the struggle against such an enemy, and under all the disadvantages under which they were forced into it, affords indisputable proof of qualifications in the Spaniards, which demand our admiration and esteem; of a patriotism, a steadiness, a zeal, a perseverance, of which no people in Europe had hitherto afforded an example.

The more I contemplate the circumstances of Spain, the more pleasure I derive from the consideration, that the honourable gentleman himself, with all the doubts and apprehensions which he professes to entertain, has not thought it wise to recommend any step to be taken with a view to peace. He feels, no doubt, that whilst there remains a chance of rescuing that country from the unjust and tyrannical usurpation of France, it would be as little politic as generous to withdraw our assistance from the Peninsula. We cannot do so, unless we be prepared to leave the Peninsula to be occupied by France: and all its means, opportunities, and resources to be immediately employed against ourselves.

It is not now a question, whether Spain and Portugal shall be suffered to return to a state of neutrality, upon our consenting on one part, and of France on the other, to retire from the Peninsula as from a field of battle; it is not now to be decided whether Cadiz shall send forth her peaceful fleets of commerce, to pass, unmolested by either belligerent, over the surface of the ocean, and to waft the products of the remote dependencies of Spain, indiscriminately to both: the only question is, whether, by abandoning the footing which we possess in the Peninsula, we shall leave France at liberty to occupy the ground which we abandon, to occupy the ports and arsenals, to seize the naval resources of Spain and Portugal, and to fit out in harbours now in our possession, or under our protection, hostile fleets destined (though destined, I trust, in vain) for the object most dear to the heart, and always uppermost in the thoughts of Buonaparte, the invasion and destruction of Great Britain.

We are engaged in the struggle, therefore, inevitably; and have no alternative but to maintain it with vigour, or, declining it, to be prepared to pay, in our own perils, and in exertions for self-defence, the price of our own pusillanimity and baseness. Is this the situation of things, in which the honourable gentleman would recommend to us to pause on our policy—to cease our efforts on behalf of our allies—and to acquiesce in the injustice and usurpation of the enemy?

But again I ask, what are the grounds of the honourable gentleman's despondency? There has been (says the honourable gentleman) no order, no plan, no combination in the military efforts of Spain: and is this wonderful? The population of universal Spain, roused by a sense of insult and injury, and actuated by the powerful and heroic determination to preserve their existence as a people, rose against their invaders, in different and distant parts of the country, rose at once, but without previous concert or combination. Who could expect to find in that unparalleled national explosion, at a time too when the French troops were in possession of all the strong places of the kingdom, all the order, all the arrangement, all that efficient organization of means, and all that wise and judicious application of them, which are to be traced in the operations of governments of regular constitution, and established authority, representing and uniting the general will, and capable of directing the general resources of a country? But these advantages of regular governments, we know, have been frequently more than counterbalanced by their inherent disadvantages in the tremendous conflicts which, of late years, they have had to sustain. And Spain, with the disadvantages which belong to her, has some counterbalancing advantages. If the old governments have fallen an easy prey before the energies of regenerated France, let it be recollected, as I have already had occasion to observe, that the principle from which these energies were supposed to spring, no longer exists; that the spirit of liberty in France has been extinguished; that its republican throes and convulsions have quietly subsided into a military despotism: while, on the other hand, the Spanish nation, rising in vindication of its invaded rights, and for the preservation of its integrity and independence, is animated by every sentiment, and impelled by every motive, which can insure a determined resistance against tyranny, and a steady devotion to the country's cause. And whilst the Spaniards, true to these motives and these sentiments, continue to maintain the struggle, can we doubt that it is the first duty, as well as the clearest interest of this country, to afford them all possible assistance?

I do not mean to deny that, if the object of this war were one of Spanish interest merely, and if it were a question as to the claims of Spain upon this country for support, there may have been—there undoubtedly has been—cause of dissatisfaction, in the conduct of the Spanish Government. The papers upon the table, the correspondence of Lord Wellington particularly, shew, that, in respect to the reception of the British army, there is great reason for complaint, and that, as between Spain and England, Spain has been much in the wrong. But the question now at issue is really of a higher order: it relates indeed, in the first instance, to the immediate existence of Spain; but it ultimately and intimately involves the most essential interests of this country—and the hopes, if hope remain, of subjugated, but yet restless Europe.

Considerations of such magnitude must not give way to the resentments—even to the just resentments—of the moment; to differences between parties whose object and whose interests are so closely united. True, we have a good cause against Spain, and could make out a very sufficient ground of quarrel, if this were the time, if we had at this moment the leisure, and if we had the inclination to bring her to account. But what is our case against Spain compared with the case of Spain, and with our own case, against France? And to whose advantage would it be, but to that of France, if we were now to separate ourselves from the Spanish cause, or to waste in complaint against our ally the season of action against the enemy? Our interests demand that we should defend the Peninsula to the last extremity; even if we were released by the conduct of Spain from all other obligation; even if honour did not bind us not to abandon her, whilst there remains a possibility of defence. Our citadel lies here, it is true, in this impregnable island: but Spain and Portugal are its outworks; and, though I can have no doubt of a glorious triumph, if we should ever have to maintain the contest in this country, I cannot consent to be a party to that chivalrous feeling, that would retreat from the outworks and admit the enemy to the gates, in order that we might have the satisfaction of defeating him under the walls of our fortress. Our obvious policy, if policy alone were in question, is to keep the war alive in every quarter where France has an enemy in arms, to prevent her from converting those enemies into conscripts for her armies, to fight our battle with combined, rather than against confederated, nations.

This, I say, would be the dictate of policy, even if we were to banish from the maxims of a great, a powerful, and a generous nation, those enlarged views of interest, and that just sense of duty, which prescribe to us to resist tyranny, even when exercised against others, and to aid the oppressed, even though our aid may be unsolicited or unacknowledged.

Let us then continue to aid Spain in spite of her weakness, in spite even of her ingratitude, if she has proved ungrateful; cautious where we have found reason to distrust her, but not eagerly seizing on every pretext, which the conduct of her government might offer for abandoning her to her fate.

But the faults of the Spanish Government, it is contended, are attributable to us—to the administration in this country, by whom no measures had been taken to procure for Spain a better form of government. Hence the mismanagement of the internal affairs of Spain; and hence also the spirit of jealousy manifested by the Spaniards towards this country!

For my own part I am desirous to claim my full share of responsibility for all the measures taken by the administration of which I was a member, with respect to Spain, and in relation to its government; a share, which must be the more ample from my having had the honour to fill that department, within the province of which it fell to advise and execute whatever measures were taken on that subject. One point the honourable gentleman will find sufficiently established by the papers laid before Parliament, that no pains were spared, even from the earliest period of our intercourse with Spain, to obtain the establishment of a supreme and central government, which should collect into one point the scattered authorities of the several provincial juntas, and controul, and guide, and give consistency and energy to, the whole. This was made the condition of the continuance of our aid: it was the express and *sine quâ non* condition of the employment of a British army in Spain.

It is true, we did not go so far as to prescribe the precise form of the government so to be constituted. And I am ready to explain, and to defend the grounds of our forbearance in this particular. But let the honourable gentleman look at Mr. Stuart's correspondence—the first British agent sent to Spain. He will find Mr. Stuart constantly insisting upon the establishment of one uniform government, and stating *that* as the condition of sending a British military force into Spain. At length this point was accomplished.

As to the characters of the persons composing the supreme government, for which the honourable gentleman would make me responsible, because I was, as he affirms, the warm panegyrist of the Spanish Junta, I beg leave, in the first place, to ask the honourable gentleman by what possible knowledge, by what intuition, rather, I could be prepared, not only to stipulate for the establishment of a supreme central government, but to dictate the selection of the members who were to compose it? What could I know of them but from the communications of the British agent? And when, in despatches received previously to the formation of the Junta, the names of distinguished persons in Spain, of Florida Blanca, Saavedra, and Jovellanos, were stated to be in the mouths of every body, as the fittest persons to be intrusted with the conduct of the government; and when I found by the first despatch transmitted after the establishment of the government, that these persons were actually appointed, not only members of the Junta, but to the leading situations of the executive government, could I possibly have supposed, that they were not, as they had been previously represented to me, the most proper persons in Spain, to whom that high and important trust could have been committed? or that the government, which had the sanction of their approbation, and the advantage of their assistance, was not the best, upon the whole, that could be put together under the very difficult circumstances of the country? The eulogium, therefore, which I am accused by the honourable gentleman of having pronounced upon the members of the Supreme Junta, was not, because it could not be, the result of personal knowledge on my part; nor was it so imposed by me upon the House: neither could it by any fair construction render me in any degree responsible for the consistency of their conduct with the tenor of my representations. What I said here, was, in fact, but the echo of the voice of the Spanish nation, conveyed to me through the medium of official reports, and repeated by me to this House and to the world. I conceived it an act of justice to the Junta, and an act of duty to my country, whose interests were so intimately connected with the existence of an efficient government in Spain, to afford every encouragement in my power, to a government professing that character, and represented to me as deserving it.

If the Junta disappointed the hopes which were entertained of it—if it either wanted the energy or the authority, which it was intended to possess—undoubtedly there is much cause for regret; but there is none for blame as to the administration here, unless it can be shown, that some other form of government in Spain would have been obviously preferable, and also could have been, with equal facility, and at an equally early period, obtained. For, let it not be forgotten how precious were the moments of this glorious and unexpected opportunity!—let it not be forgotten that, while on the one hand it was necessary for the ultimate and permanent success of the Spanish cause, that the efforts of the nation should be combined and directed by one presiding authority, it was no less necessary for its immediate safety, that the enemy, once taken by surprise, should not be allowed to recover from the first shock of the insurrection! Had we then time to pick and choose, even if we had had the means of judging, and had conceived a sound and rational preference for one form of provisional government over another? Were the feelings of the country here disposed to give us time? What would my right honourable friend (Mr. Sheridan), who has so repeatedly renewed his notice of a motion respecting the campaign in Spain, and of whose presence I should have been extremely glad on the present occasion, what would he say to the charge of the honourable gentleman, that we had too hastily acquiesced in the form of government established by the Spaniards? he, who two years ago, when no deputation had been received in this country, except from the Asturias, one of the smallest of the Spanish provinces, and consisting of a rocky and mountainous tract, though containing a brave, a loyal, and independent population, reproached the Administration with being too tardy in adopting the Spanish cause,—too timid in hesitating to give it at once every possible assistance and support? I should wish to know whether my right honourable friend, who then reproached us for having paused, before we determined to act, on the solicitation of a single province, would now condemn us for having supported the Spanish people with all the means of this country, after deputations had been received from the north, and from the south, and when we had a certainty of the whole nation having determined to rise as one man against their unprincipled oppressors? Would he, who thought us wanting to the interests of this country and of the world, because we did not send fleets and armies to the port of Gijon, when that port alone (for aught we knew), was open to us throughout the whole coasts of the Peninsula; who stimulated us to action, when a single principality had taken up arms against the French, and therewith, for aught that we could know, against the rest of Spain also; when, what turned out undoubtedly to be a faithful specimen of a general national effort, might have been, for aught that we could know, the insulated and unsupported burst of mere provincial patriotism? Would he, I say, or any rational man, have desired that when not Asturias, but all Spain had declared itself; when what might have been a partial, proved to be the universal sentiment of the nation; when the will of the whole country was expressed beyond the possibility of misapprehension, would any man have thought that it was then our duty to boggle about the precise shape and denomination of the presiding government, by which the collective will was to be provisionally represented and embodied?

In a crisis of such extraordinary novelty, and such transcendent importance; when interests so mighty were committed to the issue of the struggle; and where that issue, after all that could be done, was necessarily so hazardous and uncertain; it was impossible to take any step, or to offer any counsel, which must not at the time, be felt and acknowledged to be of doubtful and questionable policy; and to which it was not foreseen, that in the event of a disastrous result, that disaster would be, however unjustly, ascribed! But in this difficulty of choice, were we to do nothing, were we to counsel nothing, till the use of counsel and the period of action were past? Or were we at some risk, but with a determined purpose, conscious of a just end, though necessarily less confident in our means, to take the course which appeared upon the whole liable to the fewest objections?

Gentlemen talk very glibly now of what might have been, and what ought to have been, our mode of proceeding. Some would have done nothing, the safest opinion of all: but they must have found another Ministry to act upon their opinion, and another people, than such a one as the people of England were in June 1808, to countenance and support them in doing so.

Some think, that we ought to have insisted upon the immediate assembling of the Cortes; some, that we ought not to have acknowledged Ferdinand at all; others again, that we ought not to have stipulated for (in truth, we did not stipulate, they mean that we ought directly to have discountenanced) the monarchical constitution in Spain. A word upon each of these suggestions.

And first, as to our acknowledgment of Ferdinand VII., or, as it is sometimes stated, our imposition of him upon the Spanish people. On the one hand, it is said, that by acknowledging Ferdinand VII. as King of Spain, in exclusion of his father, we thereby gave a sanction to the principle and the practice of the revolutionary deposition of sovereigns; whilst on the other hand, we are accused of making the preservation of monarchy in Spain the peremptory condition of our assistance. Nothing, however, could be more unfounded than either and both of these charges. Perhaps, in any other kingdom of Europe, we should have been slow to recognize the accession of the son before the demise of the father. But in Spain, the elevation of the son by the voluntary resignation of the father is familiar to the people by the recorded transactions of some of the brightest periods of their history. There was therefore no ground for jealousy at such an event, unless there had been good cause for suspicion respecting the means by which it had been accomplished. The resignation of Charles V., their greatest monarch, and of Philip V., the founder of the Bourbon Dynasty in Spain, who subsequently resumed the reins of government on the death of his son, to whom he had transferred them, must be in the recollection of every gentleman who hears me: and with these precedents before us, and whilst there existed no ground whatever for suspicion, the Government of this country was bound to consider the resignation of Charles as voluntary, and the accession of Ferdinand as legitimate, according to the usage of the Spanish monarchy. As to the charge of imposing Ferdinand, and in his person monarchy, on Spain; why, Sir, the name of Ferdinand resounded from every corner of the kingdom; it became the watch-word of Spanish patriotism; the pledge of popular enthusiasm; the bond and cement of national union; the charm, before which all separate interests, all discordant passions and prejudices faded away. It was no suggestion, no fancy of ours; we found this symbol of Spanish loyalty interwoven with every part of the Spanish cause. It was the burden of every oral, and the stamp and sanction of every written communication, which, in my official character, it was my duty and my happiness to receive from the Spanish agents or ministers. It was not left to our option, whether Spain should be a monarchy under Ferdinand VII. If we had denied Ferdinand they would have disclaimed us; if we had stipulated against monarchy we should have been repudiated by Spain.

I say not this as matter of defence; I state the plain truth. Upon this point we have no responsibility, because we had nothing to decide. Upon every principle by which our conduct could be guided, whether drawn from legal precedent, or from the unequivocal demonstrations of national feeling, we could look upon Ferdinand VII. in no other light, than as being at once the lawful Monarch of Spain, by the established constitution of the kingdom, and the Sovereign of the nation's affections, the King of the people's choice.

But then we should have insisted on the assembling of the Cortes, the ancient, legal, recognised estates of the realm—whereas we acknowledged the weak and incapable authority of the Supreme Junta. First, as I have before argued, what right had we to criticise the form of that institution, or the pretensions of the members? Was it not enough that we were assured of its having the sanction and the confidence of the Spanish nation; and were we not justified thereby in recognizing the Junta as representative of the authority of the legitimate sovereign during the period of his most unfortunate absence and captivity? Let us only look back to a memorable instance in our own history, I mean the glorious Revolution of 1688, and judge what would have been the consequence, if the proceedings of that period had been criticised with too scrupulous nicety, or required to have been conducted with all the solemnity and precision of the most minute forms and established precedents? What might have been the consequences of such a scrupulous adherence to established ceremonials, such an appeal to ancient usage, at a period, when the novelty of the circumstances and the urgency of the case called for the adoption of extraordinary measures, if William the Third had refused to take upon himself the government before the meeting of the convention, because the address to him to do so proceeded from an irregular authority—from a few members of extinct Parliaments, gathered together in haste, with the lord mayor, aldermen, and common council of the city of London? if he had declined taking any share in administering the affairs of the kingdom, or affording any assistance to the nation, until a Parliament, summoned by regular writs, and assembled with all the forms of the constitution, should have ceremoniously invested him with the powers of the executive government. The case of Spain was still more urgent, because at the very moment, when, it is said, we should have waited for all the tardy forms and all the regular process of the old constitution of Spain for the election, and assembly of the Cortes, the French troops were in possession of all the fortresses of the country. At such a moment, it was rather to be considered as miraculous, that the Spaniards should have found in each of the several provinces a spot whereon to plant the standard of resistance, than to be expected, that they should be able to conduct the election of the Cortes with all the requisite solemnities, and with all the deliberation, which would have been necessary to find out what those solemnities were. For let it not be forgotten, that these same Cortes had been long disused; that, when last assembled, they had been assembled in mere form, and to register the edicts of the crown; that the Cortes of Arragon and Castile have never been brought to act cordially together, even if brought together at all, except by compulsory means; that many of the provinces, foremost in the great struggle against France, had not the privilege of sending representatives to the Cortes; that Asturias had never sent any, Gallicia seldom if ever—certainly not uniformly, nor of custom and right; and that to the two provinces therefore, which were the earliest in their application to us for assistance, if we had answered, "assemble the Cortes," they might have replied, "with the Cortes we have nothing to do;" that to bring into shape and into action this grand but obsolete machinery, would have required deep and laborious research into records and registers; that perhaps after all a representative might have been produced less satisfactory to the nation at large, than that which sprang from their own concurrent though irregular impulse; but that, at all events, much precious time must have been lost in the process, and that while we were discussing antiquated forms and adjusting contested elections, the enemy would have rallied from his first consternation, and effected the conquest of the country.

That the assembling of the Cortes would be a wise and salutary measure, when it could be effected peaceably and regularly, no doubt was entertained; and accordingly the Junta were advised, and had determined to make it one of their first acts. But I am not surprised, for one, that it was not earlier effected. I doubt whether a general election could be speedily accomplished here after a long disuse of Parliaments, and with an enemy occupying all the country north of Trent. And I cannot but make some allowance for the Spanish Government, when I recollect, that at almost every period since the establishment of the Junta, the French have been masters of Arragon and of the greatest part of the countries behind the Ebro.

In truth, the uniform experience of all similar revolutions shows that time only and practice can safely be relied on for modelling and perfecting the form of a government, struck out at a heat, as it were, by the immediate necessity of the occasion. The natural effect of the pressure of the immediate exigency is, in all such cases, it was in this, to unite in one body the two distinct branches of the legislative and executive authority. The equally natural tendency of experience, is to show the expediency of separating these authorities as soon as proper depositories can be found, or contrived for them. A Regent, or a Regency, for the one, and the Cortes for the other, formed obviously the natural division of the combined authorities of the Junta. And, even if we had had the right, and the leisure to prescribe the course which should be taken, I doubt whether it would have been wise to insist upon erecting these separate powers in the first instance; whether the Junta, or something like the Junta, was not a necessary stage, preparatory to the more regular distribution of the functions of the government. It is plain that the Regency could be claimed by no one, without something like the form of a choice, and something, or somebody to choose it. And it may be doubted, whether, if the Cortes had been called at once, they would have been contented with their own share of authority and power; whether the Cortes assembled in the first instance and exigency would not have been, in fact, a Junta under another name. At anyr ate, these were questions exclusively of domestic cognizance, upon which it was neither our duty, nor our right to dictate to Spain, if we had even been competent to do so. Much less should we have been justified in withholding our assistance, until this most delicate, difficult, and perplexing question should have been settled to our satisfaction, at a period so critical to the existence of Spain as a nation, that the delay of a moment might have been ruin to the cause.

Such then were the principles on which the Government, of which I was a member, acted; and such are the answers which I offer to the several clashing and contradictory charges of having been too precipitate, and of having been too dilatory; of having exacted too much, and of having exacted too little from Spain; of having dictated improperly the constitution of the government, and of having suffered the government to constitute itself.

The truth is, that we interfered to the extent, to which we had a right to interfere, and no further, when we insisted that there should be a central government formed, before a British army entered Spain.

Sir, in following the honourable gentleman next to his observations on the conduct of the war, I pass over the campaign of Sir John Moore, because it has been, heretofore, the subject of ample and detailed discussion; and because the honourable gentleman himself has very properly avoided dwelling upon it this night. I come now therefore to the operations of last summer. The honourable gentleman has condemned in strong terms the impolicy, the madness, as he calls it, of sending another army into Spain, after the dear-bought and fatal experience which we had acquired in the campaign which terminated in the battle of Corunna. But here the honourable gentleman assumes what was not the fact, in order to make his unfounded assumption the ground of a charge to which his Majesty's Government is not justly liable. The army of Lord Wellington was not sent out to penetrate into Spain; it was sent out to liberate Portugal from the yoke of the French; to provide for the security of that kingdom against any fresh attack; and, so far as could be done consistently with these objects, and so far only, upon any favourable occasion that might be presented, to co-operate with the Spanish generals and armies in the provinces of Spain, that border on the Portuguese frontier. Would the honourable gentleman then have left the British general inactive in Portugal, after having accomplished the first object of his expedition by the expulsion of the enemy from that country? or would he have restricted him from extending the line of his operations with a view to the relief of Spain, when that could be done without abandoning or endangering the other object for which the force under him was immediately destined? Would he blame Lord Wellington for availing himself of the latitude given him by his instructions, occasionally to lengthen the chain which bound him to the frontiers of Portugal? Would he have prevented him from pursuing that course which brought on the battle, and led to the brilliant victory of Talavera; a victory which covered the British arms with unfading laurels, and crowned the gallant general and his brave troops with immortal glory? But, says the honourable gentleman, that victory was barren. Barren undoubtedly it was, if you know no fruits of victory but districts overrun, fortresses taken, extent of territory acquired; yet not barren but fruitful: not unproductive, but as advantageous as brilliant, if you take into account, that it immediately opened the gates of Cadiz, and that it will hereafter open to you the ports of Spanish America. These are advantages which far outweigh the ordinary military results of a victory. But even were the effects of all our exertions confined to the prolonging the struggle against France in European Spain, so thoroughly am I convinced of the policy of supporting that struggle to the last extremity, that were the question at this moment a new and undecided question; were our armies and our fleets hitherto not engaged, nor our faith pledged in the cause, I should be of opinion, that it would be the duty no less than it would be the interest of this country, even now to begin our efforts in aid of the Peninsula, if now, for the first time, we were called upon to begin them.

It is not, however, only with respect to Spain itself, to the formation and controul of her Government, and to the conduct of the war in the Peninsula, that we are accused of great and sinful negligences and omissions, but with respect to the Spanish colonies we are said to have been criminally neglectful. We have been told to-night, in the course of a discussion upon another subject, that we should have made it a condition of our alliance with the Government of Spain, that the Spaniards should give up the slave trade in their colonies. The honourable gentleman (Mr. Brougham), who made that observation, must be aware, that it would have been much easier to declare, than to effectuate, our wishes in such a case. I am as anxious as that honourable gentleman for the total extermination of that abominable trade, and with him I am ready to allow that we ought to make every sacrifice to principle, whenever such sacrifice may be likely to advance the principle: but I very much question, whether, by such a proposition, prematurely brought forward, we might not have thrown the Spanish colonies into the arms of France, without at all advancing the object of humanity. England and the abolition, on one side, might possibly have had but an unfavourable competition against Buonaparte and unlimited slave trade on the other, in bidding for the affections of the colonies.

Sir, I have noticed this subject incidentally,

only to show, that, in the colonial no less than in the European part of this great political question, the course which the British Government have had to steer, has not been altogether plain sailing —has not been so little embarrassed with difficulties of different kinds, as to entitle gentlemen to turn round upon the King's Ministers and make it matter of charge against them, that they have not provided for every interest, and secured the operation of every principle, which they and we may concur in our desire to promote and to maintain. It is true, it is perfectly true, as gentlemen are fond of observing, that Spain is a country of prejudice and of bigotry: bigotry and prejudice, however, not without their use in such a contest as that in which they are engaged—prejudice, which exalts the spirit of patriotism by the rooted preference for their own manners and institutions —and bigotry, which, if it is akin to intolerance on one side, is allied to perseverance on the other; which, however to be deprecated as an active principle, is of powerful operation in inspiring resistance, and sustaining courage under oppression. I am not sure that, balancing the good and the evil of such qualities, I would strip the Spanish nation of them, in their present circumstances, if I could. But it is enough for my argument that I could not, if I would. And, with this conviction, nothing can be more unreasonable than to make it matter of reproach to the British Government, that they have not, at the same time that they were aiding the Spaniards in a struggle for the preservation of the mother country, been able, or attempted, to engage them to revise the whole system of their colonial polity, to adopt reformations and improvements, which, if they had been disposed to adopt them, they might have found it impossible to reconcile to the feelings of the colonies, and equally impossible to enforce against those feelings, at a time when the circumstances of the war must necessarily have loosened the ties of colonial allegiance.

Advice, however, has not been withheld, nor has the Spanish Government shewn itself unwilling to listen to the advice which has been offered to them, for extending privileges to the colonies, and uniting them closer with the mother country by community of rights and of interests. To promote this union has been the object of our policy. Some, I know, are of opinion, that we ought rather to have played a separate game with the colonies. The honourable gentleman who spoke last, has alluded to the benefits, which might be derived to this country from a connection with Spanish America altogether distinct from Spain. I have only to observe, that in my opinion, if any advantages are to result to us from a connection with the Spanish trans-atlantic colonies, we should rather wait for them as a reversion, as the reward of the success, or the consolation under the reverses of the European struggle, than consider them as a temptation to the premature abandonment of the mother country. With these feelings deeply impressed upon my mind I shall never consent that the hand of Great Britain should be laid, in untimely interference, for the sake of immediate gain upon Spanish America. I shall never be one of those, who, professing the warmest wishes for the success of Spain, would aim the most deadly blow at her existence, by robbing her of those foreign dependencies, now more than ever necessary to enable her to maintain her independence, by prosecuting to a successful issue the mortal contest in which she is engaged. Still less will I consent to starve the Spanish cause, for the sake of hastening that consummation of evil, which, if it is not to be averted, may yet be delayed; and of profiting by the rich spoil, which we may gather in Spanish America, after European Spain has fallen. I cannot bring myself to contemplate the fate of Spain, as our inimitable dramatic poet describes one of his most exquisitely drawn characters, Shylock, contemplating the fate of his daughter, who had fled from him with a heap of gold and jewels—while he is lamenting her flight, and his friends undertake to console him with the hope, that after all she may be still alive, he presently undeceives them as to the real cause of his wailing. It is not his daughter, but his treasure, that is uppermost in his thoughts. "As for her," says he, "would she lay dead at my feet, with the jewels in her ear; would she were coffined at my feet, so that my ducats were in her coffin!" So it is that the honourable gentleman and others, appear to think of Spain: they think of the money that she has cost us; they think of the little return in profit that she has made to us; they look to the advantages, which we may hope to inherit after her struggle is well over; and they are disposed rather to blame the obstinacy of that struggle, and to deplore the length of that agony, which keeps us out of our expected inheritance.

And yet, Sir, surely the coldest heart, the most calculating head, cannot but be warmed and exalted by such a spectacle as Spain affords to the world! There can surely be but one feeling in this House with regard to the character of the Spanish cause: no man can entertain a doubt that a contest of such a description ought to succeed: and, if in spite of all the difficulties, which the Spaniards have had to encounter (and formidable those difficulties have been), they have contended with unbroken spirit, though with various fortunes, against the gigantic power of France, in a manner, and for a period, to shame by the comparison the efforts of almost all the nations of the continent, I must again ask, why are we to despair? I cannot bring myself yet to despair of the ultimate success of Spain, because I would fain believe in the success of any people, that shall act upon the same principle, and persevere with the same courage, in so righteous a cause; because I would not despair of ourselves under similar circumstances.

If the enemy should pass those outworks, which the line of policy recommended by the honourable gentleman opposite (Mr. Whitbread), would level: if ever we shall have to contend against that enemy on British ground, I trust that our resistance will be signal, and his defeat certain: but I doubt how far we can expect to exceed the example which is set to us by the Spaniards. In prowess in the field, no doubt we shall, and must exceed them, because that depends upon a variety of circumstances and advantages, which the Spanish nation did not possess; not on valour only, but on skill—on discipline in the soldier—on science and experience in the officer—and above all, upon an efficient Government to organize the establishments, to provide for the accommodation, and to direct the movements of the various masses of individuals that compose an army. In these particulars, unquestionably we shall have greatly the advantage of the Spaniards; but in other qualities, not less essentially necessary for maintaining a defensive struggle—in firmness under defeat—in contentment under privations—in patience and long suffering, we may equal, but I doubt, if we can go beyond them.

Let any gentleman who hears me, ask his own mind, and ask impartially, whether he can answer for the town or city near which he lives, that if attacked in the same way, it would rival in its defence the heroic perseverance of Saragossa or Gerona? If any man, who confides (as I trust every man does) in the ability of this country to defend itself against any force of the enemy, yet hesitates how far he can answer this question in the affirmative, that man has no right to despair of the eventual triumph of Spain.

The contest is not at an end. The French, it cannot be denied, have gained very considerable advantages, and the Spaniards have on the other hand suffered most severely. But the fortress of Cadiz, containing the principal arsenal and the principal naval means of Spain, and garrisoned in part by British troops, detains before it a large portion of the French army; no impression of a serious nature has been made upon the defences of that important place; every day brings fresh accounts of the unabated enthusiasm displayed by the population of the various provinces; the French troops are harassed in their movements, and straitened in their quarters, by the desultory activity of the Spanish peasants; their supplies cut off, and their communications intercepted;—place all these things before your eyes, and then say, if it be at such a time, and under such circumstances, that we are to withdraw ourselves from the support of Spain, and to leave the Peninsula to the mercy of its ruthless oppressors?

I have said that there is a British garrison in Cadiz. I admit to the honourable gentlemen that some jealousy has been manifested by the Spanish Government upon this subject. I must, however, in this respect, do justice to the Spanish Government. It is true, that I thought it my duty to press earnestly for the admittance of a British force into Cadiz, after the failure of the first campaign, and to make that admittance the *sine quâ non* condition of ever again sending British troops into Spain. It is equally true, that the Spanish Government would not at that time consent to receive them. But it is no less true, that in such refusal, and in the explanation given of the cause of it, I did not find any just ground for supposing that it had proceeded from distrust in the British Government. A Government, depending for its existence, and certainly for its authority, wholly upon public opinion, and aware of the jealousy, (for some jealousy of us did most certainly prevail amongst the people of Spain,) with which the nation might view the introduction, at that critical period, of foreign troops into one of their most important naval stations, might feel itself obliged to decline opening the gates of Cadiz to a British corps, until an adequate and obvious necessity for that measure had arisen. But although the admittance of our troops was in the first instance refused on these grounds, I never had a doubt, but that they would be received whenever the necessity became obvious. The period of necessity has since arrived, and the event has most fully justified my expectation. Cadiz is now occupied by British conjointly with Spanish troops: the pledge of that alliance by which Spain may yet be rescued and saved. Whilst Cadiz is safe, Spain is not lost; and while all is not yet lost, all is ultimately retrievable.

The French army has achieved and may continue to achieve the conquest of province after province; but it has not been, and will not be able to maintain such conquests in a country, where the influence of the conqueror does not extend beyond the limits of his military posts! where his authority is confined within the fortresses which he garrisons, or the cantonments which he occupies; where all that is behind him, and before him, and around him, is sullen discontent, and meditated vengeance—unconquerable resistance, and inextinguishable hate.

And if the Spaniards have their sufferings to endure, at what price do the French carry on this war? At a price which no former war with the other powers of Europe has ever cost them. The honourable gentleman indeed, has lamented, that we should be parties, as he expressed himself, to the system of warfare pursued by the Spaniards, which he describes as transgressing the limits of legitimate hostility. I would intreat the House to contrast that sentiment with what fell from the same honourable gentleman in a former debate, when another honourable member detailed to the House the abominable atrocities committed by the French on their approach to the Isle of Leon. On that occasion the honourable gentleman affected to discredit the statement of crimes so shocking in the recital, and warmly deprecated the introduction of such horrible details into the discussions in this House, lest their circulation should have the effect of substituting wicked enormities of that description for the more humane spirit of generous warfare! Generous warfare! Good God! the generous warfare begun by Buonaparte against unoffending Spain! the generosity of him, —the outrageous violator of every sacred obligation, the bloody and unfeeling destroyer of the rights of sovereigns, and the independence of nations! Far am I, as far as any man, from justifying the commission, under any circumstances, of excesses, which deform the character, and brutalize the feelings of man. But the crime and the shame are in the original perpetrator. There are insults and injuries, which to have endured at the hand of an oppressor, degrades a man in his own esteem, and forces him to recover his level by a signal and terrible revenge. Such are the inflictions, which the French armies have poured out upon the Spaniards. If ever acts of ferocious retaliation might admit of extenuation, it is in such a cause, and upon such provocation as they have received, from an enemy unrestrained in his career of ambition and blood, by any law human or divine.

Such is, in my opinion, the justification of the Spaniards. Thus they defend and avenge their invaded country—their pillaged and desolated homes—their murdered parents—their violated wives and daughters—and who shall say, that such vengeance is not justified in the eyes of God and man? Who shall pretend that the assailant of unoffending and defenceless innocence is privileged from resistance or retaliation, that the invader has a right to make his inroad when he thinks fit, to commit what excesses he pleases; —but that he is only to be met in the listed field and by regular battalions—that the cottage or the altar are to be defended or avenged only by an enrolled soldiery; that the peaceful population of a country must be passive under every species of outrage and of wrong?

That our army has had any share in committing or countenancing such excesses is not pretended, and would not admit of excuse. Our business with the enemy is in the field. But that I should, therefore, whine over his sufferings and his losses —that I should deny or disguise the satisfaction which I derive from the consideration that every French soldier, who falls a sacrifice to Spanish vengeance, is one oppressor the less, for the rest of the nations of the world—would be a hypocrisy, which I disdain. Long may the struggle be! And be its course as deathful to the French armies as heretofore! One French army has already been worn down and destroyed in Spain: and I know no precept of humanity that forbids me to exult in the prospect of a similar fate awaiting those who are now the instruments of tyranny and violence.

War is unavoidably attended with calamities, as well as with glories. Its glories are sullied and darkened by its calamities: its calamities redeemed—or in part redeemed—by its glories. But if we accustom ourselves to look only at one side of the picture in the case of an enemy, and at the other in our own;—at all that is gloomy on one part, and all that is brilliant on the other—if we count for the enemy all that he gains, and all that we lose—but for ourselves only our positive gains, without admitting into the account the losses of the enemy: against such a mode of calculating results, no spirit can long stand unimpaired:—we go to the field already half subdued: we may entitle ourselves to commendation for the fineness of our sympathies; but we are utterly unfitted for continuing the contest.

I fear that I may have detained the House

to an unpardonable length upon the subject of Spain; though I feel it even now difficult to tear myself from it. I hope, however, that my excuse for having dwelt upon it so long may be found in the share which I personally had in the counsels and measures of this Government at the commencement of the Spanish struggle, and in the desire, which I naturally feel, that these counsels and measures should be dictinctly and fairly understood, but, above all, in my earnest zeal for the success of our allies, and for the continuance of our effective support of a cause involving as much our interests as our glory.

I shall now proceed to follow the honourable gentleman briefly into one or two of the other topics, to which he has alluded. As to the statements made by the honourable gentleman with respect to Sicily; to the disaffection of its inhabitants; to the probable change in the policy of the Sicilian Government, and the consequent critical situation of the British army in that island, I shall only assert, as an individual (having no official knowledge to support my assertion), that I believe his opinions and his apprehensions to be unfounded. I do not believe that there is any correspondence open between Buonaparte and the Queen of Naples. I have not seen the letter to which the honourable gentleman refers, but from the description of it, I should doubt if it be genuine.

As to the effect of the Austrian marriage upon

the politics of the court of Palermo, I cannot oblige the honourable gentleman to forego his conjecture, though I do not agree with him in it. I will only say by the way, that I am glad to miss, in the honourable gentleman's speech of to-night, the epithet of "*felix*," which he applied on a former night to this inauspicious alliance. The painter of old, when he drew the picture of the sacrifice of Iphigenia, despairing to express the workings of anguish and shame in the countenance of the father, by whom she was sacrificed, hid Agamemnon's face in his robe; so would I have the honourable gentleman deal on this occasion with the Emperor of Austria, and, at least, not insult his paternal feelings by ascribing to them the character of "felicity."

But whatever may be the soundness of the honourable gentleman's speculations in respect to the ultimate policy and conduct of the court of Sicily, I am not prepared to recommend the anticipation of treachery: I cannot agree, therefore, with the honourable gentleman to withhold the Vote of Credit, lest part of it should be expended in defeating the designs of the enemy upon Sicily, and keeping him out of possession of it too long. I am still less prepared (even if that were a cheap expedient) to seize on Sicily for ourselves.

From Sicily—declaring, that in Europe he sees nothing to require or justify so large a Vote of Credit—the honourable gentleman passes to America, and specifically objects to the Vote of Credit, on the ground, that a war with the United States is no longer probable. I hope and trust it is not. The recent proceedings of Congress have effected so much of what it was the anxious wish of the Government, of which I was a member, to attain, that I trust all our differences with America may be speedily adjusted. In truth I had never much doubt upon my mind, that America, if left to her own policy, and to the effect of those discussions, which would take place in her own legislatures, general and provincial, would at no distant period arrive at that point, at which, by the late act of Congress, she appears to have arrived. No man is more anxious than I am for an amicable accommodation with that power. But I trust, at the same time, that the change in the policy of the United States has not been effected by any improper concessions on our part; a circumstance, which I can fully disclaim, during the period that I remained in office. I should rather hope, that it has been the consequence of a determined adherence to that system, which has been so often declaimed against in this House, but which has proved as clearly beneficial to the commercial interests, as it has been consistent with the political dignity of this nation.

The honourable gentleman has introduced into this part of the discussion a reference to the instructions given to our Minister to the United

States (Mr. Erskine), upon which it was not my wish to have touched, if the honourable gentleman had not forced me to do so, because I cannot touch upon it without speaking unfavourably of the conduct of a gentleman towards whom I entertain no feeling of hostility whatever. But, as the honourable gentleman has thought proper again to advert to the subject, I am compelled, in my own defence, again to assert, as I have repeatedly before asserted, that Mr. Erskine, in the arrangement which he concluded with the American Government, did violate both the letter and the spirit of the instructions under which he acted. That he violated the letter of his instructions, is admitted by every body—by the honourable gentleman himself. Mr. Erskine was expressly directed to do certain things, which he did not do. But it was not, as the honourable gentleman insinuates, a mere formal error—a merely literal mistake. Mr. Erskine violated the spirit of his instructions, because, being authorised to concede certain points to the American Government, in consideration only of concessions to be by them reciprocally and simultaneously made, he did that absolutely, which he was instructed to do only conditionally, and thereby lowered the tone and just pretensions of his country. I am still ready, as I ever have been, to go into the full discussion of this question, whenever the honourable gentleman may think proper; but unless he should advert to it again I shall now take a final leave of it, and never again revive it.

Sir, I have now only to add, with respect to the Bill before the House, that it is not because I think that a war is to be apprehended with America, or that a question may arise as to the abandonment or seizure of the island of Sicily, that I assent to the Vote of Credit; but because I wish to enable His Majesty's Ministers to aid to the utmost extent, to maintain to the last extremity, the contest in Portugal and Spain, and also to take advantage of any opportunities which may arise for the annoyance of the enemy, and for which, without a Vote of Credit, they might be unprovided. For the application of the means, which this Vote entrusts to them, the Ministers are responsible. And I can assure the honourable gentleman, that, if he and his friends had now the conduct of the Government, for the same purposes, and under the like responsibility, I should not be disposed to withhold from them that degree of confidence (whatever it be) which this Vote may be construed to imply.

After some discussion, the Bill was read a third time and passed.

STATE OF THE NATION.—KING'S ILLNESS.

DECEMBER 20th, 1810.

THE CHANCELLOR OF THE EXCHEQUER having moved that the House resolve itself into a Committee on the State of the Nation, submitted the following Resolutions :—

"First.—That it is the opinion of this Committee, that it is the right and duty of the Lords Spiritual and Temporal and Commons of the United Kingdom of Great Britain and Ireland, now assembled, and lawfully, fully, and freely representing all the estates of the people of this realm, to provide the means of supplying the defect in the personal exercise of the Royal Authority, arising from His Majesty's said indisposition, in such manner as the exigency of the case may appear to them to require.

"Secondly.—That it is the opinion of this Committee, that for this purpose, and for maintaining entire the constitutional authority of the King, it is necessary that the said Lords Spiritual and Temporal of the United Kingdom of Great Britain and Ireland, should determine on the means whereby the royal assent may be given in Parliament respecting the exercise of the powers and authorities of the Crown, in the name and on the behalf of the King, during the continuance of His Majesty's present indisposition.

"Thirdly.—That it is the opinion of this Committee, that for this purpose, and for maintaining entire the constitutional authority of the King, it is necessary that the said Lords Spiritual and Temporal, and Commons of the United Kingdom of Great Britain and Ireland, should determine on the means whereby the royal assent may be given in Parliament to such bill as may be passed by the two Houses of Parliament, respecting the exercise of the powers and authorities of the Crown, in the name and on the behalf of the King, during the continuance of His Majesty's present indisposition."

The first and second Resolutions were agreed to with the dissent of Sir F. Burdett, but without a division.

MR. PONSONBY, on the third Resolution being moved, proposed the following Amendment:—

"That all the words after the word 'That' should be left out, for the purpose of inserting that An humble Address should be presented to His Royal Highness the Prince of Wales, requesting that he would be graciously pleased to assume and exercise the sovereign authority of these realms, during the continuance of His Majesty's indisposition, and no longer, under the title of Regent of the United Kingdom of Great Britain and Ireland."

MR. CANNING rose and said:—The Committee has now submitted to their consideration the two different courses of proceeding, severally recommended on each side of the House, as fittest to be pursued in the present unfortunate situation of the country. Upon one side—upon that of my right honourable friend, the Chancellor of the Exchequer, the whole of the plan proposed has been laid before us. Upon the other side, the general principle and introductory stage only, from which, however, we collect the nature of the intended subsequent proceedings. Thus situated, we are now to determine what course it will be best to follow under all the circumstances. The duty which devolves upon us, is to provide for a great and pressing emergency, by supplying the defect which has unfortunately taken place in the executive power.

In deciding the preference between the two modes recommended for our adoption, the committee is first called upon to exercise its judgment as to the degree of power and authority which the two Houses of Parliament can justly claim to belong to them, under the circumstances of so extraordinary an emergency. That, if not within the power of the two Houses of Parliament to supply the remedy which the exigency requires, it is not of the competence of any other existing authority, is a point agreed on all hands. Not the right, therefore, and the power, but the mode of exercising them is the question in dispute. On the one hand, it is proposed that the two Houses of Parliament should set out as nearly as possible in the ordinary manner of legislation, passing an act, which, so far as they are concerned, would be an Act of Parliament in form, and supplying by a legal fiction the place of the third branch of the constitution, for the especial purpose of giving effect and validity to the one necessary act, so passed by them, and no further. On the other hand, it is suggested that the deficiency should be remedied at once by an act, which if it be not an act of legislation, differs from it, not in being something less, but in being something more.

To object to either of these modes its own positive difficulties and embarrassments, is only in other words to say, that we are in a situation of great embarrassment and great difficulty ; and there is no course of proceeding under such circumstances but what is and must be liable to some objection. It is, however, no fault of ours that we are so situated. It is not, as in ordinary cases, to be imputed to any man, or to any measures, or to any series of measures, that they have brought us under these circumstances of perplexity. The infliction is from Providence alone. It is one which we all equally feel, and all equally deplore ; and which, while we endure it with humble and patient resignation, and indulge the consolatory hope of its speedy termination, the most anxious wish of every man's mind must be to alleviate its inconveniencies, while it endures, so far as may be possible, and in the manner least productive of inconveniencies of any other kind.

Our situation, however painful, and perplexing as it is, is not wholly unprecedented. Among the precedents which we have to guide us, and which have been referred to in former discussions, I agree with both the right honourable gentlemen who have preceded me, in not thinking it necessary for the formin g an opinion on this important question to look to those which are drawn from an earlier, and more imperfect state of the constitution, when we have it in our power to appeal to periods of a more recent, and perfect state of the constitution; not because I conceive that those former precedents might not, in the absence of better guides for the conduct of Parliament, be resorted to with advantage, but because all the lights which they afford have been so recently explored, and brought together by the industry and intelligence of those who preceded us in this House, and who had to act two and twenty years ago in that instance, which bore in its circumstances the strongest resemblance, as it is in point of time, the nearest to that in which we now unhappily stand.

Of precedents drawn from more modern times, there are three, which have been particularly dwelt upon, two of them bearing upon the case by analogy; the third, that of 1789 (to which I have just alluded) by direct similarity in all its parts. It is obvious, that a direct precedent is likely to afford a more complete and certain guidance, than one, from which one can reason only by inference, unless there be in that direct precedent, some inherent vice and imperfection, which renders it wholly unworthy of imitation. Let us see first what are the circumstances of the precedents which bear upon the question by analogy.

The first of these is that of the Restoration. In the circumstances of this I can find no similitude to the present case. By this an exiled monarch was to be restored to a situation of which he had been unjustly deprived—an acknowledged right long unjustly withholden was to be proclaimed and re-established. Can it now be said, that any right has been withheld which we are called upon to adjudicate?—that any violation has been offered which we are called upon to repair? Is there now a monarch waiting the decision of parliament to be restored to his rights and reinstated in his sovereignty? If such be the predicament in which we are placed, the Restoration is an authority to which we may properly be referred; but if it be clear, that we have now no right to adjudicate—no violation to repair—if we are not about to create a power, but to supply a temporary defect in the exercise of it, surely the authority of that precedent cannot be considered as binding, whose circumstances are shewn to be so totally dissimilar. When the right honourable gentleman says, that both houses of Parliament acted in that instance, as he has described, he in reality says nothing more than that they did what was necessary in the circumstances of that particular case, and nothing beyond it. In that particular we shall do well to follow the principle of the example set us by the Parliament, which called Charles the

Second home; but the details of the transaction appear to me to hold out no other light, which can be of any use to us on the present occasion.

We come next to the precedent of the Revolution. Splendid and cheering to the recollection of Englishmen, as the great event must always be, it will be right and wise in the committee, before they permit their feelings to hurry them away, to consider what the object was of the Parliamentary proceedings at that period? Was it to provide for the care and custody of the person of the monarch? Was it to ensure his return to the government of the country upon his restoration to health? Was it to erect a temporary authority during an accidental defect of the competence of the Sovereign? Or was it not to provide against the restoration of James, and set up safeguards and barriers against his return to defend the Crown, which they proposed to transfer against the hostile approach of its ancient possessor? Was not the throne declared vacant by James's abdication? And was not this declared vacancy the ground of all the subsequent proceedings? Is there any resemblance, therefore, or is there not rather a direct contrariety between the case of the Revolution, and that for which we are now called upon to provide? Has our Sovereign forfeited his throne? Is it our purpose to declare the throne vacant? Or is it not the first and fundamental principle of our proceeding that it is full? Is it any part of our object to retard and embarrass the resumption of the exercise of the royal authority by our Sovereign, or is it not our fervent prayer that it may be speedily resumed? I do not mean to say, that while considering what is to be done in a crisis of great difficulty, there may not be some advantage in comparing it with what was done in cases so far resembling it, as to have some of the constituent parts the same, but their arrangement and relations to each other different, and even opposite. Undoubtedly some suggestions may be borrowed—some assistance derived from such cases; but the assistance is that of analogy, and an analogy founded not upon direct inference and application, but upon a comparison of points of difference, and of circumstances directly the reverse of each other.

Some gentlemen, indeed, carry their notions of the deference which is due to a favourite precedent, to an extent so strict as, in my opinion, to be almost ludicrous. They insist upon our imitating not only the main scope and action of the great transaction of which we are speaking, but its accidental defects; and would have us create to ourselves deficiencies which those who brought about the Revolution had, but which, luckily, we have not to supply, in order that we may copy them in the manner of supplying them. Thus the right honourable gentleman (Mr. Ponsonby) has said, that there was no use made of the great seal in those acts of the Revolution by which King James was declared to have abdicated the throne, and the Prince of Orange was called upon to take the government into his hands. Certainly there was not—for how could such an attempt succeed, when there was no king in whose name the great seal could be used; when the executive power was not merely suspended in its functions, but rendered null by the absolute exclusion of the King, and the total want of the royal authority? Besides, there was this farther practical difficulty in affixing the great seal to any commission or act, as at that moment the great seal, from accidental circumstances, was at the bottom of the Thames.

The honourable baronet (Sir F. Burdett) carries this principle still farther. He is so attached to the Revolution in all its parts, whether principle or circumstance merely, that he finds a great defect in that particular of our situation which, to ordinary observers, would appear a considerable, though to be sure only an accidental, advantage. At the time of the Revolution there was no Parliament sitting. The honourable baronet, therefore, finds that the first Address to the Prince of Orange was voted, not by the Parliament, but by an assembly of persons, to which a deputation of aldermen and common-council of the city of

London had been discreetly called to give their assistance and advice. In the warmth of his zeal for the precedent of the Revolution, the honourable baronet seems to think that the accidental circumstance of an existing Parliament should be got rid of without delay; that we should immediately abdicate our authority, and dissolve ourselves at once, for the sake of assembling another body of representatives, who should have the benefit of advice and assistance from the Lord Mayor, aldermen, and common-council of the city of London.

It is surely a singular remedy for the unfortunate incapacity of one branch of the Constitution, to proceed unnecessarily to incapacitate the branches which happily remain entire. It is surely a strange application of precedents to contend, that because at the time of the Revolution there happened to be no Parliament (and that there was none was, by the way, one of the grievances which produced and justified the Revolution), because, in order to procure the semblance of a Parliament, it was then necessary to collect the scattered fragments of former Houses of Commons, of a former reign, and to eke out their numbers with a deputation from the aldermen and common-council of London; therefore a Parliament actually existing ought to be dissolved, or rather, ought to dissolve itself (for I know not what authority there is to dissolve us), merely that there may be one feature more of resemblance between the Revolution and the present time. It will not be pretended that the representation of the people was more complete in an assembly so heterogeneously composed, as that which first addressed the Prince of Orange, than in the present or any intervening House of Commons. It was, as I have said, the remnant of old Houses of Commons, not specially elected for the purpose of the time, not chosen in preference to a regular Parliament; but called together hastily for the want of any other mode of collecting any representative body whatever. To this body, so collected, were added a certain number of the aldermen and common-council; but, respectable as their authority, and useful as their advice may be, who would ever have dreamt that from such an extraordinary Convocation, arising from an extraordinary necessity, would be deduced the inference, in after times, that no House of Commons was competent to its functions without the addition of fifty aldermen and common-councilmen of London?

I prize the blessings derived from the Revolution, and respect the authority of those who conducted it, as highly as the honourable baronet or any other man: I think the proceedings of that time wise, and just, and necessary; but because they were necessary, therefore just and wise. But I do not think it an indispensable proof of my value and veneration for that illustrious precedent, that I should consider it as a rule for all occasions; that I should think the example of revolutionary times applicable to quiet times; and should consent, in the language of one, who said all things well on these subjects, Mr. Burke, "to make the extreme medicine of the Constitution its daily bread." The present case has difficulty enough, but it has nothing of revolution in it.

But after all, is not the very instance which is held out for our imitation, mistaken and exaggerated? What did this assembly, to whose likeness we are bid to conform ourselves, do? Confer the Crown on the Prince of Orange? Declare King James to have abdicated? In fact, bring about the Revolution? No, they addressed the Prince to call a Parliament, or Convocation, by letters instead of writs, since the authority for issuing writs no where existed. The Prince of Orange did, in pursuance of this Address, write letters to convoke a representation of the people, according to the usual rights and modes of election; and upon the assembly of that Convocation it was that the work of the Revolution went forward. How can it be necessary that we should go through their previous stages, being already at the point to which they were intended to lead? We have now a Parliament, full free, and so constituted as to be fully competent to provide for the exigency that exists.

Will the honourable baronet, to adopt his precedents in their full extent, contend, that we must begin by addressing the Prince of Wales to call a Parliament by letter instead of by writs? (otherwise he could not till he has the command of the great seal); and what would be gained by interposing such a stage in our proceedings but delay? Is it not rather our duty, Parliament being called together, to consider how we can best provide for the emergency that has unfortunately occurred, and remedy the mutilated state in which the Government is placed by the incompetency of the King to exercise his royal functions?

The right honourable gentleman (Mr. Ponsonby), however, does not partake in these views of the proceedings of the Revolution. He agrees that we are a Parliament competent to the discharge of the duty which has devolved upon us; and that the only question is, how we shall best discharge it? But he thinks the precedent of the Revolution binding so far as it prescribes Address as the mode of our proceeding. In the speech of the right honourable gentleman, distinguished as it was by eloquence and acuteness, no part was more acute or more eloquent than that in which he displayed the absurdity, as he conceived it to be, of doing on the King's behalf an act implying the King's personal will, for the purpose of declaring and remedying the extinction of that will by the King's personal incapacity. The fault of this argument, in my conception, is, not that it is not applicable to the case, but that it is in fact the whole of the case. To state that the King is personally incapable, and that acts nevertheless must be done in his name, and implying his will, is to state nothing more nor less than the fact; such is the difficulty in which we are, such is the absurdity (if that be the fit name for it) which that difficulty necessarily involves. To describe its contradictions is an easy task; to find a solution of it, that shall not be liable to the charge of contradiction, is perhaps impossible; to find that which has with as little contradiction as any other, less of practical mischief or danger, is, I apprehend, the task which we are this day assembled to perform. All the right honourable gentleman's eloquent amplification, therefore, though I heard it with pleasure and admiration, is merely a statement of the case, and goes not one step towards its remedy.

When he comes to state his remedy, Address instead of Bill, I do not see how he gets rid of the absurdity which belongs to the constituting a Regent by the great seal: for the great seal in the Regent's hands must still speak in the King's name, and assume to utter his will; but I think he admits other hazards to which the constituting a Regent by the great seal is not equally liable. I have said that the principle of the Revolution does not bear him out, because the Revolution was not conducted in the King's name, nor pretended, even in legal fiction, to be brought about or sanctioned by his will. But I should go farther and say, that this precedent made directly against his proposal—directly against appointing a Regent in the way in which King William was ultimately appointed King. And for this reason: the question of a Regent was in contemplation at that time. The Tories, those whose advice was not adopted, and whose course was not followed at the Revolution, contended that King James ought to be considered as still retaining his right to the Crown, still the lawful Sovereign, but as being incapable of exercising the functions of sovereignty, just as if he had been disabled by mental derangement, and that the Prince of Orange should be appointed Regent to carry on the Government in his (King James's) name. Now, if this suggestion had been made the rule of proceeding, if such had been, in fact, the settlement at the Revolution, the right honourable gentleman would indeed have a precedent directly in point. But, as it is, the precedent appears to me to operate directly against him, and the more so from the circumstance of the very case to which the right honourable gentleman wishes to apply it, having been actually under contemplation. As the notion of regency was suggested and was negatived,* the inference

* See Cobbett's Parliamentary History, vol. 5, pp. 59, 66.

certainly is not that the course then adopted would have been thought applicable to a Regency; the presumption is strongly the other way.

No argument has been offered to prove, that we should exercise less power by the mode of Address, than the one originally proposed to the House, or be likely to entail less embarrassment upon ourselves, or fewer difficulties upon the country. There certainly is one ground, and only one, upon which the mode of proceeding by Address might be considered as more applicable to the case; and that is, supposing a right in the Prince of Wales to the Regency. For such a right I have not heard any one contend, and as I am far, very far indeed, from wishing to revive the differences of former times, I will not argue it. I will say no more than that the circumstance of adopting an Address now might, in the hands of an ingenious reasoner, be made to appear like the implicit acknowledgment of the right formerly contested. I do not mean, I distinctly disclaim the meaning, that the right honourable gentleman moves his Address with this view; but I think this may be one effect of its success, and for that, among other reasons, I object to it.

In a balance of difficulties, then, how can we better make up our decision than by resorting to the most recent and the most applicable precedent? A precedent, I will not say sanctioned by the authority of great names, such as the name of the person who took the lead in this House on that occasion, weighs with me on every occasion on which it can be cited; because I am aware there are others who might naturally be swayed by the authorities which were opposed to Mr. Pitt in these discussions; I will not say sanctioned by great majorities in Parliament, because I recollect, that to a majority of two only we owe the blessings derived from the Revolution: I will say merely to a precedent which Parliament did adopt—which stands recorded on our journals, as the law of Parliament upon this question, until it shall be repealed and abrogated. Surely it must be felt that if no great benefit can be shewn to result from the abandonment of a recent precedent, it must, on the other hand, be productive of no inconsiderable evil. It must throw loose to all succeeding times a question, which we even now perceive the inconvenience of having to discuss, on conflicting authorities, and by remote and disputable references; it must give to both these opposite decisions, and ensure to those that may be to be discussed hereafter, the character of so many irregular impulses of passion, or inclination, controuled by no general principle, and conformable to no uniform system. Whereas, if we adopt now the precedent of 1789, so far as it was completed by Parliament, the concurrence of these two proceedings will settle the question for all time to come.

There is but one point more which I have to state on the subject of the proposed proceeding by Address; and it forms, I confess, in my mind an insuperable objection to it. I cannot conceive how we can, satisfactorily to our own sense of duty, provide for the care of the King's person, and for the resumption of his authority, in the happy event of his convalescence, otherwise than by bill, and by a bill which shall precede the actual investiture of the sovereign power in any other hands. That these objects should be amply provided for, is not more the duty of Parliament than it must be, and is undoubtedly, the wish of the illustrious person to whom we are all agreed in confiding the exercise of the regal authority: that they would be provided for as amply with his consent, and without Parliamentary enactment, by the mere impulse of his royal mind, there can be no question. But we are providing for all future times, and all possible cases; and we should not, I think, do our duty fully if even in an instance where, without any special provision, we might rest assured that the objects would be accomplished, we yet were not to take, upon a strict and abstract view of the case, the best security that the case admits—that is, the security of Parliamentary enactment. Other limitations or restrictions which might be thought necessary to accompany the delegation of the regal authority, might perhaps be provided by

Address. But I must take the opportunity of expressing my opinion, that, as that which I have just stated is the only provision in the nature of limitation or restriction (if it can properly be called either) which I think cannot be properly made except by bill—so it is the only one which I should wish to see, under the circumstances of the present times, attached to the exercise of the powers of the crown, in the hands in which we are about to place them, or in any hands in which it is fit that they should be placed.

My right honourable friend (the Chancellor of the Exchequer), has intimated an intention of proposing other restrictions, on the model, as I understand, of those proposed in 1789. As he has not entered into any detail upon them, and has professed to wish that the discussion of them may not be anticipated to-night, I will abstain from any detailed exposition of my view of this part of the subject. I will only say that, respecting as I do the precedent of 1789, so far as it rests in principle, and is established by authority, I do not conceive all parts of all that was proposed on that occasion to be of equally permanent obligation. What depended upon the circumstances of the time—the change of circumstances may naturally vary. And I own I cannot conceive a period less favourable than that in which I am now speaking, for the abrogation or suspension of any of the legitimate powers of the crown. If I doubted the expediency of such an experiment before this night, I have heard this night enough to convince me of its inexpediency. When the honourable baronet asked why, if such powers as it is proposed to suspend can be dispensed with for a limited time, they should not be dispensed with altogether? I do not quarrel with the justness of his reasoning; but I content myself with observing that, in 1789, there was no party in this country which would have been prepared to apply and to act upon this inference. That is in my mind a consideration indicating change enough in the circumstances of the country to warrant great caution in adopting that part of the proceeding of 1789. The time will come for stating more at large this argument, and others which appear to me to be conclusive against the policy of such restrictions at this period, as may cripple and degrade the executive authority.

I will now only add, that I have formed my opinion upon this point upon the best deliberation that I could give to it, without concert or understanding with any party, or any set of men whatever, and with no other object than the consideration of what may be best for the public service. Having formed this opinion, I have thought it candid and honest to avow it undisguisedly on the first mention of the subject of restrictions in this House; and while I may yet hope perhaps that the decision of those who have the conduct of this measure is not finally and unalterably made up. I am not one of those who think the executive power in this country too strong, or who think it can be weakened, in whatever hands, without disadvantage to the public interests.

I have now stated my sentiments upon the whole of this most anxious, painful, and distressing subject to the Committee. I do not concur with those who blame His Majesty's Ministers for not having sooner brought it under our consideration. On the contrary, I approve of the reluctance and delicacy which they have manifested; and if my right honourable friend could now assure the House and the country that a still further procrastination would not be attended with any injurious consequences to the country, I should, on that assurance, have no hesitation in agreeing to defer to a still more distant day the painful duty which we are now proceeding to discharge. Called upon to proceed in the discharge of it, we must endeavour to remember and to combine in our decisions, what we owe to public duty, and what to our feelings of affection and veneration for the exalted individual whose situation is the cause of our discussions; what we owe "*Patriæ Priamoque*," to our country and to our King, not doubting, however, that these duties, though double in their obligation, will be proved concurrent in their practical discharge. The effect of the vote in which I shall concur this night is, at the same time that we recognize and record our duty, to assert our right to execute the awful trust which is unfortunately devolved upon us. The application of the right and power which we claim, will be the subject of future discussions. But I am satisfied that in using our power liberally, we shall find that we use it wisely.

A division took place on the third Resolution.

Ayes	269
Noes	157
Majority	112

REGENCY RESOLUTIONS.

December 31st, 1810.

THE CHANCELLOR OF THE EXCHEQUER submitted the following Resolutions respecting the Regency—

"1st. That it is the opinion of this Committee, that for the purpose of providing for the exercise of the Royal Authority during the continuance of His Majesty's illness, in such manner and to such extent as the present circumstances and the urgent concerns of the nation appear to require, it is expedient that His Royal Highness the Prince of Wales, being resident within the realm, shall be empowered to exercise and administer the Royal Authority, according to the laws and constitution of Great Britain, in the name and on the behalf of His Majesty, and under the style and title of Regent of the Kingdom; and to use, execute, and perform, in the name and on the behalf of His Majesty, all authorities, prerogatives, acts of government, and administration of the same, that belong to the King of this realm to use, execute, and perform, according to the law thereof, subject to such limitations and exceptions as shall be provided.

"That it is the opinion of this Committee, that, for a time to be limited, the power so to be given to His Royal Highness the Prince of Wales, shall not extend to the granting of any rank or dignity of the peerage of the realm to any person whatever, except such person or persons as may perform some singular naval or military achievement. That it is the opinion of this Committee, that, for a time to be limited, the said power shall not extend to the granting of any office whatever in reversion, or to the granting of any office, salary, or premium, for any other term than during His Majesty's pleasure, except such offices as are by law required to be granted for life, or during good behaviour.

"That it is the opinion of this Committee, that such parts of His Majesty's private property as are not vested in trustees, shall be vested in trustees for the benefit of His Majesty.

"That it is the opinion of this Committee, that the care of His Majesty's royal person, during the continuance of His Majesty's illness, shall be committed to the care of the Queen's Most Excellent Majesty, and that, for a time to be limited, Her Majesty shall have power to remove from, and to nominate and appoint such persons as she shall think proper, to the several offices of His Majesty's household; and to dispose, order, and manage all other matters and things relating to the care of His Majesty's Royal person, during the time aforesaid; and that, for the better enabling Her Majesty to discharge this important task, it is also expedient that a Committee shall be appointed to advise and assist Her Majesty in the several matters aforesaid; and with power, from time to time, as they may see cause, to examine upon oath the physicians and others attending His Majesty's person, touching the state of His Majesty's health and all matters relative thereto."

Mr. W. Lamb, on the first Resolution being moved, submitted an amendment, "That the last words of the first Resolution 'subject to such restrictions and limitations as should be provided,' be omitted."

Mr. Canning rose and spoke as follows:—Sir, having upon a former occasion taken the liberty of intimating to the Committee the opinion that I had formed respecting the restrictions which my right honourable friend* then declared his intention to propose, and which, in a most perspicuous and able speech, he has now proposed to us, I was anxious to follow my right honourable friend, and to explain, as early as possible, the grounds upon which I differ this night from him in opinion. I was anxious to do this, before the debate could possibly have grown into asperity or contention—asperity in which I utterly disclaim any participation—contention in which,

* The Chancellor of the Exchequer.

I trust, I need not assure my right honourable friend I should be most unwilling to engage with him. I nevertheless most readily gave way to the honourable gentleman (Mr. Lamb), who has just sat down, whom, from our concurrence in sentiment on this occasion, I believe I may call, in a Parliamentary, as I am happy to call him in a private sense, my honourable friend,—and whom I can with sincerity assure, that no one has listened to him with more pleasure than I have done; more particularly from his having discussed the subject in debate with that moderation with which such a discussion ought to be commenced, and with which I hope it is to continue to be conducted.

Sir, after the various and ample discussions which the great question, upon which we are engaged, has undergone, we are now arrived at that point in our proceedings, at which the opinions of those who have hitherto generally agreed may naturally be expected to separate and diverge: at which many of those who have hitherto felt themselves bound to go along with my right honourable friend, in pursuance of the precedent which he most properly has proposed as the general rule of his conduct, may apprehend, and, in my judgment correctly, that the precedent which has kept us together thus far, ceases to apply. In short, Sir, we are arrived at that point where authority fails us, and where discretion must begin. Justly as the precedent of 1788 has been represented, as affording a rule for the conduct of Parliament in all cases of similar visitation—as the sure basis of all future legislation upon emergencies like that to which it applied—it seems obvious that it is only so far as the circumstances of the emergency are alike, and only so far as the precedent itself was completed, that there is any just ground for reasoning conclusively from its authority. To the discussion of points not decided in 1788, and of circumstances essentially different from those of that time, we come as to so many new questions; unbiassed by the authority of a precedent not strictly applicable, and unfettered in our judgments, so long as we keep the range of our respective opinions within the sphere of the constitution.

The authority attributed, and justly attributed, to the precedent of 1788, is two-fold—that which belongs to it as a proceeding of Parliament; and that which it derives from the sanction of the great names of those who devised and conducted the Parliamentary proceedings of that day. The first branch of this division—its authority as a proceeding of Parliament—is again distinguishable into two parts; that which actually received the final sanction of the two Houses of Parliament, and that which was left inchoate but imperfect. The former may be justly described in strict Parliamentary language as a Parliamentary precedent. The latter, whatever opinion we may entertain of what might possibly or even probably have been the ultimate decision of the two Houses, respecting measures in progress, but not completed, cannot be considered in the light of authoritative precedent.

It has been argued by my right honourable friend, and well and rightly argued, that the authority of what was done at that period by the two Houses of Parliament had been greatly augmented by the subsequent approbation of His Majesty after his recovery; that the royal authority having, when revived, sanctioned retrospectively the proceedings adopted during its suspension, told back upon all the antecedent stages of their progress, and gave an effect to what had been done equivalent to the royal assent to any act of Parliament. But though such may have been the effect of His Majesty's subsequent approbation upon such part of those proceedings as had received the final sanction of the two Houses of Parliament, it cannot be contended, that such approbation told equally in confirmation of those other parts of the precedent, which neither had been previously, nor were subsequently, carried into effect; which were merely the acts of the House of Commons, and had never received the sanction of the other House. On the contrary, if that which had been agreed to by both Houses is admitted to have received confirmation by being subsequently approved of by His Majesty, I am intitled to insist, by a parity of reasoning, that, whatever parts are so defective as not to have received the sanction even of both Houses of Parliament, cannot possibly be considered as of authority equally binding. If such proceedings being found imperfect and incomplete at the time of the King's recovery, because not having then received the concurrence of one of the branches of the legislature; if the Regency Bill then in the House of Lords had been carried forward to its completion, and passed with a prospective view, undoubtedly the provisions of that Bill would have been binding as the act of the whole of the legislature; and this would surely have been the course pursued had it been the purpose of the Parliament, or of the Government of that day, to make the Regency Bill of 1789 a precedent for all future occasions. But, if so far from having been approved of, adopted, and enacted into law, the Regency Bill was immediately upon the King's recovery rejected by the Lords, is the mere circumstance of its having been proposed and discussed, and formally decided upon, in one House of Parliament, to be considered as placing it on the same footing with proceedings clothed with full Parliamentary authority, and having received their confirmation from the Crown? Upon the very grounds upon which my right honourable friend contends, and I agree with him in contending, for the authority of the former part of the proceedings of 1788, which we have hitherto faithfully copied, I must deny the same validity to the remainder; unless we are prepared to exalt conjecture into precedent; to give the face of legislation to the projects of former times; and to equalize solemn and recorded acts of Parliament with the traced intentions of individuals, or, at most, of one branch of the legislature.

There is, however, another species of authority, not binding indeed, as that of the legislature, but one nevertheless of no small obligation, derived from the character of those engaged in any great political transaction. Of him who carried through this House those proceedings, which furnish the precedent for the measures now under discussion, it cannot be necessary for me to say, that I cherish his memory with as much affection and veneration as any man who is the most forward to quote or to imitate his conduct. Yet ardent as is my attachment to the character, and deep and unfeigned as is my respect for the opinions of Mr. Pitt, I still cannot think myself warranted to claim, nor can I expect that others—that the House—would allow the authority of those opinions, great as it may be, an equal weight with the positive enactments of the legislature. This I could not do, nor expect others to concur in doing, even if, in looking back to the history and progress of the proceedings in 1788, I were to find, that the course then pursued, in framing the provisions for the establishment of the Regency, had been marked from the beginning by some principle as clearly defined as that which formed the foundation of the prior part of those proceedings: namely, of the averment of the right and duty of the two Houses to provide for the exercise of the regal power. But nothing can be more distinguishable than the two different stages of the proceeding upon that emergency: that in which Parliament affirmed and established the right of the two Houses to provide, and that in which it proceeded to frame the provision; distinguishable not more in the degrees of their intrinsic importance, than in those of the authority which they respectively derive from Parliamentary or individual sanction.

The right of the two Houses was proclaimed and maintained by Mr. Pitt; that is the point on which his authority is truly valuable; on that point it was confirmed by the adoption of both Houses of Parliament: it was acted upon by them to the fullest extent; and that proceeding of the two Houses it was, which received the subsequent sanction of the Crown. The principles upon which this right was affirmed and exercised, if true at all, are true universally, for all times and on all occasions. If they were the principles of the constitution in 1788, they are equally so in 1811. The lapse of twenty-two years has not impaired—the lapse of centuries cannot impair them. But the mode in which the right so asserted should be exercised, the precise provisions to be framed for the temporary substitution of the executive power—these were necessarily, then, as they must be now, matters not of eternal and invariable principle, but of prudence and expediency. In regard to these, therefore, the authority of the opinions of any individual, however great, and wise, and venerable, can be taken only with reference to the circumstances of the time in which he had to act, and are not to be applied without change or modification to other times and circumstances. We have Mr. Pitt's authority against such an application of them, for if he had thought the Regency Bill ought to have passed as a model for future times, why was it dropped? why was it not completed and recorded together with the foregoing part of the proceedings of that day? Nor is the final fate of the Regency Bill the only argument against the conclusive authority of its provisions. In the very progress of it through this House, any man, who has read or can remember the history of that period, must know, that opinions were greatly divided with respect to many parts of that Bill, even among those who were generally favourable to its object, and to Mr. Pitt's administration; and that, in the very last stage of its progress, when the Bill was in the hands of the Speaker, and ready to take its flight to the Lords, Mr. Pitt consented to two most material alterations with respect to some of the restrictions, which we have this night proposed for our adoption: the first limiting the restriction of the prerogative of creating peers to three years, recommended, I believe, by the late Sir William, then Mr. Pulteney; the other reserving to Parliament the power of reconsidering that clause which restricted the grant of offices for life, in the case of any person whom the Regent might appoint to the office of Lord Chancellor. I am, therefore, surely borne out in my argument, that the proceedings upon the Bill are not fairly to be assimilated in authority to those previous proceedings of both Houses, which were founded on constitutional principles, applicable to all times and all circumstances; but that the provisions of the Bill were shaped and fashioned to the particular circumstances and exigency of the occasion. It follows that they are liable to be so shaped and fashioned now, without any derogation from the authority, or any dereliction of the principles of the legislature of that day; or of that great man, by whom the deliberations of this branch of the legislature were particularly guided.

Having thus cleared away from the discussion all that undue influence, which has been attempted to be raised on presumed authority, and which, if admitted, would be a bar to any discussion at all, I come now, Sir, to an impartial consideration of the nature and principles of the question immediately before us. Omitting for the present any reference to the former period, of which so much has been said, I shall take the liberty to consider the measure now proposed to us, upon its own grounds, and with reference to the time and to the circumstances in which it is proposed. What then is the nature of the duty imposed upon us by the emergency in which we stand? What steps have been already taken by us in discharge of that duty? What is the precise object of this night's deliberation?

We have already solemnly determined that it is the right, as well as the duty of the two Houses of Parliament to provide for the due discharge of the royal functions during the lamented incapacity of the Sovereign. In effecting this purpose we are all agreed, that, while we provide for the temporary exercise of the regal power, every necessary provision should be made to secure to His Majesty the effectual resumption of his functions in the happy event of his recovery. We are all agreed that the most advisable and expedient mode of carrying on the executive government during this interval will be by a sole Regent; and that the Regent so to be appointed should be no other than the illustrious individual by birth and situation nearest to the throne. The question of to-night is, what portion of the regal powers and prerogatives should be given to the Regent for the execution of the arduous trust confided to him; or what portion withholden from him, for the purpose (as I understand) of marking that it is a trust confided, and not a right adjudged to him?

Apprehensions have been shadowed out rather than expressed by my right honourable friend that if the whole prerogatives were made over to the illustrious person in question, he—but not he more than any other individual, placed in similar circumstances—might be led to regard himself in another light than that of a trustee: that, in the full and unrestricted exercise of the powers of the Sovereign, he might forget that they were exercised by him only in the name, and on the behalf of their rightful possessor; that he might consider them as an inheritance rather than as a deposit, to be restored entire and unimpaired, whenever it may be the will of Providence to re-establish the health of His Majesty. I confess I do not share in these apprehensions. The case itself—the discussions in this and in the other House of Parliament—the sentiments expressed so distinctly and unequivocally in every part of our recorded proceedings—the common sense and feeling of the whole country—all must concur to shew to the Regent the real nature of his trust and office: even if, in the absence of any or all of these indications, it were possible that he could have conceived any powers to be vested in him which would not be resumed by His Majesty at the moment of his recovery.

The quantum of power to be confided to the Regent, must then be decided by other considerations than that of the danger to be apprehended from a mistake so monstrous on the part of the Regent himself—an apprehension, in my judgment, altogether visionary. We must consider what is the task which the Regent will have to perform, and what are the powers requisite for its due performance. Having found and recorded the actual incapacity of the Sovereign; having assumed and asserted the right and the duty of the two Houses of Parliament to supply that incapacity, let us now consider what is the nature of the business, which, through incapacity, stands still, and which we are to find the means of carrying on. It is the business of a mighty monarchy. It consists in the exercise of functions as large as the mind of man can conceive—in the regulation and direction of the affairs of a great, a free, and a powerful people; in the care of their internal security and external interests; in the conduct of foreign negociations; in the decision of the vital questions of peace and war; and in the administration of the Government throughout all the parts, provinces, and dependencies of an empire, extending itself into every quarter of the globe.

This is the awful office of a King; the temporary execution of which we are now about to devolve upon the Regent. What is it—considering the irresponsibility of the Sovereign as an essential part of the constitution—what is it that affords a security to the people for the faithful exercise of all these important functions? The responsibility of Ministers. What are the means by which these functions operate? They are those which, according to the inherent imperfection of human nature, have at all times been the only motives to human actions, the only controul upon them of certain and permanent operation, the punishment of evil and the reward of merit. Such then being the functions of monarchical government, and such being the means of rendering them efficient to the purposes of good government, are we to be told that, in providing for its delegation, while it is not possible to curtail those powers, which are in their nature harsh and unpopular, it is necessary to abridge these milder, more amiable and endearing prerogatives, which bear an aspect of grace and favour towards the subject? Or are we to be told that, in depriving the Regent of the means of grace to sweeten the exercise of power, while we impose upon him all the invidious functions of Government, we are not making a most serious change in that branch of the Constitution, which we profess our desire to uphold in all its powers and prerogatives?

My right honourable friend says, that our duty, and indeed our right to act, is limited by the necessity which creates it. We should not be justified, he contends, in doing any thing but what the pressure of this necessity actually requires to be done. I adopt my right honourable friend's principle: but I apply it differently. What is necessary is, to provide for carrying on the functions of the disabled Sovereign: what is not necessary is to change their nature. What is necessary is that the Government should go on: what is not necessary is, that part of it should be arrested. We are compelled, by necessity, to delegate the exercise of the executive authority to a Regent: but there is no necessity for making that exercise more difficult in his hands than in those of the rightful possessor; for imposing new difficulties upon this arduous office—diminishing the means of its efficiency—and adding to the irksomeness of its burthen. It is neither necessary nor politic, in my opinion, to mark distrust and jealousy, when, by the free tender of a magnanimous confidence, we might alleviate at least the heavy responsibility which we impose, and furnish incitements to the faithful discharge of it, such as jealousy and distrust are little calculated to inspire.

But perhaps the prerogatives of the Crown are more than adequate to the discharge of its important duties, more than sufficient to maintain the dignity and lustre of that throne which he, to whom we are now entrusting the support of its rights and powers, will in due time himself be called to fill? Perhaps this temporary delegation affords an opportunity for trying an experiment, which in the person of the rightful occupant, could not be tried without danger.

Sir, I confess I dread the example of this experiment, not for any use which I believe to be intended to be made of it by my right honourable friend, most assuredly not, but from the manner in which it is likely to be welcomed, felt, and treasured up for future use by others, who may be disposed to employ it for purposes very foreign to his views. I am not one of those, Sir, who think the Crown already too powerful. That, I am convinced, is not the sentiment of my right honourable friend, any more than it is mine. And being of opinion that the executive power in this country does not possess too much influence, or too extensive means of rewarding public services, I must, in consistency with that opinion, contend that, whatever portion of the powers of the Crown shall be withheld from the Regent, will be so much taken away from what is necessary for the due discharge of the indispensable functions of the monarchy.

This, Sir, is my general view, with regard to the proposed restrictions, or rather, of the principle of restriction itself as applied to the munificent prerogatives of the Crown in the hands of the Regent. Thus I think of it, as compared generally with the general principles of the Constitution. But is there any peculiar consideration arising out of the times in which we live, arising out of the present circumstances of the country, which lessens the force of the objections which I have taken the liberty to urge, and renders that course safe and profitable now, which I think I have shewn to be generally inexpedient? The answer to this question is, the precedent of 1788. Sir, I will not say that in 1788 restrictions might not have been expedient. I will not go into the circumstances, because I will not revive the animosities of that period. But if not absolutely necessary then, at least they might have been harmless. I perfectly concur in the observation of my right honourable friend opposite (Mr. Lamb) as to the difference between the circumstances of the country in the year 1788, and at the present moment. I agree with him that my right honourable friend, in stating that difference to consist merely in the simple opposition of a state of war to a state of peace, has treated this argument with somewhat of levity, and greatly under-rated its force. My right honourable friend seems to think, that the only effect of such a difference in the situation of the country, is to render such of the royal functions as are particularly and directly applicable to a state of war, more necessary to be preserved in full efficiency on this occasion, than in the year 1788. Surely this is a very narrow and imperfect view of the question. When I admit that, in time of profound peace, some of the functions of the executive government might have remained in repose with little disadvantage, as compared with that which would result from suspending their activity in a time of war, do I, therefore, mean that the difference between a state of war and a state of peace, as bearing upon the question, consists exclusively in military operations? Do I mean that the powers of the executive government, which enable the Sovereign to meet the exigencies of war, are those only which are exercised in the management of fleets and armies? Do I mean that there are peace prerogatives and war prerogatives, perfectly distinct in their nature, one half of which may occasionally be suspended, so that the other half be continued in activity? No, Sir; a state of war is not merely a state implying military enterprises and military dangers, and requiring military means and exertions. It is a state of civil, as well as military hazard and difficulty. Failures, as extensive as unexpected, and as unmerited as either, must at least be contemplated as possible in the course of a war: even of one generally fortunate and well conducted, the pressure of pecuniary burdens upon all classes of the community is necessarily aggravated; trade suffers; danger is apprehended; and does my right honourable friend conceive then, that a state of war, involving the possibility of so many perils—of so much public embarrassment and national disappointment—must not materially augment the difficulties in every part of the home administration of the Government? Does my right honourable friend state the question fairly, when he supposes it to bear only on the conduct of the war itself; and on the powers directly and specifically applicable to military operations? Does it not affect the whole of the powers of the Government? And can it be expedient, is it even consistent with a just regard to the security of the nation, that the general powers of the kingly office, necessary even in time of peace for conducting the administration of the country, should be restricted at a time when the person in whose hands they are placed is called to the task of carrying on an arduous war, encompassed with all the various and accumulated difficulties, foreign and domestic, which are inevitably inseparable from such a state of things?

Do not let it be imagined, Sir, that in stating these difficulties, it is my wish to magnify them beyond their just size. I am desirous of being distinctly understood not to entertain the slightest apprehension, but that the country possesses, in ample store, both the spirit and the means to meet and successfully to overcome them. All that I mean to infer from this statement is, that difficulties of such an extensive and complicated nature, afford strong grounds of objection against imposing any unnecessary restrictions upon any of the functions of the executive government; that it is not a fair view of the nature of these functions, to suppose them capable of being separated and parcelled out—one for this purpose, one for that—one for time of peace, another for time of war—but, that the body of the prerogatives must be considered as a whole, constituting, by their assemblage and union, the aggregate power of the kingly office, not as I think greater than is necessary for the carrying on the Government well, and more indispensably necessary than ever in times of national difficulty and national exertion.

My right honourable friend, therefore, does not appear to me to have done any thing towards extenuating the obvious distinction between a season of peace, such as that of 1788, and one of war, such as the present, or towards reconciling the precedent of 1788 in its provisions and details to the exigency of the present occasion, by merely keeping alive what he is pleased to consider the warlike part of the prerogative, of making peers, for instance, while he throws that prerogative, and others, generally, into abeyance. In attempting this, he has indeed done quite enough to shew, that he himself distrusts and cannot follow out the precedent of 1788, to shew, that it is not applicable to these times; that he cannot adopt the restrictions and limitations of 1788, without restricting those restrictions, and limiting those limitations; and after a forcible and elaborate panegyric upon the Regency Bill of 1788; after holding it up and strongly recommending it to the Committee as the rule of their conduct; after intimating no small surprise, that any admirer of Mr. Pitt should presume to question any part of it as applicable to the present state of things, he concludes by presenting it in a changed and mutilated state, and, I will venture to say, in scarce one material clause precisely the same as it passed this House in 1789. This is surely a singular way of proving the veneration which he feels for this precedent himself, or of inculcating it in others.

Now, Sir, I have ventured to give it as my opinion, that the restrictions and limitations of 1789 are not applicable to the present time. My right honourable friend may, therefore, have flattered himself, that I am one of those who are to be gratified by his restrictions and limitations upon them. I do not know whether he is prepared to hear from me that I disapprove his restrictions and limitations, upon the restrictions and limitations, even more than the original ones; that thinking the plan altogether objectionable, I think this, which he intends as a mitigation and improvement, the most objectionable part of it.

Extraordinary as my right honourable friend may think this declaration at first sight, I flatter myself I shall be able to make it intelligible to him, if not to induce him to concur in it.

My sentiments are too well known within these walls, not to secure me from any imputation of wishing to shut the ranks of the peerage against those, whose distinguished merit in their country's service, by sea or land, shall hereafter entitle them to such exalted honours. The achievements of military heroism are, by the common consent of mankind, fit objects of the highest reward. Would I consent to check so legitimate and beneficial an ambition? to damp an ardour as splendid in its character as pure in its motives? to withdraw from valour and prowess the just incitement which arises from an enthusiastic hope of identifying their personal fame with the greatness and the glory of their country? What! if Lord Wellington, who has displayed so eminently, during the late campaign, those distinguished qualities of a general, which he was supposed, but falsely supposed, not to possess, should, before the conclusion of the present year, exhibit to his admiring and grateful countrymen another specimen of those more shining qualities, for which he has been uniformly acknowledged to be conspicuous; and should terminate a campaign, signalized by such consummate prudence and skill, by an achievement more congenial perhaps to his nature and habits—a brilliant victory—would I be the man to deny to him the well merited reward of more exalted rank in the peerage? Or, if a gallant admiral, with the characteristic enterprise of his profession, should rush into battle with that animating exclamation, with which Nelson led on the battle of the Nile, "A Peerage or Westminster Abbey," would I be the man to contend for closing against his hopes one part of that glorious alternative? for leaving him, indeed, the monument to cover his remains if he should fall; but for shutting the ranks of the peerage against his living glory?

I hope and trust, Sir, that no honourable gentleman will suppose such to be my feeling. I hope I shall not be so answered, when I declare that I must give my opposition to the exception, in favour of naval and military peerages, now proposed by my right honourable friend. Far, indeed, am I from wishing to exclude meritorious individuals of these descriptions from the well-earned honours of the peerage. Long may such honours be so bestowed! many be the victories in which they shall be won and worn! But the manner in which I wish such rewards and distinctions to be conferred, is in the ordinary course of the constitution—in the spontaneous and unfettered exercise of the royal prerogative—such as it has been for ages, such as it is now—such as the very exception, proposed by my right honourable friend, proves it ought to continue, but such as that exception does not leave or make it. I would accomplish this salutary and necessary object by the very simple process of leaving things as they are, not by first lopping off from the royal prerogative the power of granting peerages generally; and then turning round again for the purpose of piecing it again, and restoring its former state in part, with a view to meet the circumstances of a particular case. It is not, it cannot, be a sound or a just principle of legislation, first to undo, and, in the same breath, partially to re-establish what we have undone. This in itself is irrational; but this is not all. There are other objections much more conclusive against this exception, than even against the general limitation as it stood before the change. The necessary effect of this exception would be, not to relieve the prerogative from restraint, but to change its very nature; to strip that part of it, which would be so withdrawn from the limitation, of one half of its value. For, in what does the value of this prerogative consist? Not surely in any duty and positive obligation imposed upon the possessor of it to give or assign a certain stipulated reward for a certain definite service. He is not to adjudicate the specified and rightful earnings of valour or merit. There is a grace and favour in the reward of eminent public service; there is a discretion in selecting them for that reward, which can only be found in the free choice of the Sovereign, and in the spontaneous exertion of the royal prerogative. It is in this view that the grant of honours and distinctions is "twice blessed;" that

"It blesseth him that gives, and him that takes;"

that it endears the bestower and receiver to each other; that the stream of nobility springs, as it were, warm from the heart of the Sovereign, ere it descends upon the favoured head of a meritorious subject. Strip the prerogative of this grace, this discretionary power, and you do not only restrict its operation, but you destroy its essence. If the law were to direct such honours to be conferred, where would be the grace? Where would the gratitude be due? Where the obligation conferred? Deprived of all appearance of spontaneous bounty, the honour would be claimed as a right, not acknowledged as a favour; and the Regent would be placed in the situation of a bare trustee indeed, but of a trustee without confidence, authorised only to perform, in previously specified cases, a prescribed and indispensable duty.

Nor is this the only objection. To change discretion into necessity, and grace into obligation, would be bad enough. But how full is the prescribed task itself of difficulties in the execution? By the terms of the Resolution it would, in effect, be obligatory on the Regent to confer the honours of the peerage upon any person who may "achieve any signal naval or military services." Such words allow great latitude of construction; and may be productive, under the various interpretations that may be put upon them, of much and serious embarrassment to the Government of the Regent. If a signal and decisive victory—such as should decide the fate of a campaign; or lead to the conclusion of a peace; such as the victories of Marlborough or Prince Eugene—should be gained, there would unquestionably be no difficulty; every body would be agreed upon the merits of such a service, and would admit the indubitable claim, arising from it, to the rewards of the peerage. But such decisive actions and such unquestionable results are not to be looked for in the ordinary course of war. On the other hand, a signally disastrous defeat might possibly befal a country without any blame being imputable to the commander; nay even after he might have performed every duty that could be required of him in a most exemplary manner. Still, however, in such a case (I trust a most improbable one) there might be no great embarrassment to the Regent. No one would blame him for not marking even consummate ability, shining through unmerited misfortune, with splendid reward. But between these two extremes may probably be found most of those military services, the merits of which would become the subject of discussion, if they chanced to be performed during the interval while the honours of the peerage are exclusively appropriated, and consecrated by Act of Parliament, to military merit. Numberless cases may exist between the distant limits which I have described; and who but must foresee in the practice of this exception an endless source of embarrassing discussions, of jealousies and invidious comparisons, no less injurious to the public service, than perplexing and inconvenient to the Regent? Am I putting an imaginary case? The course of the last twelve months has furnished precisely such an instance as I have ventured to anticipate for the present year. It must be in the recollection of every gentleman present, that the glorious victory (so I must call it) of Talavera did not meet with the unanimous suffrage of this House. If that had been an "achievement" under the Regent's cognizance, to be dealt with according to the provisions of this Bill, he would have been accused by the honourable gentlemen opposite of having abused the discretion confided to him, and squandered the honours of the peerage. For I will not put the other supposition, that he could have withholden the peerage from Lord Wellington on that occasion. And who is sanguine enough to hope that all the "achievements" of the year to come will be of a character more unequivocal, of less disputable glory, than the battle of Talavera?

So far, therefore, from correcting the limitation

as it originally stood, I contend, that the exception makes infinitely worse. Whether the Regent should grant or should withhold the honours of which he is made the steward, his conduct would be equally liable to question; nor would it be any trifling practical inconvenience, that the early part of the next session of Parliament should be occupied, as it possibly might be, in inquiries how far that officer of Parliament may have made a proper use of the portion of the prerogative committed, not to his discretion, but to his responsible charge. Much better would it be to suspend the prerogative altogether, than to vest it in so mutilated a state, and on such perplexing conditions, in the hands of the Regent. Better would it be, that for one year military merit should go without its reward, or that we should at once resolve, as it were, that this year shall be barren of glory, than that the royal prerogative should be exhibited in a state so shackled and degraded—in a state so inadequate to its purposes, and so foreign to its nature.

So much, Sir, for the limitation of the limitation proposed by my right honourable friend. But now as to the limitation itself. Is it exclusively in cases of military or naval merit, that it is essential to the best interests of the state, that the person exercising the royal authority should have the unrestricted prerogative of creating peers? Are there not other instances in which the exercise of such a prerogative, unfettered by limitations, is equally necessary to enable a Regent well and beneficially to administer the affairs of the nation? I will suppose, for instance, that the eminent person now holding the Great Seal, might be desirous of retiring from office; and that the Regent might in consequence select for his successor, some one of the ornaments of the bar. Now, under the restriction, which I am now considering, the Regent could not elevate the object of his choice to the peerage. A Lord Keeper might indeed be appointed, and I am aware, that in the eye of the law, the Lord Keeper and the Lord Chancellor are the same: whether Lord Keeper or Lord Chancellor, he is, by virtue of his office, prolocutor of the House of Lords. But if he cannot be raised to the peerage, must not great inconvenience at least, perhaps more than inconvenience, be felt in the progress of public business, when he, who presides over the proceedings of the peers, not being a peer himself, can take no share in their debates, but must remain as mute as the mace upon their table?

Other cases may easily be imagined, wherein the operation of this limitation would interfere with the completion of arrangements, either for forming an administration, or for the conduct of affairs in Parliament. But I think I have stated enough to justify the opinion, that the prerogative ought to remain unfettered; and that, at all events, it would be more becoming to withhold it altogether, than to grant it under restrictions never before devised or imagined ; restrictions by which we should, in effect, reserve to ourselves the power of controuling the exercise of that part of the prerogative, which we confer, and should tell the Prince Regent, that, while we allowed him to administer the functions of royalty in the name and on the behalf of the Sovereign, we were determined to constitute ourselves "Viceroys" over him.

As to any argument to be deduced from a supposed abuse of this prerogative, or from the too lavish use of it, either in recent or former times, the fault of that argument is, that it would lead not to a temporary, but to perpetual restriction of it. It would lead to abridging the prerogative in the possession of the Crown, not to a mere partial suspension of it in the hands of the Regent. But I agree with my right honourable friend, and with my honourable friend on the other side of the House (Mr. Lamb) that the imputation of an extravagant use of this prerogative, is at least excessively exaggerated. In very late times, and by the present administration, either whilst I was connected with it or since, certainly there has been a most sparing use of the power of creating peers. But, looking back to former administrations, to which this abuse is imputed, I must say, I very much doubt, whether the House of Lords, numerous as it now is, has been so augmented as to bear a greater proportion than heretofore, to the weight and influence of the Commons, and generally to the increased diffusion of wealth throughout all classes of the community. It is true, that there is recorded in our history one instance, and one only, of a flagrant abuse of this power for political purposes—that in the reign of queen Anne—when the Tory administration, by pouring twelve newly created peers in one day into the House of Lords, established a majority in their own favour. But even this abuse, if it were likely to be imitated, could not now be imitated successfully. It must be admitted, that the addition of twelve peers, when the whole number consisted but of two hundred must have borne a considerable proportion to the whole. But now when the House of Lords consists of three hundred peers, what would be the addition of twelve, even if in the present times such a stroke were likely to be ventured; and how much greater must the addition be to make such a stroke permanently decisive! And here again the argument goes too far for the object to which it is applied. If there be this danger in the unlimited power of creating peers, the limitation, to be effectual, must be made permanent. But to all such stretches of prerogative the House well knows, that there is a limitation more operative than the provisions of a bill; more efficacious than any system of checks and balances, —the controul of public opinion.

The same objections, which I have stated to the general suspension of the prerogative of making peers, apply according to their kind and degree to the next restriction — that upon the grant of patent offices or pensions for life. Much has been said of late years, of the great extent of this patronage, and of the expediency of reducing it. I have never, any more than my right honourable friend, allowed the truth of these statements. Investigation has shewn them to be exaggerated: and even if it were possible for me to consent to any change in the system, it certainly should not be to one, that should materially diminish its amount, though it might alter the mode of administering it. But that there must, and ought to exist, in the hands and at the discretion of the Crown, means, and ample means too, for the remuneration of public service in the civil and political departments of the state, I am, and have always been, decidedly of opinion. The legitimate use of such means appears to be in the facility which they afford for winning men of ability, who may have no very ample property, into the public service. On this ground I have hitherto supported, and on this ground, I shall continue to support them. On the bench, from which my right honourable friend has spoken, may be found sufficient proof of the utility of such means of remuneration. My right honourable friend (the Chancellor of the Exchequer) himself, is a proof of their advantageous application to the public service, brought, as he was, at the formation of the Government in 1807, from an honourable profession, of which, if he had continued a member, he must unquestionably have risen to the head, to take a share in the administration of the Government. The sacrifice these prospects His Majesty had most graciously intended to compensate by the grant for life of a sinecure office, had not this House interfered an Address to His Majesty, that he would be graciously pleased to grant it only during pleasure. This vote, if the question shall ever again be brought before Parliament, I shall most heartily concur in rescinding, and so giving full effect to the principle, for the justice of which I am contending. Another instance of the proper application of such offices is to be found on the same bench, in the grant of one of the Tellerships of the Exchequer, in the last session, to another right honourable friend of mine (Mr. Yorke). When I see before me two such instances of the beneficial use of this power of calling great abilities into the public service, I cannot consent that this power should be suspended. Perhaps there are few public men less interested than I am, in any probable arrangement of a new administration. I speak, therefore, with the more freedom upon these subjects. And as to any misuse, which may be apprehended from favour and partiality in the distribution of such offices as may fall vacant, during the continuance of the Regency, I will fairly own, that, if his Royal Highness should have the power of rewarding the long and disinterested attachment, the steady and tried fidelity, and the great public talents of any individual, who even might not have strictly earned such reward by actual labour in office, I should not grudge such an exercise of the power of the Regent; nor think it more than a reasonable compensation to His Royal Highness for the cares, the anxieties, and the embarrassments of the situation the duties of which he is called upon to discharge.

One argument for these restrictions, is, that the powers and prerogatives they withhold, might, if confided to the Regent, constitute a bar to the resumption of the Royal functions by His Majesty on his happy restoration to health. The supposition, that such an effect could be produced by such a cause, appears to me in the highest degree extravagant and ridiculous. Can any man seriously believe, that all the possible chance of the falling-in of offices for life, all the various casualties, which, within a year, could occur to create vacancies (for it must be recollected that they must fall vacant before they can be given away) —or that even all the abuse which could take place in the distribution of peerages during the Regency, could so fortify the government of the Regent, within that period, as to enable him, (if so inclined) to prevent His Majesty's ready resumption of his power in case of his recovery? What tendency even have such causes to produce such an effect? Where is the man who, though neither formidable, nor mischievous, would yet, if elevated to the peerage, and made formidable by a pension or a sinecure, be enabled to stand in the breach and to obstruct the King's re-occupation of his throne?

The argument, if argument it may be called, and the apprehension in which it pretends to be founded, appear to me perfectly senseless. There is, moreover, a strange inconsistency in the different arguments respecting these powers and prerogatives. When it is proposed to us to withhold them from the Regent; they are represented as wholly unnecessary for the well carrying on of the Government. But they are at the same time, it seems, as strong to do mischief as they are weak to do good. They are strong enough to endanger the whole of the Executive Government, if abused; and by a strange perverseness, inefficacious to their legitimate purpose. They are nothing in positive activity, but every thing in prospective prevention: they would not, if properly used, tend to secure a majority in Parliament; but, with a little stretch, they might effect a revolution. By what process all that which is so powerless *in esse*, can be so formidable *in posse*, is what I am at a loss to conceive.

But here again the zeal of controversy appears to outrun discretion. For if, in fact, the powers to be withholden from the Regent can, by their abuse, be productive of such great inconvenience, and yet by their proper exercise be productive of so little good, that the Executive Government can go on very well without them, this surely would be an argument for abolishing such prerogatives altogether. A power capable of doing much mischief, and but little good, ought not to be preserved.

Fortunately, however, the argument is good for nothing either way. The apprehension of any opposition being made to the return of His Majesty to the exercise of his authority, must be felt, even by those who use it, to be in the highest degree extravagant. If I could believe that there existed a man, so lost to what is due to himself, to his Sovereign, and to society, as to harbour such an idea, I would not only not consent to give him power without restrictions, but I would not confide to him any power at all. I would not arm with "a pigmy's straw" that man, into whose mind so monstrous a design could even for a single moment find admittance. God forbid that any power should be granted, or any provision made, which could, either by perversion or by accident, obstruct His Majesty's resumption of his functions. I would have nothing to impede, nothing to retard that resumption, beyond the moment at which it should please a gracious Providence to restore him to the wishes of his people. No effort, no exertion should be necessary on his part. Like the sun, by the mere act of his appearance, he should dissolve and dissipate all the clouds and vapours by which his lustre is obscured.

But in exact proportion as we make anxious provision for the secure resumption of his power by the King, I think we should abstain from unnecessarily restricting the powers of the Regent. These, Sir, are not times in which any man can think it desirable to cripple the energies of the Executive Government, in whatever hands it may be. But we must recollect, that in the very circumstances of the King's situation, of his desired, and (thank God!) probable recovery, there is a certain source of weakness to the ephemeral and evanescent Government of the Regent, which going to repose in the possession of power, can never be certain that it may not awake and find itself dissolved in the morning.

There are some species of difficulties, Sir, which, when a man has to encounter, he feels his courage rise in proportion to the task, and is animated by the obstacles which oppose him. This is the case where he is backed by all that should be his natural support: where he brings the full use of all his means and resources to bear upon the contest in which he is engaged. But not so, if he goes into the field with his best faculties shackled, with jealousy instead of encouragement at his side. The difficulties which we are about to impose by the restrictions are of this latter description; and tend to dishearten and unnerve the executive power, at a moment, when surely all its energies are necessary to be employed.

And after all, the only reasons for proposing these restrictions appear to resolve themselves into this, that they were already proposed in 1788. To this I have answered, that there are two kinds of imitation; one, that which catches the spirit and the principle, and applies them to similar circumstances; the other that which takes the dry and dead letter, and attempts to adapt it to circumstances wholly dissimilar. My right honourable friend, indeed, has found that the precedent of 1788 did not suit his case, and, therefore, has been reduced to the necessity of endeavouring, by clipping here and stretching there, to make it fit. For myself I have truly said, and am anxious again to repeat, that I can be surpassed by no man in respect and veneration for the great man who guided the proceedings of 1788. But I am convinced that I do that precedent more honour, in considering and approving of it, with reference to the circumstances of the period in which it was proposed, than those do who contend, that the great, and fertile, and profound mind that framed it, could, if he had happily survived to the present times, have devised nothing more applicable to the emergency for which we have to provide.

Sir, as my right honourable friend has expressed a wish that no discussion should take place this night upon the last Resolution, it is not my intention to go much at length into the matter which is the subject of it. The custody of His Majesty's person, I take it to be perfectly clear, from every analogy of private life, and from all the feelings of nature, should be given to the Queen. With respect to the household, I must confess, I do not approve of my right honourable friend's proposed arrangement. I should much rather attach a large portion of that establishment permanently to the service of His Majesty, than have the whole of it attached to him for a limited period, as proposed in the Resolution, then to be revised and retrenched. I say this with as much frankness as if advising with my right honourable friend, as a member of the Government, previous to the bringing in of his measure. I should have recommended an attempt now to preserve a proper splendour to surround His Majesty's person during the whole term of his natural life, should his illness unfortunately be commensurate with his life, rather than leave the matter in prospective dependence upon the decision of some future, and, perhaps less favourably disposed period. I may be wrong or fanciful in point of feeling, but, I will own, I am not satisfied with a provision which has the appearance of fixing a time, after which there is to be no hope entertained of His Majesty's recovery. I do not wish that there should be added to the preamble of the Bill a clause stating that a period will come, and that Parliament will have to declare that period, whether it be six or twelve months, when the recovery of His Majesty will be hopeless. Notwithstanding the comments which have been made upon my former statement of my readiness to have concurred in further adjournments, if proposed, I now repeat that I should be much better satisfied, that the functions of the Crown should remain in suspense till the longest period of which the exigencies of the public service could possibly admit, than be thus reduced to the necessity of defining a period at which all hope is to be abandoned. And this appears to me to be the effect of providing a larger scale of household for a limited time, with a recorded admission that it must then be altered; of accumulating comfort and splendour upon the period of hope, with an avowed view of reducing them to a more contracted scale at the era of despair.

Sir, I would do what is right at once, and once for all: I should not think any thing right but what was ample both for comfort and for splendour; and I would settle the establishment permanently, in order that the portion of patronage, which may be withheld from the Regent, may not be given to any body else. For upon this point I perfectly concur with my honourable friend on the other side (Mr. Lamb), that it would be highly improper to set up a new political power, growing out of that influence which belongs to the appointment of the household, and which has always hitherto been joined to the Executive Government. Why should that influence subsist at all during the Regency? The Regent certainly must not have it, and why should Her Majesty be burthened with it? Why should not the Lords of the Bedchamber, and such other attendants as ought to be attached to His Majesty's person, enjoy their places during life, that is, during the continuance of the King's illness, whatever that may be, independent alike of the Regent or of any other political influence whatever? Something of this sort, it appears to me, might be done, and might spare all the jealousies and heart-burnings, to which disputed patronage and renewed discussions, may give rise: while, more than any other practicable arrangement, it would secure to His Majesty the most faithful and acceptable attendance. This is not the time, however, for going into any detail upon this subject. Generally, I will only say, that no views of niggardly economy ought to be permitted to mix themselves with the consideration of how we may best provide for the safe, the tender, and the respectful care of the King. We must not think of saving by his sickness. We must not forget that he is still our King.

We must not consider him as a remnant to be thrown aside: but as a relic to be treasured with pious devotion, to be consecrated with the prayers and the vows of all good men: to be not immured, but inshrined amidst the gratitude and veneration of his subjects.

Sir, I will trouble the Committee no further. The vote to which we are about to come to-night, is upon the restrictions to be imposed upon the Regent. I have stated my reasons for thinking these restrictions inexpedient. I have stated why I think the limitations introduced to qualify them more exceptionable even than the restrictions themselves. With these opinions I cannot do otherwise than vote for the amendment, by which both the one and the other are to be altogether done away.

The House divided upon Mr. Lamb's Amendment, when the numbers were—

For Mr. Lamb's Amendment	200
Against it	224
Majority in favour of the first Resolution	24

On a division upon the second Resolution, for Restricting the Prerogative as to the Granting of Peerages, the numbers were:—

For the second Resolution	226
Against it	210
Majority for the second Resolution	16

On a division upon the third Resolution respecting the Grant of Pensions, &c. &c., the numbers were—

For the third Resolution...	233
Against it	214
Majority for the third Resolution	19

The fourth Resolution, relative to the disposition of the King's private property, was agreed to without a division; and the discussion upon the fifth Resolution respecting the Household Establishment, was postponed till the following day.

RESOLUTIONS RESPECTING THE REGENCY.

January 1st, 1811.

The Chancellor of the Exchequer moved the fifth Resolution—(see page 72).

Earl Gower proposed, as an amendment, to omit that part of the Resolution from the words "Queen's Most Excellent Majesty," and to insert in the room of it, "together with such direction of his Household as may be suitable for the care of His Majesty's royal person, and the maintenance of the royal dignity."

Mr. Canning having observed, that the greater portion of the discussion of that night, and especially the latter part of it, had been conducted, as if the Committee had lost sight altogether of the question actually before them, spoke as follows:—

I think, therefore, that I may possibly do an acceptable service, if, studiously passing by all the extraneous topics which have been introduced into the debate, I confine myself entirely to the explaining the grounds of the vote which I mean to give this night, and so recal the attention of the Committee to the real question upon which alone we have on this occasion to decide. During the latter part of the debate, not only the question of restrictions in general, but all the various points connected with the whole complicated subject of the Regency, have been again discussed, as if the vote of to-night were to decide them all. But, in my apprehension, the question now under consideration lies within a very narrow compass. It is but a small part even of a small part of the whole subject; and, however it may be decided, it will not only not affect the other Resolutions, but not even decide finally the arrangements, to which it immediately relates. In giving my vote this night, I certainly reserve to myself the right, when the bill shall be brought in, of considering minutely the details by which the principle of the Resolution shall be carried into effect.

The question, then, immediately before us, is simply this, what degree of power, and whether any political power, should be granted to Her

Majesty, to whom, by the consent of all, the care of His Majesty's sacred person ought to be intrusted? In the settlement of this, as indeed of every other point of the Regency, I think those honourable gentlemen go too far, who recommend extraordinary caution in regard to the present proceedings, on the notion, that they are to constitute a fixed rule to guide all future Parliaments, who may be called upon to make provision for a similar emergency. In the present instance, I certainly have no hesitation in saying, that the Regency should, and ought to be committed to the Prince of Wales, and the care of His Majesty's sacred person to his Majesty's royal Consort: but I desire to be distinctly understood, that I do not consider myself as giving in this admission an opinion, that, in all future possible cases, either the Regency or the custody of the King's person must of necessity be so confided. I utterly deny, that we are, in these particulars, which are matters not of fixed principles, but of expediency and discretion, now settling an immoveable precedent for the future. This I have thought it necessary to say, in order to argue upon the present case with the more freedom.

The Resolution now before the Committee divides itself into three parts: first, that the custody of His Majesty's person shall be given to the Queen; on this point there is in the present instance no doubt or difference of opinion. The second, or rather the third point, as it stands in the order of the Resolutions, but I take it here to get it out of the way, is, that it is expedient that, for the due administration of this trust, Her Majesty should have a council; on that too, as a general proposition, there appears no difference of opinion. The intermediate proposition between these two, is that which forms the question for the present discussion; namely, whether the trust to be confided to the Queen shall be accompanied with a grant of political power; whether Her Majesty shall be enabled to remove not only the officers of His Majesty's household—of less consequence in a political view, though of great importance with regard to His Majesty's comforts—but also persons standing in the situation of great officers of state; whether we may not sufficiently provide for the comfort and dignity of His Majesty, without committing considerable political authority to hands, in which such authority has never before been constitutionally placed..

According to my view of the state of this question, if I were this night to vote for the original Resolution, I should at once decide affirmatively, that the Queen should have the power of removing sixteen great officers sitting in the House of Lords, and several others having seats in the House of Commons. The Amendment going, as I understand it, only to the object of taking care that a point of such importance shall not be hastily decided, the effect of adopting it would be, not to negative the grant of any power, but merely to decide that the whole shall not be granted, to allow sufficient time for deliberation as to the precise quantum of political power that ought to be lodged in the hands of the Queen. The Resolution goes at once to the decision of the whole case; the Amendment reserves it for more mature discussion and future decision. Between these two courses, with the doubts, which I confess I entertain upon the subject, I cannot but prefer that, which, pledging the Committee against nothing but the sweeping grant of the whole of the household, will not prevent the giving a due portion of power, even political power, to Her Majesty, by provisions to be introduced into the Bill, if, upon full consideration, it shall be thought wise or necessary to do so. Having only to choose between two propositions—one deciding the question at once, the other allowing time for consideration—and the question being in its nature and its consequences such, as neither to require nor to admit an instantaneous decision, I am disposed to adopt that alternative which affords further time for deliberation.

With regard to the exalted personage, the object for whom this provision is to be made, it is unnecessary to say, that he claims every attention, not only from his rank, but from being, as he is, so justly and tenderly endeared to the hearts of his subjects. Whatever may be the arrangement to be made for the care of His Majesty's sacred person, I hope I need not disclaim the giving any vote or opinion on the ground of any paltry and pitiful retrenchment. I would not economize upon the sufferings of my King; nor would I agree, that in the state in which he at present lies, he should be stripped of that splendour which must indicate to the world the consideration in which he is still held by his faithful and loving subjects. The royal diadem, however for the moment its lustre may be dimmed, is not to be altogether shorn of its beams. I would not in the infirmities of the man forget the station and character of the monarch. I would shade the chamber of his sickness, not with the curtain of oblivion, but with the veil of the sanctuary. I would place to guard it those, whom, if he should happily recover, he would be glad to find at his door. And that these chosen sentinels should be irremoveable by any power whatever is an opinion, which I shall submit to the House, when we come to the consideration of the details of the Bill. I think we should do our duty by taking care that the Sovereign shall have those about him whom he himself has chosen, so that, when, upon waking from his trance, he may pronounce some well known name, he may not be to be told "that he whom he calls for is not there." On this principle I should think it better to form an establishment for the Sovereign, somewhat smaller in extent, but not liable to accident or uncertainty, than to continue the household altogether on its present scale for a limited time, liable to change hereafter. I would rather take less, but have it permanent and unalterable, than have all for a limited time, subject to future retrenchment, and with a power to make any alterations in it, to whomsoever that power might be given.

It has been well observed that we do not legislate upon suspicion. Suspicion of the Prince of Wales is disclaimed by those who support the restrictions. I hope that those who may hesitate to concur in giving the whole power of the household to the Queen, will be equally free from the charge of entertaining any suspicion as to the mode in which Her Majesty would administer that trust. I can truly say, that I am not influenced in my opinions by any feeling of such a nature. The difficulty which I chiefly feel, in giving the power of removal to the Queen, is that of entrusting political power in hands where it had never formerly lodged, and thus creating an anomaly in the practice of the constitution. On the other hand, the Regent, for his own sake, if for no more weighty reasons, unquestionably ought not to have the power of removing or appointing the persons who are to surround the sick bed of the King. I see but one mode of obviating both these difficulties, namely, that of selecting that portion of the offices, the holders of which are called on more immediately to give their attendance on His Majesty's person, and fixing them immutably by law during the continuance of His Majesty's indisposition.

Perhaps I should still more completely discharge my mind, if I stated some more detailed view of this subject. First, then, my object is, that all those officers whose more peculiar duty it is to wait on His Majesty—such as the lords and grooms of the bed-chamber, the groom of the stole, &c.—should be put out of the power both of the Queen and of the Regent—should not be liable to be removed at all during His Majesty's indisposition. The expence of this establishment would be as nothing. State the whole at £16,000, of which £4,000 comes back in taxes into the coffers of the state; and what is such a sum compared with that degree of comfort, of tenderness, and compassionate and respectful care which belongs to such an arrangement?

I confess I should have been inclined to have added to the officers I have named the Lord Steward, had it not been for what has fallen from an honourable and learned member on the other side, (Mr. Adam). The details of the departments of the household form a very complicated and abstruse science, with which I do not pretend to be very accurately acquainted. I can, therefore, only state the application of the principle upon which I would act, so far as I have yet had an opportunity of acquiring information. How far the office of Lord Steward of the Household is in the situation stated by the honourable and learned gentleman, or whether it may safely be included among those which I have already mentioned, and made irremoveable, I am not at present able to form a determined opinion. At all events there would remain the office of Lord Chamberlain, an office now vacant; that of the Master of the Horse, and the two Golden Sticks; offices of pomp and show, which are necessary to the office of Regent, as having the command of the guards, to form the foundation of the Regent's household splendour. The splendour of the throne, as such, ought in my opinion to accompany the royal dignity, and be attached to the person charged with the executive power. I confess I think it is infinitely more desirable, that the Regent should exhibit himself to the country, clothed as far as possible in the insignia of his father's authority, than with any new and separate establishment, created for his new situation, and to pass away together with it.

The King's Lord Chamberlain, the King's Master of the Horse—perhaps also (but of that I feel less confident) the King's Lord Steward—officers, as they are not merely of domestic service, but of state, of pomp, and of political power, ought to be the officers of the Regent; and whoever surround his person, ought, of course, to be under his controul. On the other hand, whatever inferior officers, even in the departments of these greater officers of state, are near the person of the King, or employed in his immediate service, and generally all those of whatever rank or station who are objects of the King's personal choice —in short, who are strictly domestic, not state, and not political officers—ought to be fixed permanently and irremoveably around the King, to watch and wait his recovery. The distribution and detail of such a plan may be difficult and troublesome; but we cannot grudge the trouble, and we should surely be able to remove the difficulty. To obtain time for this purpose, I must vote for the Amendment.

But the Resolution is liable to still further objections. I cannot consent to the erecting, by a vote of one night, an independent political influence, which might by possibility be turned against the executive. I am far from thinking that the executive power is in a state in which it can admit of being diminished; but if it could afford to lose the political influence, now proposed to be transferred from it,—if this portion of the power of the executive is to be in a state of abeyance, then it ought to be in a state of abeyance entirely. What I propose would put the offices in question in a state in which, politically speaking, they could neither do harm nor good. It would render those offices of the household, whose attendance about the person of His Majesty is necessary, an independent body, not transferring the power of removing them to other hands, but making them not removeable. The right of appointing such officers should not remain in an authority co-ordinate with the Regent. If the influence belonging to such appointments does not go with the executive authority, it ought to be provided at least that it should not go against it. And if this be necessary for the power of the Regent, not less necessary is it for the comfort of the Queen. To give to Her Majesty great political power and Parliamentary influence, would be to change the very essence of her situation, to incumber her with new cares, solicitudes, and anxieties. We are not calling Her Majesty to an office of power, but delegating to her a tender, a delicate, a painful duty, which will occupy all her mind, and absorb all her attention. It would be an act of distressing generosity, a most mistaken compliment to Her Majesty, to burthen her with the distribution of political patronage; and to mix with the sacred trust devolved upon her in the custody of His Majesty's person, another trust of a totally different nature, and one which, constitutionally speaking, we are bound to consider as liable to abuse, not by Her Majesty, but by her advisers.

There is another objection, Sir, which I feel to this Resolution, which I do not know if any other gentleman feels in the same manner. My right honourable friend has said, that the period for which he proposes the present plan is short: that, till the expiration of that period, it is better to let things remain as they at present stand, and that it will then be necessary to reconsider and revise the whole plan; to retrench the household establishment of His Majesty, and place that of the Regent on a more enlarged and suitable footing. I cannot but feel that there is something not alone not soothing, but revolting, in the idea of holding out to the country two stages of proceeding, one as the period of hope, the other as the period of despair. I would much rather look to the question once for all, than again return to it hereafter, with the prospect of regarding His Majesty's disorder then as a permanent and incurable affliction. It is not the lapse of a year that can induce me to legislate for the indisposition of the King, as if it were his death. While there is life, there is hope. The arrangements which his illness makes necessary, are necessary now; what are unnecessary, ought not merely to be delayed, but ought not to be made at all. What ought to be made at all, I thought it had been agreed on all hands, ought rather to be made before the Regency is established, and while we have the power in our own hands, than left to the Regent and his advisers to propose hereafter. And surely, of all the points upon which we ought most carefully to avoid creating a necessity, or affording a plea for the Regent's interference, the royal household is the most prominent. It is that upon which our duty and our feelings most peremptorily call upon us to see justice done to the King. It is that, which, if it be not the most unsafe, is the most invidious to be left to the Regent. For all these reasons I disapprove of the original Resolution. The Amendment, as reserving for more deliberate consideration the question as to the exact proportions in which the household might be allotted to the Regent and to Her Majesty, I am bound upon my own principle to prefer. I shall therefore give my vote for that Amendment. The Committee on the Bill will be the proper stage, in which the details of the plan I have now submitted to the Committee can be discussed. I shall endeavour by that time to digest the opinions and principles which I have taken the liberty to state, into a shape in which I may venture to submit them to the House; unless my right honourable friend, or some other gentleman, shall in the mean time suggest some plan for our adoption, that shall appear to me free from the objections to which the present Resolution is liable.

The House divided—

For the fifth Resolution	213
Against it	226
Majority against the fifth Resolution . .	13

REGENCY RESOLUTIONS.

January 2d, 1811.

On the bringing up the Report of the Committee on the State of the Nation:—

MR. CANNING rose, amidst loud calls for the question, and said:—Sir, I can assure the House, that after the indulgence which I have already received during the course of these discussions, it is not my intention to trespass at any length upon their attention on this night. I do not rise merely for the purpose of expressing again the sentiments with which I have more than once had occasion to trouble them, or of declaring that I shall again vote in conformity with those sentiments. But I am anxious—I feel it due to myself—I deem it necessary for the explanation of my vote, and the justification of my conduct and motives, to protest against nine-tenths of the arguments, which have been urged on that side of the question which meets with my concurrence. My vote is governed by far other reasons than those which I have heard from the other side of the House.

If I am—as I decidedly am—of opinion, that it is not expedient to fetter the exercise of the Royal prerogative in the hands to which we are about to delegate the administration of it, by any of the restrictions which have been proposed to us, it is not because I disagree with my right honourable friends who have thought it their duty to prepare those restrictions, as to the undoubted right of this and the other House of Parliament to adopt that proposition, if it shall seem good and right to them so to do, and to couple the delegation, which it is their unquestionable province to make, with any conditions and limitations which they may think proper to annex to it. I agree, on the contrary, in by far the greater part of the able speech of my right honourable and learned friend who sits beside me (the Master of the Rolls)—in all that part of it, which went to establish the right of the two Houses to appoint a Regent, and to negative the existence of a right, or of any thing like a right in any person to claim that appointment at their hands—in all that went to prove the possession by the two Houses of a perfect and entire discretion to entrust, to the Regent of their own choice, such portion only of the executive power as they may think it necessary to entrust to him. But I differ from him wholly as to the practical application of these doctrines to the existing case—as to the fit use to be made of our discretion upon the present exigency. I am for giving the executive power as free and unfettered as possible into the hands of the Regent; but not because I think we have no right to withhold, not because I think he has any right to claim, the whole or any part of it: but simply because, in the full exercise of our right and our discretion, I think the exigency of the present times requires that no material portion of the functions of the executive government should be placed in a state of abeyance.

This is the practical question upon which the vote of this night is to decide. But surely to the decision of this question it was not necessary for those who agree in favour of the vote, in which I am also prepared to concur, for my right honourable friend, for instance, who spoke just now (Mr. Sheridan) to pursue the course of argument, which he has pursued through the greater part of his speech, and which every feeling of my heart, as well as every principle of fair reasoning, impels me to disclaim and disavow. Is my right honourable friend jealous of any concurrence of opinion upon the present occasion, except such as shall be founded on a participation in the dissensions and enmities of twenty years ago? Is it not enough for him to obtain our votes in his favour on the question of the present day? Does he consider them as not worth having unless we will also consent to go back with him to the transactions of 1789, and to enter into all the feelings and recollections of animosity connected in his mind with the discussions of that turbulent and agitated period?—unless we will join him in all that he alleges against his political antagonists of that day? Sir, I have heard these things from my right honourable friend (Mr. Sheridan) with peculiar pain: but he is not the first that has resorted to this singular species of reasoning. What advantage any man, or any set of men, can propose to themselves from substituting for argument upon the question now actually under discussion, attacks upon the characters of persons now no more, and particularly (what from my right honourable friend I should have expected less than from any other) upon the memory of that great man, who bore a principal part in the proceedings of that period, I am utterly at a loss to imagine. Can it be necessary in our present difficult and distressing situation—a situation sufficiently full of divisions and distractions—to rake up the ashes of the dead, for the purpose of kindling new flames amongst the living? For my own part I have the satisfaction to feel, that such is neither my opinion nor my practice. No man can accuse me of having ever gone out of my way, in any discussion in this House, to speak with disrespect of those who differed from Mr. Pitt when living, and who are now gathered together with him in the peace and shelter of the grave. For myself, and I hope for all those who have imbibed their political sentiments from the same master, I can confidently say, that we do not desire to erect an altar to the object of our veneration with materials picked from the sepulchral monuments of his rival. The character of him whom we reverence and regret, we are satisfied, may safely be suffered to rest upon its positive merits. It shines without contrast;—its lustre is all its own, and requires not the extinction of the reputations of others to make it blaze with a brighter flame.

I cannot—I own I cannot—conceive the feelings and policy of those who pursue an opposite system. I cannot understand the wisdom of reviving, at this moment, those party heats and political and personal animosities which the hand of death, one should have thought, might well be allowed to have closed; and which the progress of time might of itself be supposed to have obliterated. Is this the foretaste which the honourable and the right honourable gentlemen opposite think fit to give of the spirit in which their new Government is to be conducted? Entering upon a new scene of things, in which, even if they could forget and cause to be forgotten every subsisting hostility, every partiality and prejudice, by which the political men now living are divided, they would still have difficulties enough to encounter; do they think their administration requires any additional embarrassment? Or do they think that it will be a facility to it that they should array against themselves the wishes and the feelings of every man in this House and in the country who shares those sentiments, which it is my pride and satisfaction to cherish and to avow for my late illustrious and venerated friend? I doubt, Sir, if an undeserved attack upon that great man can add any thing to the strength of their future Government; I am sure it adds nothing to the force of their arguments on the question now before us.

But my right honourable friend (Mr. Sheridan) was not the first to introduce this invidious topic into our present deliberations. He has but followed the example of an honourable and learned member (Sir Samuel Romilly), who had last night the merit, if merit it can be called, of relieving the dry discussion of the question now at issue by opening an attack, as unjust as uncalled for, and as singular as either, upon the memory of Mr. Pitt. Sir, I then repressed my feelings, strong as they were at the moment, and resolved to abstain from any animadversion upon the honourable and learned gentleman's proceeding. My honourable friend opposite to me (Mr. Wilberforce) had executed that duty, in a way which left nothing to regret or to supply: and at the period of the debate at which it was my fortune to rise, I was more anxious to bring back the attention of the House to the real subject of the debate, than to lead it back to a topic which I hoped would not be reverted to again, and the introduction of which into these discussions, while I condemned it in others, I would not willingly countenance by my own example. But when I find that the honourable and learned gentleman's example is contagious—that even my right honourable friend (Mr. Sheridan) is infected by it —that it appears to be a measure of party to run down the fame of Mr. Pitt, I could not answer it to my conscience or to my feelings if I had suffered repeated provocations to pass without notice. Mr. Pitt, it seems, was not a great man. Is it then that we live in such heroic times—that the present is a race of such gigantic talents and qualities as to render those of Mr. Pitt, in the comparison, ordinary and contemptible ? Who, then, is the man now living—is there any man now sitting in this House, who, by taking the measure of his own mind, or of that of any of his contemporaries, can feel himself justified in pronouncing that Mr. Pitt was not a great man ? I admire as much as any man the abilities and ingenuity of the honourable and learned gentleman who promulgated this opinion. I do not deny to him many of the qualities which go to constitute the character which he has described. But I think I may defy all his ingenuity to frame any definition of that character, which shall not apply to Mr. Pitt—to trace any circle of greatness from which Mr. Pitt shall be excluded.

I have no manner of objection to see placed on the same pedestal with Mr. Pitt, for the admiration of the present age and of posterity, other distinguished men, and amongst them his great rival, whose memory is, I have no doubt, as dear to the honourable gentlemen opposite, as that of Mr. Pitt is to those who loved him living, and who revere him dead. But why should the admiration of one be incompatible with justice to the other? Why cannot we cherish the remembrance of the respective objects of our veneration, leaving to each other a similar freedom? For my own part, I disclaim such a spirit of intolerance. Be it the boast and the characteristic of the school of Pitt, that, however provoked by illiberal and unjust attacks upon his memory, whether in speeches in this House, or in calumnies out of it, they will never so far forget the respect due to him or to themselves, as to be betrayed into reciprocal illiberality and injustice —that they disdain to retaliate upon the memory of Mr. Pitt's great rival.

From the honourable gentlemen opposite I see we are not to expect similar forbearance—they are not so tolerant. Their feelings appear to be something like those of a catholic archbishop, of whom I have heard, in a foreign country, with which a treaty was not long ago negociating, in which treaty was inserted an article stipulating the toleration of the Protestant religion in that country. This stipulation was vehemently opposed by the archbishop; and when it was urged to his eminence that, as the catholic religion was tolerated in England, the protestant religion ought to be tolerated by the foreign prince: "The cases," he observed, "are widely different: the false religion is bound to tolerate the true; but it does not thence follow that the true religion ought to tolerate the false." It is on some such principle of reasoning, I suppose, that the gentlemen opposite, considering their creed as the only true political faith, and us Pittites as heretics, think themselves at liberty to give full licence to their attacks on the memory of Mr. Pitt, though never provoked to it by any wanton or intemperate reflections upon the character of that statesman, who is the theme of their praise and the object of their worship.

It is to me matter of equal regret and surprise, that any set of men should conceive that, by such means, they can either raise themselves, or strengthen their party. If persons of that description should become the advisers of the Regent, and if the system they mean to recommend is founded not on positive but on negative principles, not on a practical consideration of the true interests of the country, but on personal antipathies to those who have heretofore conducted its affairs, on a proscription of Mr. Pitt's foreign and domestic policy, and on a constant determination to detract from the memory of that great man (for so I hope I may still call him), my first wish is undoubtedly that His Royal Highness may disdain to act upon such advice. But even could I be brought to apprehend that His Royal Highness would adopt such a system, if recommended to him, and would act upon it, even that consideration would not alter my conduct to-night upon the question immediately before us. My principles indeed would compel me to differ from such a system of government when carried into effect; and whilst even to such a government I trust I should not give a factious opposition, I should undoubtedly feel it to be a duty to watch its measures with jealousy and suspicion. But even in the contemplation of that possibility, I would not now vote for disarming the Government of the Regent of any of those powers which are so necessary to its due efficiency, and which were originally given to the Crown as a trust for the benefit of the people. If all that the honourable gentlemen have had in view is to lessen the satisfaction with which a vote can be given, in favour of their amendment, by any man who agrees with them, not in party, but in principle, on this particular occasion, in that view they have succeeded. It is with reluctance that I concur in a vote supported by such arguments as theirs; but as the vote is in my judgment right, I must conquer that reluctance. I think it my duty to lend my feeble aid to constitute an executive government as strong as the constitution allows and the times require; confiding in the virtues of the illustrious personage to whom the power is to be entrusted, that no ill use will be made of it whoever may be his advisers; but confident that, whoever may advise him, or whatever their advice may be, the executive power cannot be so strong, but that Parliament will have strength, if necessary, to check and to controul it.

The first, second, third, and fourth Resolutions passed as originally proposed by the Chancellor of the Exchequer. Upon the fifth Resolution, which had been amended in the Committee by a majority of thirteen, (see p. 114), the Chancellor of the Exchequer divided the House, and his Amendment, which went to restore it to its original shape, was negatived by a majority of three.

For the fifth Resolution, as amended in the Committee	217
Against it	214
Majority	3

ON THE REPORT OF THE BULLION COMMITTEE.

MAY 8th, 1811.

Mr. HORNER, as Chairman of the Bullion Committee, moved the following Resolutions :—

First.—That the only money which can be legally tendered in Great Britain, for any sum above twelve-pence in the whole, is made either of gold or silver; and that the weight, standard, and denomination, at which any such money is authorized to pass current, is fixed, under His Majesty's prerogative, according to law.

Second.—That since the forty-third year of the reign of Queen Elizabeth, the Indentures of His Majesty's Mint have uniformly directed that all silver used for coin should consist of eleven ounces two pennyweights of fine silver, and eighteen pennyweights of alloy in each pound troy; and that the said pound troy should be divided into sixty-two shillings, or into other coins in that proportion.

Third.—That since the fifteenth year of the reign of King Charles the Second, the Indentures of His Majesty's Mint have uniformly directed, that all gold used for coin, should consist of eleven ounces of pure gold and one ounce of alloy in each pound troy; and that the said pound troy should be divided and coined into forty-four guineas and one half-guinea, or into other coins in that proportion.

Fourth.—That by a Proclamation of the fourth year of the reign of King George the First, it was ordered and directed, that guineas and the several other gold coins therein named, should be current at the rates and values then set upon them; *viz.* The guinea at the rate of twenty-one shillings, and other gold coins in the same proportion: thereby establishing, that the gold and silver coins of the realm should be a legal tender in all money payments, and a standard measure for ascertaining the value of all contracts for the payment of money, in the relative proportion of $15\frac{2859}{13640}$ pounds weight of sterling silver to one pound of sterling gold.

Fifth.—That by a statute of the fourteenth year of the reign of His present Majesty, subsequently revived and made perpetual by a statute of the thirty-ninth year of his reign, it is enacted, that no tender in payment of money made in the silver coin of this realm, of any sum exceeding the sum of twenty-five pounds at any one time, shall be reputed in law, or allowed to be a legal tender, within Great Britain or Ireland, for more than, according to its value by weight, after the rate of *5s. 2d.* for each ounce of silver.

Sixth.—That by a Proclamation of the sixteenth year of the reign of His present Majesty, confirmed by several subsequent Proclamations, it was ordered and directed, that if the weight of any guinea shall be less than five pennyweights eight grains, such guinea shall cease to be a legal tender for the payment of any money within Great Britain or Ireland; and so in the same proportion for any other gold coin.

Seventh.—That under these laws (which constitute the established policy of this realm in regard to money), no contract or undertaking for the payment of money, stipulated to be paid in pounds sterling, or in good and lawful money of Great Britain, can be legally satisfied and discharged in gold coin, unless the coin tendered shall weigh in the proportion of $\frac{20}{21}$ parts of five pennyweights eight grains of standard gold for each pound sterling, specified in the said contract; nor in silver coin, for a sum exceeding twenty-five pounds, unless such coin shall weigh in the proportion of $\frac{20}{62}$ of a pound troy of standard silver for each pound sterling specified in the contract.

Eighth.—That the promissory notes of the Bank of England are stipulations to pay, on demand, the sum in pounds sterling, respectively specified in each of the said notes.

Ninth.—That when it was enacted by the authority of Parliament, that the payment of the promissory notes of the Bank of England, in cash, should for a time be suspended, it was not the intention of Parliament that any alteration whatsoever should take place in the value of such promissory notes.

Tenth.—That it appears, that the actual value of the promissory notes of the Bank of England (measuring such value by weight of standard gold and silver as aforesaid) has been, for a considerable period of time, and still is, considerably less than what is established by the laws of the realm to be the legal tender in payment of any money contract or stipulation.

Eleventh.—That the fall which has thus taken place in the value of the promissory notes of the Bank of England, and in that of the country bank paper which is exchangeable for it, has been occasioned by too abundant issue of paper currency, both by the Bank of England, and by the country banks; and that this excess has originated, from the want of that check and controul on the issues of the Bank of England, which existed before the suspension of cash payments.

Twelfth.—That it appears that the exchanges with foreign parts have for a considerable period of time been unfavourable to this country, in an extraordinary degree.

Thirteenth.—That, although the adverse circumstances of our trade, together with the large amount of our military expenditure abroad, may have contributed to render our exchanges with the continent of Europe unfavourable; yet the extraordinary degree, in which the exchanges have been depressed for so long a period, has been in a great measure occasioned by the depreciation which has taken place in the relative value of the currency of this country, as compared with the money of foreign countries.

Fourteenth.—That during the continuance of the suspension of cash payments, it is the duty of the Directors of the Bank of England, to advert to the state of the Foreign Exchanges, as well as to the price of bullion, with a view to regulate the amount of their issues.

Fifteenth.—That the only certain and adequate security to be provided, against an excess of paper currency, and for maintaining the relative value of the circulating medium of the realm, is the legal convertibility, upon demand, of all paper currency into lawful coin of the realm.

Sixteenth.—That in order to revert gradually to this security, and to enforce meanwhile a due limitation of the paper of the Bank of England, as well as of all the other bank paper of the country, it is expedient to amend the act which suspends the cash payments of the Bank, by altering the time, till which the suspension shall continue, from six months after the ratification of a definitive treaty of peace, to that of two years from the present time.

MR. CANNING.—After the ample discussion which this question has undergone, I rise, Sir, not in the presumption that I am able to add any thing to the information which the Committee has already received from gentlemen the best qualified by their talents and their acquirements, by their professional pursuits and their official situations, to throw light upon the subject in all its principles and details; but simply for the purpose of stating the grounds of my own vote upon the several propositions which are submitted to our consideration.

In discharging this duty—a duty which I feel to be incumbent upon me as a Member of Parliament—I beg to be considered as speaking in that character only; as delivering freely and honestly, a sincere and unbiassed opinion, upon a question so important, that I did not think myself at liberty to let it pass without forming, to the best of my judgment, some opinion upon it; as neither adopting nor countenancing the prejudices of any set of men whatever; as neither the advocate nor the antagonist of the Bullion Committee; neither the advocate nor the antagonist of the Bank.

With respect to both those bodies, I firmly believe, that they have, each according to their measure, performed conscientiously a very difficult duty.

Of the Bank it is always to be remembered, that the condition in which they have found themselves has been none of their own seeking; that the original restriction, in 1797, was imposed upon them by Parliament, upon their own shewing indeed of their difficulties—difficulties, however, arising out of circumstances over which the Bank had no controul; and that the restriction was renewed after they had declared their readiness to resume their payments in cash. Of the necessity of the first restriction I have no doubt: of the policy of the terms upon which it was last renewed, I certainly entertain great doubts; but the error of that policy, whatever it may have been, is not justly to be visited on the Bank. Placed, as the Directors of the Bank have been by the effect of that last renewal, and by the events which have since occurred, in a situation perfectly novel; having—from the mere managers of the affairs of a great money corporation,—become, by the force of circumstances, the sole issuers and regulators of the whole currency of the country;—it is surely not to be wondered at that, in such a situation, they may have found the maxims of their original and habitual occupation either inapplicable to their new and enlarged sphere of action, or insufficient for it; and may have committed mistakes in the exercise of one of the highest prerogatives of the Sovereign, which they would easily have avoided in conducting the concerns of their constituents. If they have fallen into such errors, I am not inclined to blame them. I would correct the errors, but without imputation on the men.

On the other hand, I must as fairly confess that I think the Bullion Committee has been hardly dealt with in the course of these discussions. A stranger who had derived his only knowledge of the case from the debates of the two last nights, would almost have been led to imagine that the Bullion Committee was some strange and self-erected power, wholly extrinsic to the constitution, and independent of the controul of this House; who, without commission, and without provocation, had thought fit to intermeddle in the affairs of the Government and of the Bank, and to attempt the subversion of a system not only eminently beneficial, but confessedly without fault, without mischief, and without danger; a system with which all the world was perfectly satisfied in all its parts, until this officious Committee thought fit to disturb the general satisfaction. But what is the true history of this proceeding? A Committee was appointed last year by the House of Commons to inquire into the causes of the high price of gold bullion, and into the state of the foreign exchanges and of the currency of the country. They took these subjects into their consideration: they brought to that consideration talents and information such as have rarely been collected together in any one Committee of this House; and they bestowed upon it (that praise no man denies to the Committee) unremitted diligence and labour. The result of their investigations they submitted to the House, according to its injunction and to their duty. And because that result was to some persons unexpected, and is to others unpalatable, are we therefore justified in turning round upon the Committee of our own appointment, and rebuking them for the execution of the task which we had imposed upon them?—What would we have had them do? refuse the task allotted to them by the House?—or decline to render an account of the inquiries which we had ordered them to institute?—Or would we have had them fashion their Report, in spite of their own conviction, to the creed or the convenience of any persons or party, and recommend only whatever might best flatter our prejudices and justify our inaction?

If such were our wish, why was the Committee named? Why was not the proposal for its appointment rejected, or at least opposed? I was in the House on the day when it was proposed; and, so far as I recollect, not a single voice was raised against it. If the subject did not require investigation, it was idle, and not only idle, but mischievous, to set the investigation on foot. If it was apprehended that the possible or probable result might be prejudicial to the interests of the country, then was the time to stop. It would then have been perfectly easy to do so. A single word, the intimation of a doubt from any quarter of the House, might, at that moment, have checked the proceeding. But to institute an inquiry upon a matter of great difficulty, with a pre-determination to come to but one conclusion, is neither very creditable to those who appoint, nor very just to those who are appointed the conductors of it.

Although I do not go with the Committee (as I shall presently have occasion to explain) to the length of their practical conclusion ; and although the details of this intricate and perplexing subject are as little agreeable to my taste, or habits, as to those of any person in the House ;—although I would as gladly as any body have turned aside from the task of examining the reasonings and deductions of the Report ;—yet I cannot in justice throw upon the members of the Committee the blame of those inconveniences which are inherent in the nature of the subject referred to their inquiry. However much I may dislike the unpleasant truths which are told in the Report, I do not think myself warranted to transfer that dislike to those whose duty it has been to tell them.

The Committee, then, I say, have only done their duty. Nor can we avoid the performance of the duty which now devolves upon ourselves. Distasteful as the matter may be, it is before us, and we must dispose of it.

I do not share in the apprehensions of those persons who predict danger and mischief from this discussion. I have seldom known an instance in which more good than evil has not arisen out of the parliamentary discussion of subjects, however delicate, upon which the public mind had been previously agitated and divided.

As little do I agree with those who think that the discussion must necessarily be barren and useless. Even if it should not terminate (as probably it may not) in the adoption of the practical remedy suggested by the Committee, or in the suggestion of any other in its room, I do not think that the time and the trouble of the House will therefore have been entirely thrown away. The discussion which has already taken place out of doors, renders some decision of this House necessary. In the course of that discussion, the fundamental principles of our whole money system have been disputed and denied;—all that had long been considered as fixed and determinate in them has been shaken, or at least attempted to be shaken:—a mischief more serious than even that which the Committee has proposed to cure; and one to which a cure may be (and ought to be) administered by the Resolutions of this House, whatever may become of the practical recommendation of the Committee.

Nor is it only out of doors that these fundamental principles have been questioned. The right honourable gentleman opposite to me (Mr. Vansittart)—a gentleman for whom personally I entertain the sincerest respect as well as regard, and whose just reputation for knowledge upon these subjects entitles his opinions upon them to very peculiar attention—has countenanced, by himself adopting it, a mode of reasoning which has been much employed in the written controversy, but which I had hoped no man in this House, and least of all any man of such extensive information and such high authority would have been found to endure, much less to sanction. He has rejected altogether the established doctrine of a fixed standard of the currency of the realm; and, instead of trying the disputed value of our present circulating medium, by reference to that which has always hitherto been taken as the settled measure in all such inquiries, he has thought himself at liberty to bend and accommodate the fundamental principles of our money system to the state of our currency, such as he happens to find it.

Others who have supported the right honourable gentleman's propositions have carried this licence still farther. They have not only considered the principles of all our coinage laws, so far as they relate to the value of our money, as inapplicable to the present state of our currency, but as altogether obsolete. They appear to look upon the law by which Bank paper is made inconvertible into cash, not as an occasional law growing out of a temporary necessity, and determinable with that necessity, but as a wise and provident contrivance to substitute absolutely and indefinitely for the ancient coin of the kingdom, a currency better adapted in their opinion to the present state of the world and to the peculiar exigencies of this country. The suspension of the cash payments of the Bank had hitherto always been treated as a necessary evil; as an expedient upon which we were forced with reluctance, and of which we had the decency at least to pretend to desire and to anticipate the discontinuance: but, in the view of the subject which has been taken by these supporters of the right honourable gentleman's propositions, the Bank restriction is now become the staple resource in our pecuniary system; it is to be avowed as the standing policy of the State; and to be prized as an invention long desired, and now happily found, for supplying boundless exertion with inexhaustible and unexhausting finance.

The decision of the House, therefore, important as it would undoubtedly be, if it should either confirm the recommendation of the Bullion Committee, or substitute in its stead some other practical measure for the termination of the Bank restriction, will yet be not less (I had almost said will be more) important, if, even rejecting that recommendation, and confirming the continuance of the restriction, it shall nevertheless at the same time recognise the general principles which that Committee have laid down; and shall separate and distinguish the measure of the restriction itself, from the false and dangerous arguments by which it has been not only justified as an expedient, but recommended as a system.

To record principles which are true, and which have been called in question, is not of itself an idle nor an unparliamentary practice: and it is no paradox to say, that to record principles is never so much a matter of duty as when some over-ruling necessity obliges us to a practical departure from them. It then becomes incumbent upon us to prove that we are acting indeed from necessity, not from indifference or change of system; to take care that our deviation shall not be made a precedent to be resorted to hereafter on occasions of less urgency; to provide that the exception shall not be erected into the rule.

This then is the answer which I give to those who represent the concluding Resolution of the honourable and learned Chairman (Mr. Horner) of the Bullion Committee, as the only essential object of our deliberations; and who would persuade us that, if we are not prepared to decide with him upon the opening of the Bank, we have nothing to do with all his preliminary Resolutions but to get rid of them as quickly as possible. I, for one, am not prepared to vote with him for the opening of the Bank; I shall vote against the honourable gentleman's concluding Resolution: but I think that, according to all sound and practical views, the question, important as it is, whether the Bank shall be opened or shut, sinks into insignificance in comparison with that which has been raised with respect to the principles upon which the whole money system, and consequently the whole credit of the country, essentially depends.

Give me the affirmation by Parliament of the first ten Resolutions of the honourable and learned gentleman—those Resolutions which state (and state correctly) the principles of that money system, from which we have been compelled to depart, and the effects of our departure from them—and I would not unwillingly consent to a compromise with the right honourable gentleman opposite to me (Mr. Vansittart). I would, on that condition, adopt the two last of his propositions; adopt them in substance at least,—so far as to agree with him that this is not the moment at which our cash payments can be resumed, or at which the precise period of their resumption can be determined. The right honourable gentleman ought surely to be satisfied with this compromise. His conclusion would, to my mind, even flow more logically from the premises laid down in the Resolutions of the honourable and learned gentleman. I certainly cannot subscribe to it as flowing from his own. I am ready to do as he would have me do, if he will allow me to record the reasons of my concurrence: but it is a concurrence which, I feel, requires explanation and apology; it is a concurrence which, if I do not altogether withhold it, I certainly cannot give, except on the condition that I shall be at liberty to prove at the same time, that it is given not in consequence of the right honourable gentleman's reasons, but in spite of them. That our currency is in such a state that the Bank cannot safely open, I agree; but it is hard to insist that I should find every thing right in that state of things which forces me to come to such an agreement.

My right honourable friend, the Chancellor of the Exchequer (Mr. Perceval), has, with great dexterity, as well as eloquence, endeavoured to divert our attention from the specific object of this night's deliberation, by directing it to those circumstances in the present situation of affairs at home and abroad, upon which there is scarcely any difference of feeling or opinion. The inordinate ambition and gigantic power of the enemy, the warfare directed by him against our trade and our manufactures; these are topics upon which my right honourable friend has expatiated with a force of statement, and a warmth of language, which do full justice to his argument; and has appealed to us, whether we will wantonly aggravate difficulties already so complicated and so overwhelming? He has availed himself with equal skill of another argument, which he well knows would operate upon my mind with no less force than upon his own, and which, if I could indeed be convinced that it was legitimately applied to the question in the way in which he applies it, would lead me, I will not say to concur in his conclusions, but at least to hesitate in rejecting them. He refers to the recent triumphs of our arms; he places before our eyes the prospect of successes still more splendid; he describes the safety of this country as involved in the war in the Peninsula; and he asks us, how that war is to be maintained? how we are to find the means of keeping on foot that army which has already performed such brilliant achievements, and of seconding the exertions of the Commander who has carried the British name to the highest point of military glory? Shall such a contest—a contest for all that is interesting to this country and to Europe, be abandoned? Shall Lord Wellington be checked in his career? Shall Portugal have been liberated only to be again given up to slavery? Shall the hopes of Spain have been revived only to be finally dashed and extinguished? God forbid! My right honourable friend well knows that, in calling upon me duly to weigh these considerations, he interposes the surest impediment to any rash decision on my part, by which interests so dear to this country could by possibility be brought into hazard. He knows that I must put a violence upon myself before I can coolly calculate the real bearing of topics which come home so forcibly to my feelings; before I can dissipate the illusion which they throw round the matter in debate, and examine dispassionately the degree in which they really apply to it.

But I will not pay my right honourable friend so ill a compliment as to suppose that he is not himself perfectly aware, that in thus shaping his argument, he has, in fact, either assumed or omitted the question that is in dispute.—The question is not—whether we shall continue the war in the Peninsula with all our heart, and with all our might?—Who doubts,—who dissuades that determination? That point might have been assumed without hazard of contradiction. But my right honourable friend argues that point as if it were disputed:—and assumes without argument that which it was necessary for him to prove;—namely, that to the continuance of the war, and of our successes in the Peninsula, it is essential that the present system of our currency should remain unchanged. Just as fairly might I assume without argument, that a change in our currency is necessary to this same purpose of continuing the war;—and then retort upon my right honourable friend his own expostulations against fettering the energies, and cramping the exertions of the country. In either case the point which alone is in dispute, remains to be decided.

Why is the continuance of the present system of currency essential to the continuance of the war? Is it because that currency is in a sound state?—or that, being depreciated, a depreciated currency is the best instrument of foreign exertion? Which of these two propositions is it that my right honourable friend intends to maintain? I ask this question with the more earnestness, because throughout the whole of his speech, long, able, and eloquent as it was, I watched in vain for any sentence which distinctly expressed an opinion upon either of them. I did not hear him affirm that the currency was sound; I did not hear him admit that it was depreciated; he always stopped short of this affirmation and of this admission; and if any distinct proposition could be collected and embodied out of those topics with which he endeavoured to cover these simple questions, it seemed at most to amount to nothing more than this—that it was best to go on as we are, avoiding all inquiry on the subject.

To that proposition (if that be the proposition which my right honourable friend means to maintain)—I answer, that it comes too late. The period for acting upon that policy passed by when the House consented to the appointment of the Bullion Committee.

To the question, how shall our military exertions be best supported? I reply—By supporting the credit of the country; by ascertaining the soundness of our currency, if it be sound; by ascertaining the degree of its defect, if it be defective; with a view in the one case to apply a remedy so far as a remedy may be applicable; and in the other to fix and settle the public opinion, which of itself is no small ingredient in the financial resources of a state.

I have no right, and certainly full as little desire, to impute to my right honourable friend that he is avowedly the advocate of a depreciated currency: but this debate would end most unsatisfactorily for the public as well as for the House, if it were to end without its being clearly understood on what precise grounds my right honourable friend thinks the present state of our currency such as it ought to be.—First, whether he thinks it is not depreciated; secondly, whether, admitting it to be depreciated, he considers the depreciation as incurable, and therefore only would take no step to cure it; or, thirdly, whether he concurs with those who see in that depreciation a fertile source of wealth and blessings to the country:—these, after all, are the points in dispute,—and these points my right honourable friend appears to me to have studiously avoided.

Even in that part of his speech in which he approached the nearest to the question of depreciation, my right honourable friend so managed the course of his argument as to make it impossible that he should arrive at any definite conclusion.—With a semblance of candour which seemed as if he had adopted an inverted mode of reasoning as the best calculated in this particular instance for discovering the truth, he begins with examining the question of Excess—"Prove," says my right honourable friend, "that there exists an excess, and then I will be ready to go with you into an inquiry whether that excess has produced depreciation."—Now, it cannot be necessary to remind my right honourable friend, that to reason from effect to cause has always been the course of sound philosophy.—The Committee affirms the existence of depreciation; and, as that depreciation cannot arise from any doubt of the solidity of the Bank—of its ability to meet its engagements, they attribute it (unanswerably, as appears to me) to excessive issue. "Prove this excessive issue," says my right honourable friend. But how is positive excess (if I may use that expression) susceptible of proof? How is it possible to prove, that too many bank notes are issued, so long as there is a single applicant willing to receive them? The comparison of the amount of bank notes in circulation with that of the aggregate pecuniary transactions of the community, would of itself afford no certain criterion of the sufficiency or excess of that circulation—even if it were possible to state that comparison with any thing like accuracy. But who shall pretend to state the actual aggregate amount of all the pecuniary transactions of the community ? So far as a pretty general increase of prices is any symptom of excessive currency, that symptom undeniably exists. But I acknowledge it to be no more than a symptom. I admit further, that the mere amount of bank paper in circulation, however large it may be, does not of itself necessarily constitute excess. I admit that there is not excess, unless there be depreciation. Whether depreciation does exist or not, is, therefore, the question which must necessarily have the precedency in our examination.

The right honourable gentleman opposite to me (Mr. Vansittart), when he opened his counter-propositions to the House, put to my honourable friend near me (Mr. Huskisson), the question—"What do you mean by depreciation?" He put this question, rather irregularly, in the middle of his own speech; and seemed to think it matter of triumph that he did not receive, at that moment, an answer in a single word. An answer he has, however, since received, and I should imagine (in one sense at least) to his complete satisfaction. "By depreciation, do you mean discredit?" said the right honourable gentleman. If by "discredit," the right honourable gentleman means a doubt of the solidity of the Bank, a doubt whether the outstanding demands upon the Bank do not exceed the amount of their assets; unquestionably no such doubt exists, and consequently "discredit" enters for nothing into the "depreciation" of Bank of England paper.

But when the right honourable gentleman has obtained this concession, it appears to me that he has obtained nothing at all towards overthrowing the arguments of his antagonists, or towards establishing his own. For the same concession would be equally true with respect to a paper currency which should represent to its full amount the whole moveable and immoveable property of the country. There would be assets in existence adequate to the redemption of that paper. Of a paper issued to such an amount, although resting on such unquestionable security, it is probable that my right honourable friend (Mr. Perceval), who spoke last, would not dispute the excess; yet how could that excess be indicated except by depreciation? That depreciation, in the case which I have supposed, the right honourable gentleman (Mr. Vansittart) could not deny; but he must acknowledge that it would arise from other causes than discredit. The argument, therefore, or rather the suggestion (for it has not been distinctly argued), that there can be no depreciation unless arising from, or accompanied with, discredit; and the inference which is covertly insinuated, that they who affirm bank notes to be depreciated, intend to attack the credit of the Bank, entirely fall to the ground.

The alleged depreciation of bank notes consists in this—that, whereas they did in fact represent heretofore the real as well as the nominal value of the coin which constitutes our lawful money, they now represent its nominal value only. This is the answer to the question of the right honourable gentleman.

In return, my honourable friend proposed a question to the right honourable gentleman, to which I think he has not yet given any answer. "If you affirm," said my honourable friend, "what I deny, the equivalency of bank notes to money, tell me, what is the common standard by which you measure that equivalency?" This question the right honourable gentleman has altogether evaded. He has given no answer to it.—Does he mean to acquiesce in those which have been given for him by others who have taken the same side with him in this debate, or by some fanciful writers, who, under the guise and garb of practical men, have indulged themselves in the wildest theories and imaginations, upon this subject of the standard?

"The coin," says a noble Lord, "is, or was, the standard of the paper." But this description does not advance us a single step? for the question still remains, "What is the standard of the coin? What is that common measure to which coin and paper may be equally referred for the purpose of ascertaining their agreement, or disagreement, with it, and with each other?"

The noble Lord has indeed devised a singular definition of this measure, in which I should be exceedingly curious to know whether the right honourable gentleman concurs. He defines it to be "a sense of value in reference to currency as compared with commodities."—I hope I do not misquote him. To the best of my recollection, these were the very words—"A sense of value!" But whose sense? with whom is it to originate? and how is it to be communicated to others? Who is to promulgate, who is to acknowledge, or who is to enforce it? How is it to be defined? and how is it to be regulated? What ingenuity shall calculate, or what authority control its fluctuation?—Is the "sense" of to-day the same as that of yesterday, and will it be unchanged to-morrow? It does fill me with astonishment that any man, of an accurate and reasoning mind, should not perceive that this wild and dangerous principle (if principle it can be called) would throw loose all the transactions of private life, all contracts and pecuniary bargains, by leaving them to be measured from day to day, and from hour to hour, by no other rule than that of the fancies and interests of each individual conflicting with the fancies and interests of his neighbour.

A "sense of value!" It is not many days since an experiment was tried upon this "sense," which may serve to illustrate the probable course of its operations, if left exclusively to its own guidance. The artisan who on the Thursday night had exchanged a one-pound note with his neighbour for four dollars, found in the morning that he had, insensibly to himself, become two shillings richer by the exchange. I am not, here, about to enquire whether the Bank were right or wrong in raising the denomination of the dollar; I refer to this operation merely as an illustration of the argument: and I ask, Where would be the end of such operations if every individual's "sense of value" were to be his only guide in his dealings with his neighbours? In this instance the authority of the Bank sanctioned and limited the degree of the rise in the current value of the dollar, or, to put the same thing in other words, the degree of the loss which the bank note should sustain in exchange against the dollar. But, is it to be imagined that,—if they had merely sanctioned the principle of such alteration, without limiting the degree,—two shillings in the pound, or ten per cent., is the precise amount of the rise on the one hand, or of the depreciation on the other, which all the holders of bank notes, and of dollars respectively, would have agreed to fix by a common "sense of value?" Is not such a supposition utterly absurd? Is it not clear that something wholly extrinsic to that capricious "sense," is necessary to regulate the ordinary dealings between man and man; and that the course of those dealings could not be left without a guide, but at the hazard, or the certainty rather, of immediate and inextricable confusion?

If, however, we were persuaded to leave the proportions and prices of all commodities to be adjusted by this "sense of value," we ought at least to be consistent in our theory and practice. This "sense of value," which is now proposed to be erected into an universal measure, has been occasionally adopted as such by individuals. There is a man now expecting the judgment of the law, whose "sense of value" led him to exchange for guineas a proportion of Bank of England paper, which he considered as no more than an equivalent. Of what crime was this man guilty, but of obeying that natural and instinctive impulse which the noble Lord is now prepared to set up as a substitute for the standard of our money? If there be nothing more fixed and stable than individual feeling, to which the estimate of values can be referred, let us at least refrain from punishing the exercise of that individual feeling. If the law shall decline to fix a standard measure, it cannot reserve the right of visiting erroneous measurement as a crime. This would be an injustice like that of the eastern monarch who called upon the soothsayers to interpret his dream, but refused to tell them the dream of which he required the interpretation.

No dream, it must be owned, could be more extravagant than the visions of those practical men who have undertaken to refine away the standard of the currency of the realm into a pure abstraction. There is indeed something perfectly ludicrous in the inconsistency and injustice with which they impute a love of abstraction to their opponents, while they are themselves indulging in the most wanton departures from substance and reality. "Beware of abstract theories," say they to the Bullion Committee, when they find fact and law laid down as the foundation of its Report. "Beware of abstract theories," say they to the honourable and learned Chairman of the Committee, when they find, in his first seven Resolutions, nothing like theory or imagination; but a clear, concise, a dry and faithful, recapitulation of those rules which the statutes of the country have established for the weight and fineness of its coin. Nor has the speech with which that honourable and learned gentleman introduced and enforced his Resolutions—a speech which, remarkable as it was for eloquence and ability of every kind, was by nothing so distinguished as by its perpetual appeal to acknowledged principles and established law,—even that speech has not rescued the honourable and learned gentleman from the imputations of flightiness and romance.

The same caution, to "beware of abstract theories," is addressed to my honourable friend near me, whose intelligence, whose accuracy, and whose official knowledge, digested and assimilated by a powerful and really practical understanding, make him perhaps, of all men, the least proper object of such an admonition. And this admonition comes from whom? from the inventors and champions of "abstract currency;" from those who after exhausting, in vain, every attempt to find an earthly substitute for the legal and ancient standard of our money, have divested the *pound sterling* of all the properties of matter, and pursued it, under the name of the "*ideal unit,*" into the regions of nonentity and nonsense!

When the ingenious sophistry of Dr. Berkeley, to prove the non-existence of matter, was quoted to Dr. Johnson as a fallacy not easy to be refuted, Dr. Johnson stamped his foot with force against a stone, and exclaimed, "I refute it thus." Unluckily, I know no process of reasoning that can reduce one of these practical men to the necessity of admitting, that a pound sterling is not a creature of the imagination: one cannot appeal even to their senses, because that sense of theirs, which I suppose is the most conversant with this subject, the "sense of value," is enlisted on the other side. But one may appeal from their theories to ancient records, to positive institution, and to existing law. On those authorities, I contend that a certain specified weight of gold, or silver, of a certain fineness, is the only definition of a pound sterling which an Englishman, desirous of conforming to the laws of his country, is bound to regard or to understand.

Here then it is that I should pause for the answer of the right honourable gentleman opposite to me to the question of my honourable friend.— Does he admit or deny this definition of standard? does he admit or deny the existence of a standard at this moment conformable to this definition? If he admits it, then it is possible not only to answer his question with respect to the meaning of the word "depreciation," but also to demonstrate that a depreciation, in the sense in which that word is used, does exist. Grant but the lawful standard as the instrument of mensuration, and nothing is more easy than to assign the exact proportion in which coin and bank notes differ in value from each other. But while the right honourable gentleman denies the existence of any such instrument, how can he reasonably require that the accuracy of such a measurement should be proved to his satisfaction?

A pound sterling is either $\frac{20}{62}$ of a pound of standard silver; or, $\frac{20}{21}$ of a guinea weighing not less than 5 dwts. and 8 grs. This is the simple and the only definition which the practice of our ancestors recognises, and the law of the country allows. Does a one-pound note represent this portion of the precious metals, or does it not? If it does, the legal coin of the country, and the notes of the Bank, are equivalent. If not, either the law is mis-stated, or the depreciation is proved.

"Oh! but," says the right honourable gentleman, "the bank note represents the coin itself, *quatenus* coin; and has no reference or relation to the quantity of gold or silver which that coin contains." But does not the right honourable gentleman see that it is impossible for him to avail himself of the law in one instance and to deny its operation in the other?—The King's proclamation confirmed by Act of Parliament has fixed the denomination of the coin; which denomination it is admitted on all hands, the bank note continues to represent: but the same Act of Parliament has fixed the weight of the coin as the sole and indispensable test of the value which that denomination implies. The law (as the right honourable gentleman well knows) watches with such scrupulous anxiety over the weight of the guinea, as to consider the loss of a single grain as sufficient to destroy its character as a legal coin. When the law evinces this anxiety about weight, is it not a little too much to assume in argument that its only care is denomination?

But what is the proposition for the sake of which this assumption is hazarded? Not simply that bank notes are a convenient symbol of coin, but that they are actually equivalent to it. In proof of this equivalency it is contended that the law has bound them together.

First, this argument would prove too much: it would undoubtedly get rid of all the embarrassing considerations of standard, of weight, and of intrinsic value; but, on the other hand, those who maintain it would be involved in absurdities, which even the ingenuity of the right honourable gentleman could not reconcile. They would have to maintain, for instance, that in the year 1695, when, previous to the resolution taken to reform the silver coinage, arguments something like those which are now used on the right honourable gentleman's side of the question, prevailed upon the Legislature to try the experiment of a statute by which it was made penal to receive or tender the unclipped coin at any higher price than the clipped coin—they would have to maintain, I say, that from the passing of that act, the clipped and unclipped coin of the country became precisely equivalent; in other words, that an ounce of silver in the one became, by the operation of the statute, equal to an ounce and a quarter of the same silver in the other. Unquestionably this cannot be what the right honourable gentleman is prepared to maintain as true; though I must admit, on the other hand, that a subject of this country might at that time have been punished for acting as if he thought it false. But is the relation which was thus produced by law between two things, obviously of different values, equivalency? Or is it to be imagined, that so forced and unnatural a state of things, call it by what name you will, could be maintained by any law, that any law could continue long in force whose purpose it was to maintain it? The consequence of this state of things in 1695, was the disappearance, that is to say, the hoarding, the melting, or the exportation of the perfect coin: the further consequence was, that, after a short trial of the compulsory law, Parliament found itself obliged to go to the root of the evil, and to reform the depreciated part of the currency.

But, moreover, the right honourable gentleman's assertion of the equivalency of coin and bank notes, is in direct contradiction with admissions of his own. In the course of this debate he has admitted (though others have denied) that in the year 1804 the paper of the Bank of Ireland was depreciated. I might here ask him in what sense he understands the word depreciated, when he so applies it; and he would have to answer me, as it has been answered to him, that the Irish bank note did not then represent the intrinsic value of the coin with which it was interchangeable.

This is a most important admission on the part of the right honourable gentleman; and it has a bearing upon the present question, of which one would almost apprehend he could not have been aware, but which nevertheless he will find it difficult to deny. The premium, as I understand, in 1804, was about one shilling and sixpence on the guinea. At that period Irish Bank paper, as interchangeable with English, was at a discount which pretty nearly corresponded with its depreciation in reference to the coin. The premium now openly paid in Ireland upon guineas is from three and sixpence to four shillings. But Irish Bank paper is now exchangeable with English nearly at par. Whence is it that English Bank paper, which had an advantage over Irish Bank paper in 1804, when Irish paper was depreciated only about seven and a half per cent. should be now nearly on a par with it, when it is confessedly depreciated almost twenty per cent. If indeed English Bank paper has suffered a depreciation to the same amount, this phenomenon is perfectly intelligible: but upon the hypothesis of the perfect and unchanged equivalency of English Bank paper and coin, it admits of no solution.

To my mind, I do confess, here is one decisive proof of depreciation.

But, is not the case of the dollar (to which I have had occasion to refer with another view in a former part of the argument), itself a conclusive proof, not only of the existence of a depreciation of Bank paper, but of the opinion of the Bank, and of the Government, that such depreciation does exist? Why was the bank note, which was equivalent to four dollars on one day, worth two shillings less than four dollars the next? Those who claim to themselves exclusively the title of practical men, take a subtle distinction, and say that it is not the bank note which is worth less, but the dollar which is worth more: and they treat as theorists and visionaries all whose faculties do not enable them to enter into this distinction. But, however the variation arose, why did the Government and the Bank think it necessary to sanction and promulgate it? Why? but because the dollar, being a coin circulating in this country by sufferance only, a currency of convention, would, according to the admission, or rather the declaration of the Bank, under the authority of the Privy Council, have been driven out of circulation, that is to say, would have been hoarded, or melted, or exported, if it had not been allowed to pass at the marketable value of the silver which it contains.

With this example before their eyes—with this admission and declaration still recent before the eyes of the public, there are yet some persons who contend, that the disappearance of our legal coin—the guinea—is no proof of the depreciation of bank notes, in respect to that coin; but is entirely owing to the balance of trade and of payments, and to the wiles of our inveterate enemy. The bank note, which, confronted with the dollar, shrunk from twenty to eighteen shillings, preserves, as they affirm, in face of the guinea, an unaltered, and unalterable equivalency. And what is it, according to their theory, that occasions this peculiarity? The law. The law, which does what? The law, which makes it criminal (if indeed it be criminal) to exchange the guinea for more than its denominative value in bank-notes; and which prohibits the exportation of the legal coin of the realm.

Let us see what is the mode in which these powerful and beneficial laws are now actually operating. The result which they were intended to obtain confessedly was to keep our legal coin at home, and to maintain it in circulation. The result actually is, that such coin has vanished from domestic circulation, and that it is exported to all parts of the world. The dollars were sent into circulation, unprotected by any law which should prevent their exportation to foreign countries: for a time they circulated in abundance; at length they began to disappear. By what process has it been attempted, and successfully, to check their disappearance? By the same process which it so wisely contrived to prevent the disappearance of guineas? By forbidding more to be given for them than they had hitherto been exchanged for in bank notes? No, but by a precisely contrary process—by allowing the dollars to pass at, or above, their value. The consequence is, a continued circulation of dollars in this country, in spite of the balance of trade and of the wiles of the enemy.

Here, then, are two metallic currencies, one of which continues in circulation, while the other vanishes from it. The distinctive differences between them are: First, that of one the exportation is permitted, and of the other prohibited. I acknowledge the perversity of human nature, and its proneness to do what is forbidden: but I cannot think that principle alone sufficient to account for the exportation of the coin, which it is illegal to export, and for the continuance in circulation of that which might be exported without offence. Secondly, the one is exchangeable for its full marketable value in our domestic currency, whereas the law enforces (or is supposed to enforce) the exchange of the other at no more than its denominative rate. The bank note is the common measure both of the guinea and of the dollar, of the exportable and unexportable coin: the guinea it is allowed by law to measure only according to its denomination; the dollar, by the ordinance of the Bank, it is allowed to measure according to its marketable value. What is the result? The coin, which is by law unexportable, flies to another market, while the exportable remains at home.

But let it, for argument's sake, be conceded that the rise of the dollar is not a proof of depreciation in the bank note. It follows then, that if the bank note, which would heretofore have purchased four dollars, is not depreciated in respect to the dollar, because it is now obliged to call in in two shillings to its aid in order to make the same purchase, neither would the bank note, which heretofore purchased a guinea with the aid of one shilling only be depreciated in respect to the guinea, if it should now be allowed to make the same purchase with the aid of four or five shillings. I think I may defy the most practical of men to quarrel with this proposition.

Well, then, if this be so, and if it be indeed an object to keep our guineas at home, why is not the operation, which has been so successful with respect to the dollar, applied to the guinea? What difference is there in the principle? and what difference in the practical policy of the transaction, but such as would preponderate in favour of the guinea? If it be answered, "that the guinea is a legal coin, which the dollar is not; that the dollar might be treated as arbitrarily and unceremoniously as we pleased, but that the same experiment could not be tried upon the guinea, without an alteration of the law, and that alterations of the law are dangerous;" I reply, that the law is much less in our way on this point than gentlemen seem to apprehend. It is true that the dollar is a foreign coin, of which our laws take no specific cognizance; but it is equally true that there is another coin in the country not a legal coin—a coin of which the law takes no notice, except to put it out of its protection; which no man is obliged, or even permitted, to receive from another in payment; which, in short, is as completely devoid of the qualities of British coin as the dollar, and indeed more completely so, since it is expressly stripped of those qualities by statute. Now, if such a coin as this can be found, where is the harm of trying upon it the same experiment which has been so happily applied to the dollar; especially if it be, as fortunately it is, a gold coin, and therefore capable of supplying that share which dollars do not supply towards the completement of a metallic circulation? The coin to which I allude is one which my honourable friend near me (Mr. Huskisson) is accused of having treated in his pamphlet with exaggerated respect, but which, in the course of this debate, has, I think, been too much disparaged—I mean the light guinea.

The light guinea is not, any more than the dollar, a legal coin. A guinea having arrived by wear at a certain degree of lightness, is at once divested by law of all its qualities of coin, and is reduced to its intrinsic value, whatever that may be, as bullion. It happens to be sure, at the present moment, that this reduction, as measured in bank notes is a promotion. But that is equally true in respect to the dollar. The rate at which the dollar now passes is not only higher than it was some time ago, but higher than that which it bears, from its intrinsic value, in comparison with the legal coin of the country. Whether it was right to raise the denomination of the dollar, I do not think it necessary to give an opinion :—that is done. But upon the principle, whatever it was, on which the denomination of the dollar was raised, there can surely be no objection to suffering the light guinea to go for what it is worth, and thereby obtaining an anomalous gold currency to correspond with the anomalous silver currency, each alike independent of the legal coin of the realm.

The legal coin — the guinea of full lawful weight—would still remain, in the eye of the law, in that of the imagination, and in the argument of the right honourable gentleman, as the equivalent for bank notes. It would not often come forth indeed to afford a practical illustration of his argument: but he might continue to enjoy the satisfaction of maintaining, as he does now, as an abstract proposition, that bank notes and guineas are equivalent in law.

Meantime the advantage derived from the marketableness of light guineas would be, either to retain at least that portion of our metallic circulation at home, or to make the foreigner or the enemy pay its full value for it on exportation.

It is on all hands acknowledged—by the right

honourable gentleman and his supporters it is earnestly contended, that our gold finds its way out of the country, either in discharge of the balance of payments, or into the coffers of the enemy. That enemy is by some persons represented as sitting like a great spider in the midst of its web, and drawing along the living lines and fibres of its net all the gold of Great Britain, into an abyss from which it is never to return. By what process this can be effected, except by that of a trade of some sort or other, we are not told, and I am at a loss to conceive. Among all the dangers of the country, many of them real and formidable, a danger happily more visionary than this was never apprehended by a disordered imagination.

That our gold, however, goes from us, is generally asserted and believed; and whether by a natural efflux, or by some unheard-of power of magnetic attraction in Buonaparte, is, in regard to the question which we are considering, of little moment. It goes, and we wish to stop it. It can be stopped effectually only by being retained in circulation at home. It can be retained in circulation (as those who raised the denomination of the dollar, and who gave the reasons which were given for raising it, must of all men be the last to deny,) only by allowing it to pass for what it is intrinsically worth, or what it will fetch in the market.

Here, however, I shall be met by an argument which has been urged with much vehémence and solemnity by the right honourable gentleman (Mr. Vansittart), that the law absolutely prohibits the exportation of our coin, and that any reasoning, therefore, which is founded upon the supposition of that exportation, is not only incorrect, but is of a most immoral and dangerous tendency, as holding out encouragement to perjury and fraud. Let us examine this argument.

We are all agreed upon the fact, that gold bullion is at a high price in the currency of this country. We are all agreed, that either as the consequence of this high price or as the cause of it, or both, there is a great scarcity of gold bullion in this country. We are all agreed that the gold coin has nearly vanished from circulation; and nobody doubts, so far as I have heard, and nobody has asserted more strenuously than the right honourable gentleman and those who side with him, that this high price and scarcity of bullion, and this vanishing of our gold coin, are infallible indications of a large exportation of gold; of which exportation a large part must, as infallibly, have consisted of coin, either melted or unmelted. Upon these facts, I say, we are all agreed. Now I ask, is it not idle, is it not absurd, to assume for the purpose of argument a supposed obedience to the law, which notoriously has no existence; and to deny for the purpose of argument, a fact which is acknowledged by all to be the surest symptom, and contended by many to be the origin and cause, of the evils which have brought us to the necessity of the present discussion? Is it not wholly unworthy an assembly of legislators, to pretend an ignorance in our legislative capacity of that, which every one of us, in his individual capacity, perfectly believes to be true? Is the existence of a statute which, as we know, is openly violated (and for the most part with impunity) every day in the week, to be pleaded as a bar against any attempt to remedy the evils which confessedly result from its violation?

What then can be more unjust, or more ridiculous, than to represent those persons as countenancing and encouraging perjury and fraud, who only tell you what you yourselves avow, that perjury and fraud are and have always been committed under your present system of law; and who, inferring that they always will be committed under that system, suggest to you the expediency of amending it? Who are the encouragers of crimes?—they who, finding the existing law notoriously inadequate to counteract the temptation to commit them, propose either to change the law or to remove the temptation;—or they who content themselves with whimpering over the depravity of human nature, and, instead of endeavouring to prevent the commission of crime, console themselves with the reflection that the mischief to the public is only in proportion to the guilt of the criminal?

He was not an unwise or unjust judge, of whom it is recorded; that—

> "He sent the thief who stole the gold away,
> And punish'd him who put it in his way."

Undoubtedly it is neither wise nor just to place temptations in men's way, which we know by constant experience to be sufficient to overpower the positive enactments of law. It is neither politic nor moral to resort on every occasion to the obligation of oaths as supplementary to a defective legislation. This policy unfortunately pervades too many of our statutes; and it is but rarely successful in its object, never perhaps where considerable gain and great facility conspire to tempt to perjury. The exportation of coin, or of bullion melted from coin, when the exchanges are unfavourable beyond a certain limit, is looked upon as so much in the natural course of things, that most writers, who have treated of coinage and of trade, have laid it down as a consequence not to be disputed, and not even necessary to be proved. According to the concurrent opinions of such writers, the efflux of bullion from one country to another is governed by causes nearly as steady and uniform in their operation, as those which govern the seasons or the tides. As well might you pretend to fix a limit on the shore, and bid the flowing ocean advance no farther, as attempt by the interposition of a statute to stop the tide of the precious metals in whatever direction it is made to flow by the influence of commercial necessity and commercial demand.

The right honourable gentleman, and those who adopt his views of the present question, acknowledge the force of these principles: they attribute, in fact, the whole of our difficulties to their operation. There is, indeed, a slight difference of opinion among them as to the cause of the export of our gold; some attributing it to the demand for gold in the market of the continent, others to the necessity of remitting it from hence, in payment of the balance of trade; but all concurring that, whatever may be the degree in which either of these causes, separately or jointly, operate, the result is an irresistible attraction of the gold of this country to the continent. Is it not, then, with marvellous inconsistency that these same gentlemen oppose the mere existence of a powerless law, and a high-coloured description of the crimes which it occasions and constitutes, as an answer, and the only answer, to those who contend, that, if the evil which the law is intended to prevent, be indeed one which it is important to check, and if the efflux of our gold be certain, so long as the force of the temptation is stronger than the restraint of the law, it is necessary, and it would be as wise as humane, either to alter the law, or to diminish the temptation?

I may, perhaps, be inclined to believe, that the repeal of this law would be in itself no unwise measure. That belief might be supported by the opinion of many able writers and experienced statesmen, and by the example of many of those states in which commerce has been most flourishing, and credit and coin most abundant. I admit that the immediate, the momentary effect of this repeal, (if unaccompanied by any other measure), might be to increase the exportation of our gold, by removing the scruples of such persons as may now, perhaps, be wavering between temptation on the one hand, and obedience to the law on the other. Even so, however, it would have the benefit of saving all that perjury and fraud which shock, so justly, the moral feelings of the House; and of extending to the honest trader a convenience which is now exclusively reserved for the dishonest one. But in the long run, I certainly do not believe that the repeal of this law would swell, by a single guinea, the amount of the export of our gold.

It is true that the repeal of this law alone would not have a necessary tendency to bring gold again into circulation in this country, either by recalling what has been exported, or by enticing what is now hoarded, out of its hiding places. That would be the effect of the other alteration to which I have already alluded, of suspending the law and the proclamation which limit the current rate of the guinea, and permitting it to pass according to its intrinsic value.

I have, indeed, stated this proposition hitherto only as applicable to the light guinea; of which the purchase, at its intrinsic value, is certainly no infringement either of the letter or the spirit of any existing proclamation or statute. I do not know whether I might, without presumption, say, that the law is by no means clear on this point, even with respect to guineas of full legal weight. Guineas of legal weight, however, I left out of my proposition in the former part of my argument, expressly, as I said, in the hope of conciliating the right honourable gentleman, by leaving untouched, in respect to guineas of full weight, his proposition of the equivalency of bank paper and legal coin. But, if the right honourable gentleman should be disposed to concur with me at all, I trust, upon reflection, he would not be prevented from doing so by the contemplation of this trifling advantage to his argument. If he will consent to let guineas go for what they are worth in the market, he will have a gold currency; he will prevent the exportation of our coin; he will get rid of fraud and perjury: and all this benefit he will purchase at no greater expense, than that of being one argument out of pocket. It will then, to be sure, be vain for him to contend, against the daily evidence of men's senses, that bank paper and guineas are, at their respective denominations, equivalent to each other: but at least we shall have them both, and they may circulate amicably together.

That by no other possible means the coin of the country can be retained in circulation, so long as the precious metal of which it is composed, is intrinsically of a value so much higher than the rate at which it is estimated in our currency, is a proposition of which all experience, as well as all reason, establishes the truth. The present state of the law in the present state of our currency, operates, in fact, as a bounty upon the exportation of our coin.

Of the two causes of the export of gold, which are admitted by the right honourable gentleman and his friends, the supposed demand for gold on the continent, and the supposed necessity for exporting it to set right the balance of our trade, the first will undoubtedly have an uncontrolled operation, so long as there is no counter-demand for gold in the market at home; so long as the Bank do not purchase, and as no one else purchases here, except for exportation: the second would, in a natural state of things, find its limit far within the amount of the balance to be set right; it would cease to operate, whenever the scarcity of gold, produced here by exportation, and the plenty produced on the continent by its importation, rendered gold less eligible for transmission abroad than any other merchantable commodity. But this limit it can never find, so long as gold is the only merchantable commodity for which the consumption of this country affords no market.

Independently, however, of these causes, the difference between the real value of the precious metal and that at which it is rated in our currency, would be itself sufficient to ensure us against the continuance of a guinea in circulation. Demand on the continent might be counteracted by demand here; and gold would cease to be a preferable article for transmission abroad, from the moment at which it, like other articles, could be sold for its real value at home. But, imprisoned in the coin, and degraded by its imprisonment, gold has an unconquerable tendency to escape from a situation so unnatural: and it would make its escape from such a situation, even although you do not owe the continent any thing; and although there were no more demand on the continent for gold, than for any other article of merchandize.

But this, I may be told, is the language of theory. Is not the principle, then, recognized by any sober practical authority? Let us hear the statute-book itself. "Whereas it has been a practice," says the preamble to the Act 14 Geo. III. c. 70, "to export the new and perfect coin of the realm for private advantage, and to the great detriment of the public; and the like practice will continue," (adds this theoretical and visionary preamble), "while pieces, differing greatly in weight, are current under the same denomination, and at the same rate of value."

The persons who framed this Act, and framed it for the express and practical purpose of restoring the credit of our currency, could not be ignorant of the penalties under which the exportation of coin was prohibited; yet we see, that in spite of these penalties, they take for granted as inevitable the "continued" exportation of the coin, so long as the temptation to export it continues. We see further, that, in their opinion, conformity to standard weight is the distinctive quality by which the value of money is to be estimated. We see, lastly, that, without any reference to demand for gold on the continent, without any reference to an unfavourable balance of trade, the certain result of an attempt to circulate together, "under the same denomination and at the same rate of value," two descriptions of currency, differing in intrinsic value from each other, is to drive that which is of the higher intrinsic value out of circulation.

This is, in fact, as I understand it, the whole of the Bullion Committee upon this subject; and so far from having the guilt or the merit of novelty, we find it assumed six and thirty years ago, in the preamble of an Act of Parliament, as a doctrine established and self-evident.

Of this doctrine, thus adopted by Parliament in the year 1774, there is an earlier and not less authoritative recognition in the Report of Sir Isaac Newton, in the year 1717, of the existence of which Report I was surprised to hear a right honourable friend of mine, (Mr. Rose) declare himself entirely ignorant. A person so distinguished as my right honourable friend unquestionably is, by great knowledge and indefatigable research, I should have thought, could hardly have missed a document of such interest and importance, and so immediately bearing upon the subject before us. This Report was made by Sir Isaac Newton in his capacity of Master of the Mint, and is to be found in our Journals.*

It is too long for me to trouble the House with reading it; but gentlemen will find, upon looking into it, that upon a reference made to him by the Lords of the Treasury, as to the best method of preventing the melting down of the silver coin, Sir Isaac Newton represents the temptation to melt and export it as "arising from the higher price of silver, in other places than in England, in proportion to gold;" that is to say, from the

* Vol. XVIII. p. 664.

circumstance, that the silver coin, then our standard currency, was, by the regulations of our Mint, exchangeable with the gold coin at a rate somewhat lower than that at which it was exchangeable, as bullion, with gold in the general market of Europe. So small was this difference, that the taking of sixpence from the current rate of the guinea was estimated by Sir Isaac Newton as sufficient to cure the evil; and yet, small as this difference was, during its continuance, and by its operation alone, the silver coin of standard weight was daily vanishing from circulation.

In this Report of Sir Isaac Newton, and in the principles which are laid down for it, is to be found the answer to many of my right honourable friend's (the Chancellor of the Exchequer's) observations upon that part of the Report of the Bullion Committee, which refers to the re-coinage of the silver currency in the year 1696. The subsequent disappearance of the new silver coin, is not, as my right honourable friend seemed to insinuate, a proof that the re-coinage at that time had been unadvisedly undertaken; or that it was not the only cure that could be applied to that depreciation of the currency, which Parliament had attempted in vain to remedy (as I have already had occasion to state) by a penal law. It is true that, by a slight error in the valuation of the two precious metals with respect to each other, the silver coin was rated a small degree below its just proportion to gold; and that, in consequence, it began to disappear not long after the re-coinage was completed. But this technical error does not in any degree vitiate the principles on which the re-coinage had been adopted. It in no degree diminishes or affects the merit of those who had the courage to undertake, and the firmness to carry through that important work, in spite of the prevalence for a time, even in this House, of prejudices very much akin to those of the present day.

Those prejudices were sufficiently strong to defeat for a considerable time the intentions of the Government, after they had upon mature deliberation convinced themselves of the absolute necessity of the measure; but the good sense, temper, and perseverance of that Administration triumphed in the end, and it is no disparagement to my right honourable friend to recommend the example of the Administration of 1696 to his serious consideration.

The war in which King William was then engaged against France, may not have been equal with the present war in magnitude of exertion. Yet if we compare the means of the country at that period with its present means, and consider the exertions which were then made, it would perhaps be difficult to say that any excuse could be offered now, which was not in a great measure applicable then, for sparing, amidst the burthens of war, any internal effort which was not absolutely indispensable. But the restoration of the currency to a sound state was then deemed to be indispensable; and the war was considered not as a reason for postponing the required effort, but as an additional reason for making it with as little delay as possible.

The high price of gold was then, as it is now, one striking indication of the deteriorated state of the currency. The indication might, indeed, be at that time more undeniable; because, gold not being then our standard coin, and the guinea not being limited by law as to the rate at which it should pass current, the high price became immediately visible in the gold coin as well as in bullion, the guinea being actually exchangeable for as much as thirty shillings of the clipped silver. The unfavourable state of our exchanges with foreign countries afforded then, as it does now, the other most unerring proof that all was not sound in the currency of this country; a proof of which my right honourable friend the Chancellor of the Exchequer clearly admits the validity, when he admits that the unfavourableness of the exchange might probably now be corrected by correcting the excess, or (if he objects to the word *excess*) diminishing the abundance of our paper currency. This admission I understood my right honourable friend to make in the most unequivocal terms; not meaning thereby that I understood him to admit that it was advisable to diminish the paper currency for the sake of correcting the unfavourableness of the exchange, but simply that such a correction of the exchange would be the effect of such a diminution of paper.

This leads me to consider the subject of the exchanges, as it bears upon that of depreciation. I shall treat it as concisely as I can; both because I must confess, that with all the attention which I have bestowed upon it, I am perfectly conscious that I have not been able to unravel all the intricacies of the subject; and also, because it appears to me that the whole question as to depreciation is disposed of by the preceding part of the argument; that is to say, by the comparison of currency with bullion. The state of the exchanges may add some illustration to that argument, but is not wanted for the purpose of establishing it.

If that which constitutes the par of exchange between any two countries be (as, if I am not mistaken, it is) an equal quantity of precious metal in their respective currencies, this definition alone sufficiently shews, that whatever other considerations there may be, whether growing out of law or out of opinion, which regulate and sustain the rate of a currency at home, its value can be estimated abroad by no other criterion than that of the quantity of precious metal for which a specific portion of it is exchangeable. The foreigner knows nothing of the value of the currency of any other country except that a certain portion of that currency represents, and will procure in his own country a certain quantity of precious metal.

The question of the exchanges would therefore be as simple as the question of depreciation, if there were not confessedly other causes which operate upon the exchange, and the operation of which may sometimes be concurrent with that of the relative values of the respective currencies, and sometimes may tend to counteract it.

A country which imports from another more than it exports to it of all other articles of commerce, is supposed to make up the difference by a transmission of bullion. In point of fact, this transmission takes place in much fewer instances than the theory supposes; but the necessity of making it either actually or virtually, causes a variation in the rate of exchange in favour of the creditor, and to the disadvantage of the debtor country; the amount of which variation is measured by, and expresses, the cost of making the transmission.

Supposing the currencies of two countries, each in a perfectly sound state, any variation from the par of exchange between them can be produced only by the one country having a debt to discharge to the other. Supposing the debts and credits of two countries to be exactly balanced, any variation from the par of exchange between them can only be produced by a depreciation in the currency of one of them. These causes, however, may both exist at the same time; and they may exist, either on opposite sides, or together; in the one case aggravating, in the other counteracting each other.

A country might be largely in debt to another, and yet, if its currency were sound, and the currency of the creditor country deteriorated, the course of the exchange would exhibit only the difference between the contending effects of such deterioration on the one hand, and such debt on the other: and it might happen that these effects might be so precisely balanced, as exactly to neutralise each other. But when a country is in the situation of being indebted to another, and at the same time of having a depreciated currency, the depression of the exchange exhibits the combined effect of both causes

This last may, or may not, be our present situation. For I am far from taking upon myself to assert, that the balance of the payments from us to the Continent, enters for nothing into the amount of the unfavourable exchange against this country. I only deny that it can be the sole cause of that unfavourableness. Still less do I pretend to define the share which this cause may have in producing the effect. But as it is obvious that the depression of the exchange from this cause can never, for any great continuance of time, very far exceed the expense of transmitting bullion for the liquidation of the balance of payments; as it is not only acknowledged but contended, that bullion for this purpose is in fact transmitted; as the expense of the transmission is perfectly known, in all its several parts of price, freight, and insurance; and as their collective result is notoriously very far within the limits of the actual depression of the exchange, there will remain of that depression a large share to be accounted for, after every deduction that can be made on account of the balance of payments, and that remainder can no otherwise be accounted for than by the deterioration of our currency.

The state of the exchanges, therefore, is a proof, though I do not admit it to be a necessary proof, still less could I allow it to be the test, of a depreciated currency. I do not admit it to be a necessary proof; because, the price of bullion in the currency, is proof sufficient without it. I do not allow it to be the test; because, under certain circumstances, a currency might be depreciated to a limited degree, without producing a visible depression of the exchange; nay, it might coexist with an exchange positively favourable. These cases would arise whenever the effect produced upon the exchange by the balance of payments in favour of the country whose currency is depreciated in the one case exactly equalled, or, in the other exceeded, the degree of the depreciation. But though a depreciation of the currency might thus exist without inducing an unfavourable exchange, a state of the exchange unfavourable to a great degree, and progressively growing worse for a great length of time, is an infallible indication of a depreciated currency.

This is all the use that I think it necessary to make of the arguments to be drawn from the exchanges; and so far as this goes, I cannot understand how any one can doubt as to their bearing. We do not doubt with respect to other countries, that a sound or unsound state of their currency influences the state of their exchanges. When we see the exchanges between Hamburgh or Amsterdam on the one hand, and Russia or Austria on the other, unfavourable in a great degree to either of the two latter countries, we have no hesitation in at once ascribing that unfavourableness, in great part at least, to a depreciation of its currency.

My right honourable friend (the Chancellor of the Exchequer) has taken what I must think not a very fair advantage of an argument of an honourable gentleman opposite to me (Mr. Sharp), when he has represented him as having recommended the general policy of Holland and of Hamburgh as an object of imitation for this country; because, the honourable gentleman stated that by not issuing a paper-money, the currencies of Holland and of Hamburgh had been preserved from depreciation. The honourable gentleman certainly did not guard and qualify his statement with all the circumstances which were nevertheless obviously connected, in his mind, with the proposition which he was advancing; but it is quite as clear that nothing but the strong temptation of flying from argument to declamation, could have led my right honourable friend so far to mistake the honourable gentleman's meaning. The meaning of the honourable gentleman evidently was not to hold out Holland as having been wise in its submissions and compliances towards France, and as enjoying the reward of her prudent obedience in a state of enviable happiness and prosperity. Still less could he intend (how is it possible that any rational being could be for a moment suspected of intending?) to extol the prowess of Hamburgh. "Prowess" was, I think, the word which my right honourable friend did not disdain to put into the honourable gentleman's mouth, for the sake of making an indignant comment upon it. The scope of the honourable gentleman's argument I understood to be simply this:—that if Holland, impoverished by an exhausting war, and preyed upon by an exacting despotism—if Hamburgh, in the very clutches of the French power—if these unhappy states, stripped of their commerce and independence, could yet maintain their respective currencies undepreciated, it would seem to follow that a state of war, however expensive and burthensome—that stagnation of commerce—that even the oppression of a conquering enemy—were not sufficient justifications, much less necessary causes, of such a system of currency as that which (according to the honourable gentleman's argument) now existed in this country, and of which my right honourable friend and others seemed prepared to justify the continuance, so long at least as the war shall continue, as our commerce shall be embarrassed, and as our enemy shall persevere in his present system of measures. This is what I understood the honourable gentleman to contend; and, whatever might be the worth of his argument, it surely was not open to the imputation which my right honourable friend found it convenient to attach to it; as if the honourable gentleman had been guilty of the egregious absurdity of proposing for the imitation of this country the political courage of the Dutch, and the military prowess of the Hamburghers.

I am not, however, disposed to deny the assertion which my right honourable friend has grounded upon this argument, that inferences are not to be conclusively drawn from the establishments of other countries, whether political or commercial, to our own. The principles of public credit are so much better understood, and so much more religiously observed in this country, the line of separation between the financial operations of the State, and the concerns of the National Bank, confounded too often by arbitrary governments, is here so distinctly marked, that it cannot be doubted but many general propositions are true of paper currencies abroad, which would be utterly inapplicable to the system of the Bank of England.

The depreciation of the Austrian paper money, therefore, which has been cited and commented upon by my honourable friend near me (Mr. Huskisson), is not precisely an example; it is not a counterpart of our actual situation; but it does afford a most useful warning, it shews how rapidly paper money sinks in value, when once power has been in any degree substituted for confidence; and how tremendously, when once the first impulse has been given, the force of descent accumulates and increases. The depreciation of Austrian paper was not, in its origin, like that which we are now discussing; there was, in its origin, something of discredit, of a distrust (that is) of the solidity of the funds upon which the paper was issued.

If solidity of funds, however, were alone sufficient to keep up the credit of a paper, even the assignats of France would not have fallen so soon and so rapidly in value. The rulers of France by whom that paper money was coined, affected to be surprised at the depreciation of securities, resting, as they contended, on foundations more solid than those of the Bank of England—and calculated, like the paper of the Bank, to promote the prosperity of the country in which it circulated. Well and wisely did Mr. Burke, when, in the language of an orator, and in the spirit of a prophet, he foreshewed that series and succession of calamities, which the principles of the French Revolution, in all its parts, must inevitably produce—well and wisely did he describe those essential qualities of the paper of the Bank of England which constitute its real value.

"They (said he, speaking of the National Assembly) imagine, that our flourishing state in England is owing to bank paper, and not the bank paper to the flourishing condition of our commerce, to the solidity of our credit, and to the total exclusion of all idea of *power* from any part of the transaction. They forget that in England not one shilling of paper money of any description is received but of choice; that the whole had its origin in cash actually deposited; and that it is convertible at pleasure, in an instant, and without the smallest loss, into cash again. Our paper is of value in commerce, because in law it is of none. It is powerful on Change, because in Westminster Hall it is impotent. In payment of a debt of 20l. a creditor may refuse all the paper of the Bank of England. Nor is there among us a single public security, of any quality or nature whatsoever, that is enforced by authority. In fact, it might easily be shewn, that our paper wealth, instead of lessening the real coin, has a tendency to increase it; that instead of being a substitute for money, it only facilitates its entry, its exit, and its circulation; that it is the symbol of prosperity, not the badge of distress. Never was a scarcity of cash and an exuberance of paper a subject of complaint in this nation."

These were the characteristics of the paper of the Bank of England, when Mr. Burke contrasted it with the assignats of France. Its convertibility into specie upon demand, was suspended by the Act of 1797, on grounds which it is not now necessary to discuss. The suspension was, for a series of years, unattended with any symptoms that indicated depreciation. And it must be our wish, as well as our interest, to believe (what from reasoning also appears most probable), that this suspension alone, if not followed up by excessive issue, might have endured, as long as the political circumstances of the state might have rendered its endurance necessary, without producing that effect. But if that effect has been produced, as seems to be established beyond the possibility of contradiction, let us not, instead of attempting to correct it, endeavour rather to palliate its evils, and to reconcile ourselves to its consequences. Even under the change produced by the temporary suspension of cash payments, let us remember, that the essential and fundamental principles upon which the character and the utility of bank paper rest, are those described in the extract which I have just quoted from Mr. Burke. Let us not, under the pressure of what has been always considered as a temporary necessity, and in the despair of meeting what I trust is no more than a transitory, and, as yet, a curable evil, abjure this language and these doctrines of Mr. Burke, and adopt in their stead the cant and sophistry of those against whom his arguments were directed.

Far be it from me to imagine that between the notes of the Bank of England and the assignats of the National Assembly, there now exists that resemblance of which Mr. Burke, in 1791, denied and disproved the existence! But in proportion as I am satisfied that the bank note is of a different nature from the assignat, in that proportion do I dislike to hear them defended by the same arguments. "*Ce n'est pas l'assignat qui perd, c'est l'argent qui gagne,*" was the motto and the doctrine of a treatise, published in Paris during the reign of the National Assembly, for the purpose of maintaining the credit of assignats, by accounting for the difference between their nominal and exchangeable values. "It is not the bank note which loses, but the dollar which gains," is the argument by which we have heard the rise in the denomination of the dollar explained: "It is not paper which has fallen, but gold which has risen," is the argument which has filled all the pamphlets and all the speeches which we have read and heard upon the subject. The arguments are identically and undistinguishably the same. I wish that any of my honourable friends, who maintain the undepreciated state of our paper currency, could satisfy me and the country that there is some essential difference in their mode of applying them. I wish they could shew me that the doctrine of the French pamphlet might be false, while that of the English pamphlets and of their own speeches is true.

I do not need to be reminded of the many essential differences in the circumstances of the two paper currencies. I am here speaking, not of the causes of depreciation, but simply of the fact. That assignats were discredited in all sorts of ways, no person doubts. But the price of the precious metals in those assignats was, after all, the evidence and the measure of their depreciation. The high price which other commodities bore in assignats, afforded, to be sure, strong suspicions of depreciation; but it proved the fact, and established the degree of that depreciation only as compared with the price for which the same articles could be obtained in gold or silver. I say this to guard myself against the imputation of disparaging bank notes by comparing them with a currency so notoriously worthless and fraudulent. Paper currency may be depreciated from various causes, which have no resemblance to each other; but whatever may be the causes of depreciation, the test of it is in all cases the same.

On all these grounds, I own my entire, though unwilling conviction, that a depreciation of our paper currency does actually exist;—that the permanently unfavourable state of the exchanges with foreign countries, is an indication—and the long continued high price of bullion at home, the proof—of it. I can at the same time most truly say, that I shall hold myself infinitely indebted to any man who, by reasoning and argument, by reference to admitted facts and established principles, can bring me back from this most unsatisfactory conviction. No man set out in the examination of the subject with less disposition to arrive at this conclusion: and no man would more gladly find reasons that could satisfy his own mind for receding from it.

I confess, however, that although I can make full allowance to others for the same unwillingness which I have felt myself, to believe in the fact of an existing depreciation, I am more alarmed than encouraged by the apparent disposition rather to escape from the avowal of this fact, than to controvert it. I cannot see, without concern, the constant flight from the point at which the controversy really lies, to the war, to the harvest, to Portugal, and to Buonaparte; in short, to every imaginable topic, except those on which the discussion essentially turns. This may confuse and perplex the argument, by raising a crowd of images, with which it has no relation. But as to the point at issue, it seems to me a confession of weakness, rather than a display of strength.

Still greater is my apprehension, when I hear what are the motives assigned for continuing the present state of our currency, whatever it may be, rather than making any attempt to decide what that state really is, and, if necessary, to correct or to improve it. Some persons there are indeed so sanguine and extravagant, as to deny altogether that either improvement or correction is necessary; or, that the ideas which these words convey, can be applicable to a system which they consider, not as an evil, but as a benefit. We have been told of "localised" currency, of an "insulated" circulation, as a blessing far outweighing all the other advantages arising from our peculiar local situation; as something analogous to them; something which was wanting to complete the perfection of our insular character, and which we have fortunately stumbled upon by accident; for I think no man has been hardy enough to say, that we could have or ought to have established it by design.

One honourable gentleman (Mr. Baring) only,

I think, has gone back to the origin of the Bank restriction in 1797, and has imputed to the great man who was the author of it, an intention of laying in that measure the foundation of a system of fraudulent finance, and of providing for an indefinite extension of the public expenditure abroad, by retrenching the just value of the payment to the public creditor at home. This is the imputation brought forward by that honourable gentleman: and, while I fully acquit my right honourable friend (the Chancellor of the Exchequer) of any participation in this sentiment, I cannot but express my regret that he should not have distinctly disclaimed it; especially as he thought proper to bestow such lavish and unqualified commendation upon the speech in which it was contained, and to declare, in more large and positive terms than I think he would upon reflection be disposed to confirm, his concurrence in the general views and doctrines of that speech.

But acquitting my right honourable friend altogether of the wildest and most extravagant of the tenets which have been advanced by persons who admit and admire a depreciated currency, I see cause of sufficient alarm in those which he has avowed and maintained. If the causes of the present state of our currency be, as he says, the unfavourable balance of our trade, and the necessary extent of our war expenditure; if, so long as those causes continue to operate, gold must, as he contends, continue to flow out of the country;

if nothing can contribute to recal it, except a turn of the exchanges in our favour; if that turn can never be produced, except either by the previous turn of the balance of trade in our favour, or by the reduction of our paper currency; if the balance of trade, having been turned against us by the anti-commercial decrees of our enemy, must continue against us till those decrees are repealed; and if, of the only other expedient for correcting the exchanges (viz., the reduction of our paper currency), my right honourable friend, while he admits the efficacy to be probable, denies the application to be possible;—I am afraid the result of this series of propositions, every one of which I collect from the speech of my right honourable friend, is, not only that we have no remedy for the present evil, but that we are likely to arrive at a term, when all our exertions for the safety of the country must cease, from our absolute inability to maintain them.

The precious metals are necessary to feed and sustain our military operations abroad. In all former wars, what went out in bullion for military purposes, was replaced in the course of trade by fresh importations. But now, according to the argument of my right honourable friend, our commerce itself is but another drain for our bullion, and must continue so long as the enemy pleases. The time, therefore, must come when the stream—always flowing, and never replenished—will be exhausted; and when, consequently, all the operations, whether of war or of commerce, to which it gave motion, will stand still. This, I beg it may be remembered, is not my statement: it is that which I collected from the speeches of those who profess to see nothing requisite to be set right in the present system of our currency. It would be a statement of complete despair, if there were absolutely no check in nature for the course and progress of the mischief. One check, one only check, there is—a check, as I should think, safe as well as effectual. But while we are comforted with hearing from my right honourable friend that such a check might, in his opinion also, be effectual, we hear from him, at the same time, that it would be absolute destruction to resort to it.

In addition to these motives of policy, there are—as I have heard this night, not without astonishment and dismay—considerations of justice, which preclude any systematic reduction of the amount of our paper currency. Such a reduction, it is argued, would change the value of existing contracts, and throw into confusion every species of pecuniary transactions, from the rent of the great landed proprietor down to the wages of the peasant and the artisan. Good God! what is this but to say, that the system of irredeemable paper currency must continue for ever? What is it but to say, that the debts incurred, and the contracts entered into, under the old established legal standard of the currency, including the debts and contracts of the State itself, are now to be lopped and squared to a new measure, set up originally as a temporary expedient; and that the sacredness of public faith, and the obligation of legal engagements, are to be conformed to the accidental and fluctuating derangement, and not to the ancient and fixed rule of our currency?

If this be so, there is indeed no hope that we shall ever return to our sound and pristine state. This objection is of a nature to propagate itself indefinitely. Every day new contracts must necessarily be made; and every day successively (as it is of the essence of depreciation to go on increasing in degree), at rates diverging more and more widely from the real standard from which we have departed. Every day, therefore, must interpose additional impediments to a return to the legal standard. Never did the wildest and most hostile prophesier of ruin to the finances of this country venture to predict that a time should come, when, by the avowal of Parliament, nominal amount in paper, without reference to any real standard value in gold, would be the payment of the public creditor. But still less could it ever be apprehended that such a system was to be built on the foundations of equity and right—that it would be considered as unjust to give to the paper creditor, the real value of his contracts in gold, but just to compel the creditor who had trusted in gold, to receive for all time to come the nominal amount, whatever that might come to be, of his contract in paper.

This proposition appears to me so monstrous, and shews so plainly to what an extravagant and alarming length we are liable to be hurried, when once we have lost sight of principle, and given ourselves up to the guidance of expediency, that I am sure this House ought to lose no time in pronouncing its opinion as to the maxims by which, for centuries, the currency of this country has been preserved in eminent purity and integrity; and in declaring its determination to acknowledge no others in the theory of our money system, and to look to a practical return to that system, not only as advantageous to the state, but as indispensable to its justice and its honour.

For these purposes, it is in my opinion necessary, in the first place, to enter a distinct record of what is, in our opinion, the legal standard of our currency. I know not how this can be done with greater clearness and correctness, than by adopting the first* seven of the Resolutions proposed by the honourable and learned Chairman of the Bullion Committee.

To these seven Resolutions are opposed, and for them it is intended to substitute, the first of

* See Res. 1 to 7, of Mr. Horner.

the Propositions of the right honourable gentleman opposite to me.*

I should have no hesitation in affirming these first seven Resolutions, if they stood simply and positively on their own merits: but when I find that we cannot get rid of them without admitting into their place a Proposition so exceptionable as the first Proposition of the right honourable gentleman, and one which, when admitted, will bring in its train other Propositions still more exceptionable—one in particular (I mean the third) absolutely repugnant (as it seems to me) to common sense—I consider the affirmation of the original Resolutions as doubly important, not only from what it will establish, but for what it will exclude.

This is not the time to discuss the Propositions of the right honourable gentleman; otherwise it would be easy to shew that the doctrine of his first Proposition, which, referring every thing relating to the money of the country exclusively to the prerogative of the Crown, states, as altogether equal and indifferent, the exercise of that prerogative by the will of the Crown alone, or with the concurrence of the two Houses of Parliament—that this doctrine, if not absolutely false in principle and in theory (a question which I will not now discuss), is, at least in any practical view, and to any practical purpose, unsound: it is incomplete, delusive, and dangerous; it states the

* See Res. 1, of Mr. Vansittart.

prerogative, indeed, but it does not state it as defined and regulated by law. This, however, is a part only of the objections to the right honourable gentleman's Propositions. There are others which I shall reserve till the moment, if unhappily that moment shall arrive, when it becomes itself the subject of substantive discussion. What I have now said, in my opinion, is sufficient to disqualify it as a substitute for the precise and unimpeachable definition of the monetary system of this country as established by the joint authority of the Crown and Parliament, which is contained in the honourable and learned gentleman's first seven Resolutions.

If I do not go at large into those Resolutions for the purpose of explaining and defending the vote which I shall give in favour of them, it is because, in the whole course of this debate, I have not heard a single objection urged against them. It is singular that the whole skill of his antagonists should have been exhausted, not in attacking, but in evading his statement; that, of a chain of reasoning, which, if it could be loosened in a single link, would, I admit, fall to pieces, not a single link has been attempted to be loosened. It remains entire and unbroken, and connects undisputed premises with an inevitable conclusion.

The eighth and ninth Resolutions * of the

* See Res. 8 and 9 of Mr. Horner.

honourable and learned gentleman contain truisms which no man disputes; and which the right honourable gentleman, in proposing to substitute for them his second Proposition, only makes less completely true by the omission of one essential circumstance. The eighth Resolution states, that the notes of the Bank of England are stipulations to pay *on demand*. The right honourable gentleman's second Proposition omits the words, *on demand*. Why this omission? It can hardly be accidental; it can hardly be without some meaning: and yet the right honourable gentleman, so far as I have heard, in the speech with which he introduced his Propositions, did not offer any thing to account for so singular an alteration. Is it possible that he can mean to say, that bank-notes are *not* stipulations to pay *on demand*? It is perfectly true that the restriction law of 1797 suspends the fulfilment of this stipulation, and protects the Bank against the consequences of a refusal to fulfil it: but does not the right honourable gentleman see the danger of confounding two things so different as the temporary suspension of the effect of an obligation, and the actual annulment of the obligation itself? I am almost sure that the right honourable gentleman must, upon reflection, be aware of the perilous tendency of such a confusion. But, in the mean time, forasmuch as a correct and complete definition is preferable to one which is undeniably and dangerously defective, I cannot hesitate to vote for the eighth and ninth of the original Resolutions, to the exclusion of the right honourable gentleman's most unnecessary and most suspicious amendment.*

The tenth† of the original Resolutions contains a clear, indisputable, and (as I have before described it) inevitable conclusion, from the state of the law, as accurately laid down in the preceding Resolutions, coupled with the notorious and undisputed fact of the high price of bullion. The truth of the averment contained in this Resolution is not directly denied. The dispute is only whether that which is admitted to be true is not nevertheless unfit to be recorded. It is not denied that the exchangeable value of bank notes is at this moment considerably less than their denominative value, if those values respectively be measured in gold or silver; but it is disputed whether gold or silver be the fit measure of the value of Bank notes. This is in effect the whole of the argument, not upon this Resolution only, but upon the whole in dispute. It is the single point on which all our discussions turn.

I have already discussed this point so much at length, and have so nearly (as I am afraid) exhausted the patient indulgence of the Committee, that I do not think myself at liberty here to recapitulate the arguments upon it. I will content

* See 2d Res. of Mr. Vansittart.

† See Res. 10, of Mr. Horner.

myself with asking of those who maintain a contrary opinion, and particularly of the right honourable gentleman (Mr. Vansittart), " If the precious metals, and particularly that one which is the legal standard of the currency of the country, be not the proper measure of the value of that currency, what is? The right honourable gentleman has his answer ready in his third Proposition: and a most curious one it is.* "Public estimation" is, according to the right honourable gentleman, the true standard measure of the value of a currency; and the common measure of the two parts of a currency as compared with each other. If I felt upon this question with the spirit of a partisan—if I had been a member of the Bullion Committee, and were responsible for their Report, I should say, that the right honourable gentleman's third Proposition was absolutely beyond my hopes. Speaking impartially, I must say, that if I had seen this third Proposition any where but where it is, fairly printed and numbered in the right honourable gentleman's series, I should have thought it an invention of his antagonists, calculated to place the fallacy of his doctrine in the most glaring and ridiculous point of view, but carrying the license of exaggeration rather beyond pardonable limits, and defeating its purpose, by the grossness of the caricature. I

* See 3d Res. of Mr. Vansittart.

would have taken no other person's word than the right honourable gentleman's own, that he, a man of science, a man of practical knowledge and experience, was the author of this Proposition.

This Proposition, however, is not now regularly before us. I think it absolutely incredible that it should ever be brought before us for our direct consideration and adoption. It is now only to be viewed as the contrast and contradiction of the tenth Resolution of the honourable and learned gentleman; as intended to divert us by the prospect of something better from sanctioning that Resolution. And how does it effect that purpose? By shewing us that, if we will let that Resolution alone, and not unsettle the public mind by resolving any thing at all about the measurement of the value of Bank notes, there is already a sufficient rule for the just estimation of their value. What is that rule? "Public estimation." Good. And who is the party whose opinion is to be settled? The public. To whom do they appeal? To the House of Commons. The public opinion is divided; the public appeal to the House of Commons for judgment; and the House of Commons, after gravely hearing the arguments on both sides, delivers, not its own decision of the question in dispute, but a decree that the opinion of the public has already decided it.

Is this (I do not say) wise, judicious, satisfactory? I ask if it be intelligible; if it be not a mockery of the public; a degradation of our own character, and an abdication of our own functions?

Again I say, I cannot, will not believe, that we shall ever be seriously called upon to vote this third Proposition.

But even so, we must not leave this main point of inquiry undetermined, nor our determination upon it unrecorded. The tenth of the original Resolutions contains the just and indisputable inference from the known law and the acknowledged facts of the case. Till the indentures of the Mint be altered, and the statutes which sanction them repealed, definite weight of precious metal constitutes the true standard of our currency. By that standard, while it subsists in law, every species of our currency must be measured. Measured by that standard, Bank notes have not at present a value equal to their denomination. Unless the premises can be denied, it is vain to dispute the conclusion. And this conclusion, if it be true, it is our bounden duty solemnly to record.

These ten Resolutions, therefore, expound the law of our currency; and establish the fact of the actual depreciation of that part of it which consists in paper.

Here I confess I should be contented to leave the matter: conceiving that the remedy to be applied to the evil may best be proposed by the

Executive Government; and that the causes of it, though to my mind obvious and manifest, yet are not as capable of certain and demonstrative proof, as the fact of its existence.

I have myself no doubt of the truth of the honourable and learned gentleman's* eleventh Resolution. But I am not prepared to affirm it by my vote. I think that, unlike, in this respect, to those which have preceded it, it asserts more than it proves; and I think it implies a degree of blame upon the Bank, which I am not ready to impute to that body.

When it is stated that the depreciation of Bank notes is owing to an excessive issue, and that the excessive issue has been produced by a want of check and control, it is difficult not to construe such a statement as imputing to the Bank a heavy responsibility both for the excess of their issues, and for a neglect of those precautions by which such excess might have been prevented. But the check and control which are said to have been wanting, may have been, and in point of fact were, in part at least, extrinsic to the Bank. The main check was the payment of their notes in specie upon demand: for the discontinuance of this check the Bank is obviously not responsible. If indeed I could agree with my right honourable friend (the Chancellor of the Exchequer) in con-

* See Res. 11, of Mr. Horner.

sidering the question of excess as independent of that of depreciation, and as capable of being satisfactorily proved or disproved, otherwise than through the depreciation, I could not affirm the fact of an excessive issue without imputing to the Bank the blame of having intentionally produced that excess. But the check of cash payments once removed—which was, as I apprehend, the only infallible guard against excess, I know of no test by which the Bank could ascertain the fact that their issues had become excessive, except by that of their paper having become depreciated. The degree and the long continuance of the unfavourableness of the exchange strongly indicate —and the high price of bullion incontrovertibly proves—the depreciation; the depreciation proves the excess. But such being the order of the demonstration, it is not till the fact of depreciation was established that I could consider that of an excessive issue as proved: and it would not be until such excess should have been persevered in against better knowledge, that I should think it just to animadvert upon the conduct of the Bank in the sense of this Resolution.

Besides, I confess I think it unnecessary. I cannot help being satisfied, that without any specific resolution on the subject of excess, the effect of this debate, should the first ten Resolutions be adopted—nay, I cannot help hoping that the effect of the debate itself—will be to correct that evil.

For this purpose, however, it is undoubtedly desirable, that the Bank should be disabused of some notions which it appears to entertain, and of others which have been suggested in this debate; at least if those notions are, as they appear to my understanding, entirely erroneous. "It is impossible that there should be an excess in the issue of bank notes," say the Bank, "because those notes are never issued except upon solid security —the security of real mercantile transactions." Surely it cannot be necessary to shew that, although this may be an adequate precaution against loss to the Bank, it is none against an excessive issue. It surely cannot be contended, that every mercantile transaction, that is to say, every object of commerce, may be represented to its full value in the paper currency of the country—and represented not once only, but as often as it changes hands—without any inconvenient augmentation of the mass of that currency. A. sells to B. a bale of cloth, or a hogshead of sugar, and receives from B. a bill of exchange payable in two months. Here is a bill founded upon a real mercantile transaction. A carries B.'s bill to the Bank for discount; and a Bank note to the amount of the bill is sent into circulation. Next day B. transfers his goods to C., and receives from C. a similar bill of exchange. Here is another bill founded on a real mercantile transaction. Like the former, it is carried to the Bank; and, like it, is the cause of adding a Bank note of the same amount to the circulation. Is it not plain that this transaction may be almost indefinitely repeated, till the bale of cloth or the hogshead of sugar is represented a hundred fold in the currency of the country? The security of the Bank is not in the rule of its issue, but in the solvency of the several parties. This may guard their notes against depreciation from discredit; but what tendency has it to secure them from depreciation by excess?

"It is impossible," others have said, "that there should be an excess, when the mass of property to be circulated in this country—the rents of land, the profits of trade, the expenditure of the state, and the receipt of the revenue—are grown and daily growing to an amount so much beyond all former experience." "The amount of the circulating medium," it is said, "so far from having increased in a ratio equal to that of these several enormous demands for its employment, bears an infinitely smaller proportion to those demands than it has done at former periods of our history. It cannot therefore be in excess." This proposition has been much dwelt upon by many gentlemen who have spoken in this debate; and the difficulty of dealing with it lies in this—that on neither side of the comparison are what it assumes as *data*, fixed and certain; that, on the one side, the total amount of the currency of the country, including paper of all kinds, is necessarily unknown; and on the other side, who is there (as I have before had occasion to ask) that shall pretend to estimate with accuracy the aggregate amount of all the private transactions of the country? The peremptory inference that excess is impossible, is surely not to be drawn with confidence from premises necessarily conjectural.

In one sense, indeed, which, however, I can hardly suppose to be intended, it may be true that there never can be any such thing as excess or superabundance of currency in a country: it cannot be superabundant, if you do not care for its depreciation. Suppose, for instance, ten millions sufficient to carry on all the transactions of the country—fabricate fifteen millions of paper instead of ten, the whole fifteen will circulate:—the only consequence will be, that the commodities for which it is exchanged will rise fifty per cent. in their nominal price. Make those fifteen millions twenty; the addition will in like manner be absorbed into the enhanced prices of commodities. Excess of currency cannot be proved to the conviction of those who will not admit depreciation to be the proof of it.

But again, if we were to allow the accuracy and certainty of all the data that are assumed by those persons who have relied on this argument; to allow whatever amount they please for the pecuniary transactions of the country, public and private; to allow them to fix where they please, the amount of the currency; and to assume that its actual amount at the present moment, consisting, as it does, almost exclusively of paper, is not greater—is even less—than when it consisted in part, and in great part, of gold;—still it would remain for them, before they could infer the impossibility of excess, to shew, that there was no improved mode of carrying on the transactions of the country, which facilitated and quickened all pecuniary transfers, and made a less quantity of currency perform what had required a greater amount before;—it would remain for them to shew that the very substitution of paper for gold did not greatly contribute to this facility; that a Bank note of one hundred pounds would not perform in a given space of time an infinitely greater number of operations in exchange of commodities, than an equal sum in the more bulky and less transferable shape of guineas.

That these or any other arguments can disprove the possibility of excess, I utterly deny—and I trust that the Bank has, by this time, ceased to believe. On the other hand, that the existence of excess can be proved by the converse of these arguments, or that any conclusive inference can be drawn from the positive amount of paper in circulation, or from the comparison of that amount, either with the amount of currency in circulation at any former time, or with that of the pecuniary transactions, revenue and expenditure of the country—I do not pretend.

The currency might be increased or diminished in any assignable degree, without affording any inference fairly conclusive upon the point in question, unless that diminution or increase were accompanied by a variation of its value. Whether that value has or has not varied, is therefore the sole question. It is the point from which we set out, and that to which we must return. And as it is one which is capable of being either proved or disproved directly, they who argue about it analogically, instead of directly, afford a strong indication of their own distrust in the soundness of their reasoning.

That excessive issue has therefore been the cause of depreciation, I entertain no doubt. And although, for the reasons which I have given, I do not think it necessary to declare this fact in a distinct Resolution, I trust that the statement of principles in those Resolutions which precede, and those which follow, is sufficient to answer every practical purpose of such a declaration.

The twelfth Resolution simply records a fact, about which there is no dispute—the unfavourable state of the exchanges.

The thirteenth Resolution attributes this unfavourable state of the exchanges, in a great measure, to the depreciation of the relative value of the currency of this country, as compared with that of other countries; without however excluding the operation of other causes.

The fourteenth* declares it to be the duty of the Bank, under the present circumstances, to take the state of foreign exchanges, as well as the price of bullion, into their view, in regulating the amount of their issues.

The twelfth Resolution requires no comment.

To the thirteenth and fourteenth, however the right honourable gentleman opposite to me (Mr. Vansittart) may object, my right honourable friend (the Chancellor of the Exchequer) must agree. He must agree, at least, unless he thinks either that the depreciation of our paper currency is a good thing in itself; or that, being an evil, it is productive of good by which it is more than counterbalanced. He must agree to these Resolutions: for he admits that the reduction of the amount of Bank paper would have a tendency to set right the exchanges. The state of the exchanges, therefore, is not in his opinion, as it is in that of others, wholly independent of the amount of the Bank issues, and unaffected by it. If the exchanges are affected by the issues of the Bank, and affect in their turn, as they undoubtedly do, and as by some they are

* See Res. 12, 13, and 14, of Mr. Horner.

thought to do exclusively, the price of gold, and the general commercial interests of the country, the state of the exchanges cannot be altogether a matter of indifference in any question respecting the amount to which the Bank issues should be carried. But the Bank have told us distinctly, that they do not advert to the exchanges with a view to regulate their issues. Their reason for not doing so, they state to be, that they do not consider the amount of their issues, and the state of the exchanges, as having any connection, or bearing in any degree upon each other. In this opinion, my right honourable friend (the Chancellor of the Exchequer) thinks, as I think, that the Bank is wrong. He must, therefore, naturally agree with me in the necessity and expediency of correcting their error on this subject. Consequently, I can anticipate no objection on his part to the twelfth, thirteenth, and fourteenth Resolutions.

The fifteenth* Resolution cannot be opposed by any man, who is not prepared to go the full length of the argument, that excess of paper currency is a thing of itself physically impossible, or who is not desirous of converting the temporary suspension of cash payments into a permanent system. With these exceptions, every man must concur in the opinion, that the convertibility upon

* See the 15th Resolution of Mr. Horner.

demand of paper into coin, is the only permanent and certain security against excess in the issue of paper; and must be anxious that this principle, having been called in question, should be unequivocally affirmed. More especially must those persons be anxious for such an affirmation, who are prepared to vote for the last but one of the propositions of the right honourable gentleman opposite to me (Mr. Vansittart); in which the expediency of returning to cash payments as quickly as possible, is so clearly and properly recognised. I have already declared that I am one of those who concur in that proposition; and who would not object to voting, at the same time, for the concluding proposition of the right honourable gentleman, which declares the inexpediency of reverting to cash payments at the present moment: but to those propositions, the Resolutions of the honourable and learned gentleman (Mr. Horner), which I have already discussed, and especially this fifteenth Resolution, appear to me to form the best and most natural introduction.

I now come to the concluding Resolution of the honourable and learned gentleman,* and that with respect to which alone I differ from him to the extent of being compelled to vote against it. Agreeing with him as I do in all the main principles of

* See Res. 16, of Mr. Horner.

his argument; admitting, as I do, that the evil which he has denounced, exists, and that he and his fellow-labourers have traced it to its source; admitting also that it requires remedy, I am certainly bound to explain why I cannot go along with him in his practical conclusion: and I will endeavour to explain myself upon this point, I hope, to his satisfaction.

The object of this Resolution is to change the term of the restriction upon cash payments at the Bank; and to ascertain, though not necessarily to shorten, the period of its duration.

I have already said, that, throughout the whole of this business, I consider the Bank as entirely passive. The restriction was originally imposed upon them by Parliament. By Parliament it was renewed more than once during the continuance of the former war, after the Bank had declared its readiness to pay in cash;—by Parliament it was re-enacted at the recommencement of the war;—and with a policy, which I deeply regret, but for which the Bank is no way answerable, was made commensurate in its continuance with the continuance of the war. If, therefore, the error has prevailed of considering this as a war measure, it is not to the Bank, but to the Parliament, that this error ought to be imputed. The Bank was taught by Parliament so to consider the subject; and it is hard to visit upon the Bank the consequences of our own error.

Nothing can be more obvious than that, considering its own interests as a commercial corporation, the Bank may have thought itself not only warranted, but obliged to adopt a different course of conduct, with a view to prepare for the resumption of cash payments at a period of six months after a definite treaty of peace, from that which they would have adopted with a view to a different period, definite in point of time, but independent of the consideration of peace or war. It is possible that, taking the colour of their opinions from Parliament, and considering the war as the cause of the restriction, and peace, whenever it should be made, as certain to supersede the necessity of it, they may have thought that the six months which are to intervene between the conclusion of the definitive treaty and the call upon them for cash, would be sufficient to enable them to replenish their coffers; however they might have exhausted them in the mean time, by a liberal assistance to Government, and however they might have omitted to replace their issues by the purchase of gold in the market. I do not say that such has been the conduct of the Bank: I say, that if such has been their conduct, it is perfectly natural and excusable. We know, indeed, in point of fact, that they have omitted to purchase bullion. I regret this—because I think that continued purchases, on their part, would have tended to keep their notes and the precious metals more nearly on a par. But we have nothing to do with the policy on which the Bank conducts its own private concerns; we have no right to examine into the state of its coffers; and it would be highly improper and mischievous to do so. We had a right to require, before the Bank restriction, payment of their notes in specie on demand: that right we have voluntarily foregone for purposes, and with a view to interests, not of the Bank, but of our own; and all that we have now strictly a right to require of the Bank is, that it should be ready to resume its cash payments at the period which Parliament has fixed for that resumption.

It would, therefore, in my opinion, be unjust to shorten, by any compulsory measure, the duration, or to change the nature of the term for which the restriction has been enacted.

But I also think the change would be impolitic, as well as unjust. I am for adhering to our bargain; although I do not think it a very wise one. I am afraid, that if we propose to alter it for our own convenience, we should not only not obtain our object, but by throwing loose the terms of the existing agreement, should risk the non-performance of that agreement when the period for exacting it arrives.

That our first object might be defeated by the Bank—if we could suppose that the Directors of the Bank (which, however, I am very far from believing) were capable of defeating it by design,—is sufficiently obvious. But even innocently, and with the sincerest desire to conform themselves to the express wish of Parliament, the Bank Directors, suddenly driven out of the course which they may have adopted in reliance upon the former act, by this new and unlooked-for interposition, might, by the very measures which that interposition rendered necessary, create a state of things which would oblige us hastily to recall it.

We read in the Report of the Bullion Committee of the alarming effects of a too sudden and violent contraction of the Bank issues. We feel at the present moment the ill effect of an uncontrolled augmentation of them. The result of the present discussion must and will be (I cannot doubt but it will) to check the latter evil: but I am afraid, that, by fixing peremptorily a new period for opening the cash coffers of the Bank, we should incur a danger of the former kind to an extent of which the consequences cannot be foreseen. Of these consequences, that which I most apprehend, which I think the most certain, and consider as the most to be deprecated, would be that, the act under which the restriction is now limited being repealed, the new limitation would be found impracticable; and that we should thus be left without the prospect of any definite period for the restoration of the sound and natural state of our currency.

In the present state of this discussion, I shall be well contented if we come out of the Committee with the principles of our money system unequivocally recognised, and with the prospect of our return to the practice of them only not impaired. Of that issue I will not despair. For the rest, I am willing to leave to the good sense and good intentions of the Bank, and to the suggestions of the executive government, that gradual retrenchment of the excess of our paper currency, which can alone correct those evils, the existence of which we all agree in acknowledging. I impute nothing to the Bank for whatever has taken place amiss; I rely confidently on their disposition to amend it. As to the Government, I am quite sure, that whatever may be the present feelings of my right honourable friend, no obstinate attachment to preconceived opinions will prevent him from looking at the whole subject with impartiality, or from setting himself, with that solicitude which its importance demands, to review and to re-consider all the facts and arguments connected with it, and to adapt his conduct (his counsel, rather—for it is in that way alone that he can properly influence the Bank) to whatever may, after full deliberation, be his own final and sincere conviction. I think that, after full deliberation, he cannot be convinced but aright.

If I am asked, "What, will you then be satisfied, after all, with doing nothing?—with leaving things as they are?" I answer—We the House of Commons do perhaps as much as at this moment we can do; we do something practical, something essentially useful and important, if we strengthen, by a declaration of our opinion, the foundations of the money system of the country; if we re-establish the credit of the true standard of our currency, at a moment when it is attempted to be brought into doubt and disrepute.

The Bullion Committee will not have sat in vain, if its report shall have recalled the attention of Parliament to that system, and that standard, which it was never the intention of Parliament to abandon. Nor will this House have mis-spent its time, if, at the conclusion of this long and anxious investigation, it shall give its sanction to the principles of the Bullion Committee, so far as the system of our money and the standard of our currency are concerned, even although it may withhold that sanction from the practical measure which the report of the Committee recommends.

The Committee then divided on the first of Mr. Horner's Resolutions—

Ayes	75
Noes	151
Majority against it	76

The fourteen next resolutions were then put and negatived without a division; and on the sixteenth resolution the Committee again divided:—

Ayes	45
Noes	180
Majority against it...	135

BULLION COMMITTEE.

May 13th, 1811.

Mr. Vansittart moved the following Resolutions :—

First.—Resolved, that it is the opinion of this Committee, that the right of establishing and regulating the legal money of this Kingdom, hath at all times been a royal prerogative, vested in the Sovereigns thereof, wh have from time to time exercised the same, as they have seen fit, in changing such legal money, or altering and varying the value, and enforcing or restraining the circulation thereof, by proclamation, or in concurrence with the estates of the realm, by Act of Parliament: and that such legal money cannot lawfully be defaced, melted down, or exported.

Second.—That it is the opinion of the Committee, that the promissory notes of the Governor and Company of the Bank of England, are engagements to pay certain sums of money, in the legal coin of this kingdom; and that, for more than a century past, the said Governor and Company were at all times ready to discharge such promissory notes in legal coin of the realm, until restrained from so doing on the 25th February 1797, by an order of council, confirmed by Act of Parliament.

Third.—That it is the opinion of this Committee, that the promissory notes of the Company have hitherto been, and are at this time, held in public estimation to be equivalent to the legal coin of the realm, and generally accepted as such in all pecuniary transactions to which such coin is lawfully applicable.

Fourth.—That it is the opinion of this Committee, that, at various periods, as well before as since the said restriction, the Exchange between Great Britain and several other countries have been unfavourable to Great Britain; and that during such periods, the prices of gold and silver bullion, especially of such gold bullion as could be legally exported, have frequently risen above the mint price; and the coinage of money at the mint has been either wholly suspended or greatly diminished in amount: and that such circumstances have usually occurred when expensive naval and military operations have been carried on abroad, and in times of public danger and alarm, or when large importations of grain from foreign parts have taken place.

Fifth.—That it is the opinion of this Committee, that such unfavourable exchanges, and rise in the price of bullion, occurred to a greater or less degree, during the wars carried on by King William the Third and Queen Anne, and also during part of the Seven Years' war, and of the American war, and during the war and scarcity of grain in 1795 and 1796, when the difficulty of procuring cash or bullion increased to such a degree, that on the 25th of February 1797, the Bank of England was restrained from making payments in cash, by an Order of Council, confirmed and continued to the present time by divers Acts of Parliament; and the exchanges became still more unfavourable, and the price of bullion higher, during the scarcity which prevailed for two years previous to the peace of Amiens.

Sixth.—That it is the opinion of this Committee, that the unfavourable state of the exchanges, and the high price of bullion, do not, in any of the instances above referred to, appear to have been produced by the restriction upon cash payments at the Bank of England, or by any excess in the issue of bank notes; inasmuch as all the said instances, except the last, occurred previously to any restriction on such cash payments; and because, as far as appears by such information as has been procured, the price of bullion has frequently been highest, and the exchanges most unfavourable, at periods when the issues of bank notes have been considerably diminished; and they have been afterwards restored to their ordinary rates, although those issues have been increased.

Seventh.—That it is the opinion of this Committee, that during the period of nearly seventy-eight years, ending with the 1st of January 1796, and previous to the aforesaid restriction, of which period accounts are before the House, the price of standard gold in bars had been at or under the Mint price twenty-eight years and five months, and above the said Mint price forty-eight years and eleven months; and that the price of foreign gold coin has been at or under *3l.* 18*s.* per ounce thirty-six years and seven months, and above the said price thirty-nine years and three months; and that during the remaining intervals, no prices are stated. And that, during the same period of seventy-eight years, the price of standard silver appears to have been at or under the Mint price three years and two months only.

Eighth.—That it is the opinion of this Committee, that during the latter part, and for some time after the close of the American War, during the years 1781, 1782, and 1783, the exchange with Hamburgh fell from 34. 1. to 31. 5. being about eight per cent.; and the price of foreign gold rose from *3l.* 17*s.* 6*d.* to *4l.* 2*s.* 3*d.* per ounce, and the price of dollars from 5*s.* 4½*d.* per ounce to 5*s.* 11¼*d.*; and that the Bank notes in circulation were reduced between March 1782 and September 1782, from 9,160,000*l.* to

5,995,000*l.* being a diminution of above one-third, and continued (with occasional variations) at such reduced rate until December 1784; and that the exchange with Hamburgh rose to 34. 6., and the price of gold fell to 3*l.* 17*s.* 6*d.* and dollars to 5*s.* 1½*d.* per ounce before the 25th of February 1787, the amount of Bank notes being then increased to 8,688,000*l.*

Ninth.—That it is the opinion of this Committee, that the amount of Bank notes in February 1787, was 8,688,000*l.* and in February 1791, 11,699,000*l.*; and that during the same period, the sum of 10,704,000*l.* was coined in gold, and that the exchange with Hamburgh rose about 3 per cent.

Tenth.—That it is the opinion of this Committee, that the average amount of Bank notes in the year 1795 was about 11,497,000*l.*, and on the 25th of February 1797, was reduced to 8,640,000*l.* during which time the exchange with Hamburgh fell from 36. to 35. being about 3 per cent.; and the said amount was increased to 11,855,000*l.* exclusive of 1,542,000*l.* in notes of 1*l.* and 2*l.* each, on the 1st of February 1798, during which time the exchange rose to 38. 2. being about 9 per cent.

Eleventh.—That it is the opinion of this Committee, that the average price of wheat per quarter in England in the year 1798, was 50*s.* 3*d*; in 1799, 67*s.* 5*d.*; in 1800, 113*s.* 7*d.*; in 1801, 118*s.* 3*d.*; and in 1802, 67*s.* 5*d.* The amount of Bank notes of 5*l.* and upwards, was—

		£.		£. £.		£.
In 1798,	about	10,920,400,	and under 5,	1,786,000,	making together	12,706,400
In 1799	.	12,048,790	.	1,626,110,		13,674,900
In 1800	.	13,421,920	.	1,831,820,		15,253,740
In 1801	.	13,454,370	.	2,715,180,		16,169,550
In 1802	.	13,917,980	.	3,136,470,		17,054,450

That the exchange with Hamburgh was, in January

1798, 38. 2.; January 1799, 37. 7.; January 1800, 32.; January 1801, 29. 8.; being in the whole a fall of above 22 per cent.; in January 1802, 32. 2.; and December 1802, 34., being in the whole a rise of about 13 per cent.

Twelfth.—That it is the opinion of this Committee, that during all the periods above referred to, previous to the commencement of the war with France in 1793, the principal states of Europe preserved their independence, and the trade and correspondence thereof were carried on conformably to the accustomed law of nations; and that, although from the time of the invasion of Holland by the French in 1795, the trade of Great Britain with the Continent was in part circumscribed and interrupted, it was carried on freely with several of the most considerable ports, and commercial correspondence was maintained at all times previous to the summer of 1807.

Thirteenth.—That it is the opinion of this Committee, that since the month of November 1806, and especially since the summer of 1807, a system of exclusion has been established against the British trade on the Continent of Europe, under the influence and terror of the French power, and enforced with a degree of violence and rigour never before attempted; whereby all trade and correspondence between Great Britain and the continent of Europe has (with some occasional exceptions, chiefly in Sweden and in certain parts of Spain and Portugal) been hazardous, precarious, and expensive, the trade being loaded with excessive freights to foreign shipping, and other unusual charges; and that the trade of Great Britain with the United States of America has also been uncertain and interrupted; and that in addition to these circumstances, which have greatly affected the course of payments between this country and other nations, the naval and military expenditure of the United Kingdom in foreign parts has, for three years past, been very great; and the price of grain, owing to a deficiency in the crops, higher than at any time whereof the accounts appear before Parliament, except during the scarcity of 1800 and 1801, and that large quantities thereof have been imported.

Fourteenth.—That it is the opinion of this Committee, that the amount of currency necessary for carrying on the transactions of the country, must bear a proportion to the extent of its trade and its public revenue and expenditure; and that the annual amount of the exports and imports of Great Britain, on an average of three years, ending 5th January 1797, was 48,732,651*l.* official value; the average amount of revenue paid into the Exchequer, including monies raised by lottery, 18,759,165*l.*; and of loans, 18,409,842*l.* making together 37,169,007*l.*; and the average amount of the total expenditure of Great Britain 42,855,111*l.*; and that the average amount of Bank notes in circulation (all of which were for 5*l.* or upwards) was about 10,782,780*l.*: and that 57,274,617*l.* had been coined in gold during His Majesty's reign, of which a large sum was then in circulation.

That the annual amount of the exports and imports of Great Britain, on an average of three years, ending 5th January 1811, supposing the imports from the East Indies and China to have been equal to their amount in the preceding year, was 77,971,318*l.*, the average amount of revenue paid into the Exchequer, 62,763,746*l.*, and of loans, 12,673,548*l.*, making together 75,437,294*l.*; and the average amount of the total expenditure of Great Britain 82,205,066*l*; and that the average amount of Bank notes above 50*l.* was about 14,265,850*l.*, and of notes under 5*l.* about 5,283,320*l.*; and that the amount of gold coin in circulation was greatly diminished.

Fifteenth.—That it is the opinion of this Committee, that the situation of this kingdom, in respect of its political and commercial relations with foreign countries, as above stated, is sufficient, without any change in the internal value of its currency, to account for the unfavourable state of the foreign exchanges, and for the high price of bullion.

Sixteenth.—That it is the opinion of this Committee, that it is highly important that the restriction on the payments in cash of the Bank of England should be removed, whenever the political and commercial relations of the country shall render it compatible with the public interest.

Seventeenth.—That it is the opinion of this Committee, that under the circumstances affecting the political and commercial relations of this kingdom with foreign countries, it would be highly inexpedient and dangerous now to fix a definite period for the removal of the restriction of cash payments at the Bank of England prior to the term already fixed by the Act 44 Geo. III. c. 1, of six months after the conclusion of a definite treaty of peace.

Mr. Canning.—I should not have thought it necessary, Sir, to trouble the Committee with the expression of my sentiments in this night's debate, after the able and lucid speech of the honourable gentleman who spoke last (Mr. H. Thornton), if I had not been desirous of addressing myself more particularly than he has done to the propositions now brought forward, in the shape of Resolutions, by the right honourable gentleman opposite to me (Mr. Vansittart), which are the immediate subject of this night's deliberation.

I should, indeed, be unpardonable, if, after having already trespassed at so great length on the indulgence of the Committee, when the original resolutions were under discussion, I should again expatiate upon the general subject which I conceive to have been disposed of by the vote of the former night. The present, however, is a very different question from that which was then decided. We decided by our former vote, not to adopt the practical recommendation of the Bullion Committee. In that vote I concurred. We decided farther, not to sanction and record the declaration of the principles of our money system, on which the recommendation of the Bullion Committee was founded. In that decision I did not concur, and it is one which I deeply regret; because those principles were, as I think, correctly defined in the original Resolutions; and because I think that a declaration of them, under the sanction of this House, would have been eminently useful at the present moment.

But the House having thought otherwise, and having rejected all the Resolutions of the honourable and learned gentleman; my next wish would have been, that with that rejection the whole discussion should have terminated. Why pursue it farther? The Bullion Committee is defeated; its doctrines are, at least for the present, set aside. Why could not its antagonists be contented with this negative victory? Why must they aim at the unnecessary and perilous triumph of substituting their own doctrines in the place of those which they have discomfited?

In the majority of the former night were numbered many persons who profess to disapprove of abstract propositions. Those persons must, in common consistency, oppose the propositions of the right honourable gentleman, which are to the full as abstract as the original Resolutions. In that majority were many who not only did not agree with the right honourable gentleman opposite to me, in denying the existence of a depreciation of the paper currency; but who distinctly declared their entire conviction of the existence of that depreciation, and only thought it too notorious and undeniable to require the formality of a parliamentary affirmation. Can those persons be expected by the right honourable gentleman to concur in the Resolutions which he is now bringing forward? Others again there were, who, neither admitting nor denying the depreciation, were desirous only of escaping from the necessity of a decision either way: contending that no result could be so satisfactory, as the discussion itself was mischievous. Will those persons thank the right honourable gentleman for reviving a discussion which, if it had finally closed on Friday night, would have left them in quiet possession of their doubts,—doubts which any man might very reasonably prefer to a decision in support of the right honourable gentleman's third Resolution?

Independently of this violence to the feelings and judgments of his supporters, has the right honourable gentleman no consideration for the reputation of the House of Commons itself, when he calls upon us, by voting that Resolution, to affirm a proposition, which, I will venture to say, there is no man who, without the doors of the House, could affirm with a grave countenance?

The third Resolution is the essential part, the soul and spirit, of the right honourable gentleman's system. Of the other Resolutions, the first and the fifteenth are the only two, which, in my view of the subject, appear to require particular observation. The remainder, from the fourth to the fourteenth, inclusive, contain a vast variety of statements, historical, political, commercial, financial, and agricultural; some accurate, some inaccurate; but all valuable rather from their intrinsic erudition, than from any very near connection with the subject before us. With none of these, therefore, shall I presume to meddle.

But, before I proceed to the three Resolutions in which the whole of the right honourable gentleman's argument lies, I must say a word or two in answer to a challenge of the right honourable gentleman as to his sixteenth and seventeenth resolutions.* He states, and states very truly, that I had declared myself ready to vote for those two Resolutions, provided they were prefaced and introduced, not by his own preceding Resolutions, but by the first ten of the original Resolutions moved by the honourable and learned Chairman of the Bullion Committee. The right honourable gentleman triumphs in this declaration of mine, as if it had been a concession to his argument, instead of an exposition of my own. He has caught me in a great inconsistency it seems. And what is this inconsistency? That I am ready to affirm two things irreconcilable with each other? That I would vote premises that did not bear out their conclusion, or a conclusion contradictory to its premises? No such thing; but, simply, that I am ready to adopt the premises suggested by one man, and the conclusion drawn by another. This is what he considers as an inconsistency; as if consistency had reference not to the compatibility of doctrines, but to the identity of persons holding them.

It is true that if the first ten of the original Resolutions had been carried, I should not have objected to adding to them the two concluding propositions of the right honourable gentleman. But I cannot consent to vote for them by them-

* See Res. 16, 17.

selves, nor if introduced by his own preceding propositions.

I am not, any more than the right honourable gentleman himself, for changing the period now fixed by law for the repeal of the Bank restriction. I could therefore have been contented to vote for the sixteenth and seventeenth of the right honourable gentleman's propositions, if those principles, respecting the standard of our money, which were luminously and accurately developed in the Resolutions moved by the Chairman of the Bullion Committee, had been previously recognised and sanctioned. The truth of these principles once admitted, there might have been comparatively little danger in deciding either way the question, whether the period for returning to the strict practical application of them should be accelerated. But to decide that question in a way which should imply a denial of the truth of those principles, would be productive of a mischief than which none can be greater, except indeed that of adopting the right honourable gentleman's Resolutions, in which the truth of those principles is denied, not by implication, but directly.

To have abstained from adopting the original Resolutions, provided no others were agreed to in their room, would be to leave the true principles of our money system unvouched indeed, but not discredited, and to leave the Bank restriction precisely as it stands. To declare the continuance of the Bank restriction, by adopting the right honourable gentleman's sixteenth and seventeenth resolutions only, without adverting at the same time to the principles laid down by the Bullion Committee, would be to leave it matter of doubt whether the restriction was continued because those principles were false, or only because their force was overborne by considerations of expediency. This result would be unsatisfactory enough. To adopt and record the right honourable gentleman's premises as the foundation of his own conclusion, would be, in his view, no doubt, perfectly consistent; but it would be a consistency obtained at no less an expense than that of abrogating, so far as the Resolutions of this House can abrogate it, the whole system under which the currency of this country has been hitherto regulated and preserved in a state of purity and integrity, equally creditable to the character of the state, and to the increasing vigilance and anxiety of Parliament.

In matters which have been frequently the object of parliamentary revision, it is no light thing to come to Resolutions of a general and abstract nature without taking the former proceedings of Parliament for our guide.

If they who dissented from the doctrines of the Bullion Committee thought the errors of that Committee the more formidable on account of the authority by which they were inculcated, how much more cautious ought we to be in ascertaining, beyond possibility of doubt, the truth of those doctrines which we are now called upon to promulgate by the much higher authority of the House itself?

A declaration of the law by one of the branches of the Legislature ought not to be made at all but for a grave and adequate object; and, at least, ought to be unimpeachably correct.

Let us examine the right honourable gentleman's first Resolution, in this double view. First, let us see how far it is positively correct; and secondly, what is the object to which it is directed, and how far it attains that object.*

That the right of establishing and regulating the legal money of this kingdom is a prerogative of the Sovereign, is most undoubtedly true: that the Sovereigns of this kingdom have at different times altered the value of such money, is also true—if by value be intended only the denomination of such money, that is, the rate at which any given quantity of gold or silver should be current within these realms. But "value," absolutely stated, is by no means a correct expression. To alter the positive intrinsic value of the precious metals, or make it other than it is by nature, and by the relation which those metals bear to other commodities, is a power, which neither kings nor parliaments have hitherto, so far as I know, arrogated;

* See 1st Resolution.

but the existence of which, to be sure, would at once put an end to all dispute, and give to the right honourable gentleman, and those who side with him, a complete triumph. If value were, indeed, the offspring of authority, there is no doubt but that paper or pasteboard, or any viler material, might be raised by that authority to a level with gold. But the only power which Sovereigns have ever yet exercised or claimed, has been to fix the rate or "current" value of coin within their own dominions.

Nor is it merely an inaccuracy of expression to omit this qualification of the word "value." It is an inaccuracy which may lead to serious misconception in a case where the whole controversy turns upon this single question, "whether there be or be not an inherent inextinguishable value in the precious metals estimated according to their relation to other commodities generally, throughout the world; and independent of any arbitrary valuation, which positive edicts or enactments can affix to them?" The right honourable gentleman's proposition, as it stands, without the addition to the word "value" of the epithets "current" or "denominative," would go to favour the notion that edicts and enactments have this power: a notion so wild that it might seem almost unnecessary to guard against it, if it, or something very like it, were not in fact the foundation of almost all the right honourable gentleman's arguments.

He cannot, however, intend to avow such a notion. He will, therefore, I presume, have no objection to qualify the word "value," by the addition of one or other of the epithets which I have suggested. So qualified, the proposition, that the Sovereign has at different times varied the "current" or "denominative" value of the coin, would be true, and perfectly harmless.

The Resolution proceeds to state, that this has been done by proclamation, "or" by Act of Parliament. This is also a true proposition; but upon this also I must observe, that it is not stated with sufficient qualification. The Resolution seems to imply that the option between the two modes of proceeding is perfectly arbitrary; that Parliament may be either admitted into, or excluded from, a share in the operation, exactly according to the will and pleasure of the Crown. But, I would take the liberty of suggesting to the right honourable gentleman, that it was not enough to state the abstract principles and theory of the constitution; it was incumbent on him to state them as they have been acted upon, as they are modified by practice, as they are to be found, not in the proclamations of Henry the VIIIth, but in the statute book; in statutes of the last century; in those of the present reign.

The Sovereign (says the right honourable gentleman) can alter the value of the coin—but can he do that at the present moment, without consent of Parliament? Can he do it against existing Acts of Parliament? Can he, except by the aid and concurrence of Parliament, repeal the Acts of the 14th of the present reign, which were passed on occasion of the last recoinage of the gold; and which must be repealed or amended, if any alteration should be made in the current value of the guinea? Unquestionably the King, according to the theory of the prerogative, can, by his proclamation, reduce or raise the denomination of the current coin. But, if by doing so, he would place his subjects in the dilemma of either disregarding his proclamation, or acting in contravention of an Act of Parliament, would it be in that case a sound or a safe statement of the law, to give a naked definition of the prerogative, without reference to the practical restrictions by which the exercise of it must necessarily be controlled?

Are the opinions of lawyers so settled and uniform upon this subject as to warrant the right honourable gentleman's sweeping and unqualified assertion? Do lawyers agree that there is no limit to the power of the Crown in this respect? that the Crown may give what current value it pleases to coin, which it may debase at its pleasure?

I do not mean to assert that all such authorities are uniformly the other way: it would, perhaps, be difficult to name that branch of the prerogative which has not been exalted to an excess in the speeches or writings of some one or other of the great Crown lawyers who have spoken or written upon the prerogative. But such opinions, even if they were more general than they will be found to be, surely could not avail against positive statute:

"The *denomination*" (says Blackstone), "or the value for which the coin is to pass current, is likewise in the breast of the King; and if any unusual pieces are coined, that value must be ascertained by proclamation. In order to fix the value, the weight and the fineness of the metal are to be taken into consideration together. When a given weight of gold or silver is of a given fineness, it is then of the true *standard*, and is called sterling. Of this sterling metal all the coin of the kingdom must be made by the statute 25 Edw. III. cap. 15; so that the King's prerogative seemeth not to extend to the debasing or enhancing the value of the coin below or above the sterling value: though Sir Matthew Hale appears to be of another opinion."

The right honourable gentleman may perhaps tell me that his opinion agrees with that of Sir Matthew Hale; to which Judge Blackstone here refers as seemingly more favourable to the prerogative than his own. But if he will look into that elaborate and instructive treatise, which contains an abstract of all the learning and all the history relating to our coinage—I mean the Letter of the late Earl of Liverpool to the King—he will there find in what respects the Legislature has limited the exercise of that prerogative, since the death of Sir Matthew Hale. He will find it stated that, even in Sir Matthew Hale's opinion, "though this great prerogative is unquestionable, it is certainly advisable that in the exercise of it, whenever any great change is intended to be made, the King should avail himself of the wisdom and support of his Parliament." "Sir Matthew Hale observes," says Lord Liverpool, "that it is neither safe nor honourable for the King to imbase his coin below sterling; if it be at any time done, it is fit to be done by the assent of Parliament: and he concludes, that on such occasions '*fieri non debuit, factum valet.*'"

Even if such were still the state of the prerogative, would it justify a Resolution of the House of Commons, which describes that prerogative as absolute and indefinite, and describes "the assent of Parliament" not as that with which, according to Sir Matthew Hale, "it is fit" that such alteration should be made, if made at all; and without which, according to the same authority, "*fieri non debuit*;" but merely as that which it is optional with the Crown to ask or not to ask, according to its good pleasure? Would such a Resolution have befitted the House of Commons, even at the time when Sir Matthew Hale wrote? Is it possible to pass it now; when that prerogative, which by Sir Matthew Hale was considered as unfit to be exercised without consent of Parliament, stands actually limited by statute?

Let us now consider what is the object with a view to which this exposition of the law is made, and how far that object is attained by it.

The question in agitation is, whether our paper currency be or be not depreciated? The price of gold in that paper currency is adduced in proof of the depreciation. What answer is it to this question—what refutation is it of this proof—to say, "The King's prerogative can alter the value of the coin?"—Granted that it can. At least it has not done so in the present instance. The coin is not varied in value: the paper currency, it is contended, is. The King's prerogative has nothing to do with the paper of the Bank. The paper of the Bank is not (God forbid it ever should be!) the legal money of the realm. How, then, does the King's prerogative decide—how does it even affect—the question as to the depreciation of Bank paper? It can by no possibility affect it at all, unless the right honourable gentleman be prepared to address us in something like the following manner—"The King has a power to make whatever he pleases money; and to make that money of what value he pleases. If you murmur at this supposed depreciation of Bank notes, beware that you do not provoke an exercise of the prerogative, which shall make those Bank notes to all intents and purposes legal money; or which shall cure that pretended disparity between paper and gold about which you clamour so loudly, by raising the denomination of the coin."

Is this what the right honourable gentleman means to say? If so, though I do not think that there would be much wisdom in the measure, I admit that his Resolution is an apt and natural introduction to it. I can at least understand its application to the subject. I can see what is meant by it. But unless this be his meaning, I am at a loss to conceive how the assertion that the paper currency is actually depreciated, is disproved, or even touched, by the assertion of the King's prerogative to establish and alter at his pleasure the legal money of the realm.

The Resolutions on the subject of the coinage laws, which we rejected on a former night, and for which this of the right honourable gentleman is intended as a substitute, had a direct and sensible bearing upon the question in dispute. In affirming the depreciation of the paper currency, it was necessary to define the standard by which such currency was to be measured. The honourable and learned mover of the original Resolutions did define it, and, as I think, with perfect truth as well as precision. Can it be the right honourable gentleman's intention, by stating with such laxity the absolute and indefinite power of the

Crown over the legal money of the realm, to imply that, where every thing is liable to such arbitrary fluctuation, there can be no fixed standard by which to measure the value of the currency? If his argument be good for any thing, it can only be so by being pushed to this extent: but even then it affords no answer to the Resolutions of the honourable and learned gentleman. Those Resolutions asserted that the paper currency is in a state of depreciation, if measured by the existing standard of our legal currency. The right honourable gentleman does not contradict this assertion; he passes it by; he says nothing at all as to what the standard of our currency really is; but contents himself with disparaging its fitness as a measure of value, by insinuating that, whatever it may be at the present moment, the King has, by his prerogative, an unlimited power of changing it.

But, again, even if the King has this power, it is not pretended that he has in point of fact thought fit to exercise it. If any part of our currency has been varied in its value, either in respect to another part of it, or in respect to the standard, it is not pretended that this has been done by the interposition of the Crown. The complaint is, however, that such a variation has in fact taken place in the value of Bank paper. What answer is it to this complaint, to say, that though the King has not, yet he might, if he pleased, have made a like variation in the current value of the coin?

There is, however, another operation of the prerogative, which, to make his definition complete, the right honourable gentleman ought to have noticed: but which he has altogether omitted, perhaps because he saw that it would bear inconveniently upon his argument: I mean the King's power of giving currency to foreign coin within his own dominions. Now one of the plainest illustrations of the actual depreciation of our paper currency has been derived from the change which has been recently made in the current value of the dollar.

"The King," says Mr. Justice Blackstone in the same part of his work to which I have already referred, "may also, by his proclamation, legitimate foreign coin, and make it current here; declaring at what value it shall be taken in payments. But this, I apprehend, ought to be by comparison with the standard of our own coin; otherwise the consent of Parliament will be necessary."

"This great prerogative," says Lord Liverpool in his Letter to the King, "which the Kings of this realm have immemorially enjoyed and exercised, of giving currency to the coins made at their mint, and sometimes to foreign coins, at a determinate rate or value, and of enhancing and debasing them at their pleasure, is of so important and delicate a nature, and the justice and honour of the Sovereign, as well as the interests of the people, are so deeply concerned in it, that it ought to be exercised with the greatest judgment and discretion."

We here see the limitations in point of law, which, in the opinion of so able a lawyer as Blackstone,—and those in point of prudence and discretion which, in the opinion of so profound a practical statesman as the Earl of Liverpool, would have governed the exercise of the prerogative of the Crown in giving currency to the dollar. Have these limitations, has this caution, been observed in fixing the rate at which the dollar now circulates? The intrinsic value of the dollar "by comparison with the standard of our own coin,"—as compared, for example, with the British crown piece—is nearly in the proportion of nine to ten. The current rate at which the dollar circulates, as compared with the crown piece, is now in the proportion of eleven to ten.

By what authority has so strange an anomaly been introduced into our money system?—an anomaly which, according to Blackstone, the Crown, in the exercise of its prerogative, is bound to avoid. By an ordinance of the Bank. The prerogative of the Crown, we have seen, might have given currency to the dollar: but it could only have done so at a rate proportionate to its intrinsic value, as compared with the standard of the realm; or for any deviation from that standard it must have obtained the concurrence of Parliament. But the thing is done. It is one of the main features of our present system. It makes one of the grounds of the complaint which the right honourable gentleman proposes to answer by the authoritative language of his first Resolution. And how does he answer it? By referring to the prerogative of the Crown as the authority by which alone the currency can be regulated; and yet omitting altogether a part of that prerogative, so essential to the present subject, as the power of giving currency to foreign coin! He omits it—Why?—Evidently because he could not state it, without ackowledging, at the same time, that the rules by which the exercise of that part of the prerogative has always been governed, have been entirely neglected in the issue of the dollar at its present rate; and because he could not make that acknowledgment without avowing the depreciation of our currency.

Before the late ordinance of the Bank, nine crown pieces would have exchanged for ten dollars. Now, ten dollars cannot be had for less than eleven crowns. If this be not depreciation, what is it? Perhaps I shall be warned that this argument proves too much; for that the depreciation here established would be that of the lawful coin of the realm,—not of the paper currency, of which alone the depreciation is asserted.

I answer—the depreciation of the lawful coin in respect to the dollar is effected through the medium of the paper. If the crown piece and the dollar circulated together without the intervention of the paper, it would be impossible that they should bear to each other any other relation than that which arises naturally from their respective intrinsic values. It is by the intervention of the paper, which measures the one according to its nominal, the other according to its intrinsic value, that this relation is forcibly inverted, and the more valuable is degraded below the less valuable coin.

I shall probably be told, however, that the dollar is a mere token; it is no more than a promissory note in silver, which no man is bound to accept in payment This is perfectly true: but it is a singular argument to be relied upon by the practical school, since it is no less true that the dollar, such as it is, constitutes in fact by far the greater part of the metallic currency now in circulation. In the same way it has been argued, that a Bank note is not a legal tender—that no man is bound to take a Bank note from his neighbour in satisfaction of a just debt. This also is true: but it is no less so that the public creditor is bound to receive Bank notes, or at least can get nothing else, in payment of his demand upon the state; and it seems to be no great consolation to the public creditor to be assured that what he is compelled to take from the Government, nobody is compellable to take from him.

This being then practically the state of our currency, what satisfaction, I must again ask, does the first Resolution of the right honourable gentleman afford to those who complain of the depreciation of Bank paper, by stating, and stating, as it appears, incorrectly, the money prerogatives of the Crown?—prerogatives, which, in respect to the bulk of our currency, the paper, have no operation at all; and which in respect to the small portion of metallic currency which we possess, have been suffered to lie dormant and passive, while that currency has been regulated, by another authority, on principles directly contrary to those by which the Crown must have been guided in giving currency to a foreign coin.

This Resolution therefore the House of Commons cannot but reject: first, because it is defective as a definition of the prerogative which it affects to define; secondly, because it is wholly inapplicable to the only points about which there is any dispute,—namely, Bank paper, which is out of the province of the prerogative; and the foreign silver currency, of which in fact it has taken no cognizance; and lastly, because it is calculated, by implication at least, to exclude Parliament from all share in the regulation of a subject, in which, in all good times, Parliament has claimed it as a right, and felt it a duty, to interfere, whenever the occasion has called for its interference.

It is impossible to pass over the second Resolution without observing, that it remains liable to the objection which I took the liberty of making to it in a former debate.* The words "on demand" are still omitted: I trust, the right honourable gentleman intends to supply this omission. I must say, that the persisting in it would afford just ground of serious suspicion and alarm.

I now come to the main Resolution of all, the third. This it is that contains the sum and substance of all the right honourable gentleman's arguments and doctrines; and to which I cannot believe it possible, until the vote shall actually have passed, that any assembly of reasonable men can be persuaded to give their concurrence. The Resolution is as follows:

III. That the Promissory Notes of the said Company have hitherto been, and are at this time, held in public estimation to be equivalent to the legal Coin of the Realm, and generally accepted as such in all pecuniary transactions to which such Coin is legally applicable.

The right honourable gentleman, in stating what he considered to be the effect of this Resolution, made use of an expression which does indeed most truly describe its character, and the character

* See Second Resolution.

of that assent which he reckons upon obtaining to it. By this Resolution, said the right honourable gentleman, we "pledge ourselves to believe the equivalency of Bank notes to coin." Pledge ourselves to believe! This is perhaps more than any man ever before avowed of himself; but certainly more than any man ever openly declared his intention to exact from others. Belief is not usually matter of volition; therefore, one should think, it cannot reasonably be made matter of undertaking and engagement. Of all martyrs of whatever faith, I have always conceived the just praise to be, that they adhered stedfastly to a belief founded on sincere conviction, not that they anticipated that conviction by pledging themselves beforehand what their belief should be. The right honourable gentleman's martyrdom is of a superior description: it not only professes its faith, but creates it: and to say the truth, it does require a faith, rather of the will than of the understanding, to believe the doctrine which the right honourable gentleman has promulgated in this third Resolution.

The right honourable gentleman, however, has not done full justice to his own Resolution. The pledge which it contains goes much farther than he describes. It is not we, the resolvers, that are pledged by it to the creed of the right honourable gentleman: it pledges all mankind, except ourselves. It is so contrived, that even I might consistently vote for it, denying as I do every syllable of the doctrine which it contains. Whatever other merit the Resolution may want, this is at least ingenious, and I think I may venture to say it is altogether new in parliamentary proceeding.

The object of the right honourable gentleman is to settle the public mind on a question on which there is great division of opinion. There are various modes in which the public mind may be settled in matters depending on positive authority. The first is a proclamation by the King, where the subject matter is one to which the Royal prerogative is of itself competent; and such the right honourable gentleman contends this matter to be. A second mode is by Act of Parliament, in which the united wisdom of the two branches of the Legislature is sanctioned by the authority of the Crown. A third mode is by concurrent resolution of the two Houses of Parliament, declaring their joint opinion. A fourth mode is, by resolution of one or other House of Parliament, declaring its opinion alone. But to these four recognised modes, it remained for the ingenuity of the right honourable gentleman to add a fifth—that of a resolution of the House of Commons, declaring, not its own opinion, but that of the litigants themselves.

Are Bank notes equivalent to the legal standard coin of the realm? This is the question which divides and agitates the public opinion. I, says the right honourable gentleman, will devise a mode of settling this question to the satisfaction of the public. By advising a proclamation? No. —By bringing a Bill into Parliament? No.— By proposing to declare the joint opinion of both Houses, or the separate opinion of one? No.— By what new process then? Why, simply by telling the disputants that they are, and have been all along, however unconsciously, agreed upon the subject of their variance; and gravely resolving, for them, respectively, an unanimous opinion. This is the very judgment, I should imagine, which Milton ascribes to the venerable Anarch, whom he represents as adjusting the disputes of the conflicting element:

> "Chaos umpire sits,
> And by decision more embroils the fray."

That the public would have bowed in reverence and submission to the pronounced opinion of the House of Commons, cannot be doubted: but when the House of Commons speaks, not as a judge but as an interpreter, it can hardly expect to be regarded as infallible by those whose sentiments it professes to interpret.

"In public estimation," says the right honourable gentleman's Resolution, "Bank notes and coin are equivalent." Indeed? What then is become of all those persons who, for the last six months have been by every outward and visible indication evincing, maintaining, and inculcating an opinion diametrically opposite? Who wrote that multitude of pamphlets, with the recollection of which one's head is still dizzy? What is become of the whole class of readers of those pamphlets, of whom to my cost I was one; and a great number of whom at least were convinced, like me, of the actual depreciation of our paper currency? Were these writers and readers no part of the public? or does the right honourable gentleman apprehend that his arguments must have wrought their conversion? Far be it from me to say that, whatever I may think of his arguments, the authority of his name would not have great weight with me and with the public. Therefore do I regret that, if he does not think fit to frame his Resolution in the name of the House of Commons, he should not at least resolve in his own name the equivalency which he is so bent upon establishing. A Resolution, importing that "in the estimation" of the right honourable gentleman individually, "Bank notes are equivalent to the legal coin of the realm," though I do not pretend to say it would carry all the force of a decision of the legislature, would yet be a prodigious comfort even to those who are hardened in their disbelief of that equivalency; as it would shew them in what quarter to apply when they wished to make an exchange on equal terms.

Nor would such a declaration of individual

opinion, though unusual, be wholly without example. I saw the other day an address to the public from a patriotic lottery-office keeper, which in truth I should think had not escaped the right honourable gentleman's notice, since his third resolution is nearly a transcript of it. This worthy distributor of the favours of Fortune disclaims, in the most indignant terms, the intention to "make any distinction between Bank notes, and the current coin of the realm." He is "at all times ready," he says, "to serve the public with tickets or shares, on equal terms for either." Why should not the right honourable gentleman give a similar demonstration of the sincerity of his own opinion? It is obvious that if the lottery-office keeper, instead of speaking for himself, had only declared that "in the estimation of the public," Bank notes and coin were equal, his assurance would have gone but for little: and I really cannot see why, in adopting, as he has done, the very words of the lottery advertisment, the right honourable gentleman should decline adopting the advertiser's test of his sincerity.

I must, however, observe, that the right honourable gentleman carries his doctrine somewhat farther than his prototype, the lottery-office keeper. The advertisement is much more cautiously worded than the resolution. The advertisement only affirms the equivalency of Bank notes to the "current" coin of the realm. The resolution says, that they are equivalent to the "legal" coin. Now the assertion of the advertisement may be perfectly safe from contradiction, forasmuch as "current" coin of the realm, there is at this moment none. But the "legal" coin of the realm, though driven out of circulation, is capable of strict definition. The right honourable gentleman's proposition therefore admits of a test, which the advertiser's does not. To make his proposition perfect, the right honourable gentleman ought to define both those things which he declares to be equivalent to each other. Bank notes he has defined in his second Resolution: they are "engagements to pay certain sums of money in the legal coin of this kingdom." But he has omitted to define the "legal coin."

With his leave, I will venture to remind him that one pound in sterling money of this realm, is either $\frac{20}{21}$ of a guinea, weighing not less than $5^{dwts.}$ $8^{grs.}$ standard fineness; or it is $\frac{20}{62}$ of a lb. of standard silver. Does the right honourable gentleman object to either of those definitions? If not, does he maintain his proposition of equivalency? Does he maintain that a one-pound note is equivalent to $\frac{20}{21}$ of a lawful guinea, or to $\frac{20}{62}$ of a lb. of standard silver? Does he not know that a guinea is intrinsically worth not a one-pound note, with one shilling in addition, but with the addition of four or five shillings, at the present moment?—and that so far from purchasing nearly the third part of a lb.

of standard silver, a Bank note of one pound would now purchase little more than the fourth part of it?

But the right honourable gentleman warns us, that we overlook the force and real meaning of the word "legal" as employed in his Resolution. He alludes not to the laws which have fixed the standard, and which ensure the weight and purity of our coin; but to those which provide by wholesome penalties against the influence of its real upon its denominative value. The gold of a guinea may be worth what we will; the Resolution applies only to the gold in a guinea. It does not say that a Bank note is worth as much as a guinea. It says only that the guinea can pass for no more than the Bank note. It ties the living to the dead, and then pronounces them equal to each other. The gold which is necessary to constitute a guinea, may be worth twenty-six or twenty-seven shillings. The right honourable gentleman's business with it commences only when it has received the stamp and sanction of the Sovereign. It is then that, degraded by this distinction, and restricted by this guarantee, it loses about a fifth of its value, and becomes worth only a one-pound note and one shilling.

Be it so. This then may be the state of the law: but how does this prove "public estimation?" If the Resolution had purported merely that by law the guinea could pass for no more than twenty-one shillings, perhaps the right honourable gentleman may have the law on his side. But this proposition he had the sagacity to see would not answer his purpose. It would do nothing for the Bank note. It would settle the proportion between gold and silver coin; but not between either of those metals and Bank paper. Bank paper, until it is made the paper of the state, and a legal tender (which as yet happily it is not), must depend upon confidence for its value; and I am afraid that confidence may rather be impaired than restored by such a Resolution as the right honourable gentleman's.

There is, however, yet one addition, which qualifies the right honourable gentleman's proposition. Bank notes are not only "equivalent to legal coin," it seems, but are "generally accepted as such;" which to be sure it is natural to expect they should be, if equivalent. They are so accepted, however, not in all transactions. No—only in "transactions to which such coin is legally applicable." There are transactions, then, it seems, in which they are not accepted as equivalent? Yes; but those transactions are not legal ones. Is the purchase of gold bullion a legal transaction? I presume it is. A pound of gold bullion is at this moment worth about 58*l.* 16*s.* in Bank notes: 58*l.* 16*s.* in guineas, according to their current value, makes fifty-six guineas. Now forty-four and a-half of these guineas, we know, weigh exactly one pound. The right honourable gentleman, therefore, means gravely to affirm that there exist persons who will with equal readiness give 58*l.* 16*s.* in Bank notes, or fifty-six golden guineas, in payment for a commodity which is intrinsically worth exactly forty-four guineas and a-half. It warms one's heart to hear such heroic instances of more than Roman virtue: but I must be permitted to doubt whether they can be truly stated to be as "general," as the right honourable gentleman supposes. I doubt whether even the patriotic lottery-man, from whom the right honourable gentleman has borrowed his third Resolution, would make such a sacrifice as this to the laws of his country. I doubt whether the right honourable gentleman himself does not stand the single instance of such striking self-devotion: and would again submit to him, therefore, whether his third Resolution, instead of affirming any thing about the public, ought not to run singly in his own name.

But, after all, is the right honourable gentleman sure that he is prepared to define exactly, at this moment, the legality or illegality of interchanging guineas and Bank notes, at any other than the nominal current value? What cognizance does the law take of the rate at which Bank notes shall pass? Is there any law which touches this matter? If any body had such a fancy for Bank notes, and differed so entirely from the Bullion Committee, and from the right honourable gentleman, as to think them not only not depreciated in respect to coin, but as worth being bought up in coin at a premium; is there any law which would prevent him from gratifying his taste in this particular? If for more, might he not also buy them for less, than their nominal value? Is there any law to prevent that? The man who has been convicted, and is now expecting judgment for buying guineas at a premium, might he not justly aver that he had only sold Bank notes at a loss? Is there any law which forbids that? The right honourable gentleman may tell me, that this question is at this very moment before the judges of the land, by whose determination the conviction to which I have referred, will be either confirmed or reversed. And so I tell the right honourable gentleman; and from that very circumstance, from the law on that subject being in such a state of uncertainty as to require a reference to the judges, it is, in my opinion, unseemly, and must be most unsatisfactory, for the House of Commons to assume the law to be such as the right honourable gentleman's Resolution declares it.

But, supposing the declaration of the law by the right honourable gentleman's Resolution to be correct, how does it bear out his assertions as to "public estimation?"—Does he not know—is it not notorious—has it not been admitted in the course of this debate—that in one part of the United Kingdom, at least in Ireland, so far are Bank notes from being "equivalent to the legal coin in the public estimation," that a premium is openly given for guineas? Does the right honourable gentleman forget, that the House of Commons, to which he proposes his Resolution, is the House of Commons of Ireland as well as of Great Britain? And can he conceive a proceeding more likely to bring that House of Commons into contempt with the people of Ireland, than that, with the perfect knowledge which we have that they are every day exchanging Bank notes against guineas at a discount, we should come to a Resolution that—not in our estimation, but in theirs—Bank notes and guineas are equivalent?

When Buonaparte, not long ago, was desirous of reconciling the nations under his dominion to the privations resulting from the exclusion of all colonial produce, he published an edict, which commenced in something like the following manner:—"Whereas sugar made from beet-root or the maple-tree is infinitely preferable to that of the sugar-cane...." and then proceeded to denounce penalties against those who should persist in the use of the inferior commodity. The denunciation might be more effectual than the right honourable gentleman's Resolution; but the preamble did not go near so far; for though it asserted the superiority of the maple and beet-root sugar, it rested that assertion merely on the authority of the state, and did not pretend to sanction it by "public estimation."

When Galileo first promulgated the doctrine that the earth turned round the sun, and that the sun remained stationary in the centre of the universe, the holy fathers of the Inquisition took alarm at so daring an innovation, and forthwith declared the first of these propositions to be false and heretical, and the other to be erroneous in point of faith. The Holy Office "pledged itself to believe" that the earth was stationary and the sun moveable. This pledge had little effect in changing the natural course of things: the sun and the earth continued, in spite of it, to preserve their accustomed relations to each other, just as the coin and the Bank note will, in spite of the right honourable gentleman's Resolution.

The reverend fathers, indeed, had the advantage of being enabled to call in the aid of the secular arm, to enforce the acceptance of their doctrines. I confess, I am not wholly without apprehension that some of the zealous advocates for the right honourable gentleman's doctrine may have it in contemplation to employ similar means of proselytism. There is something ominous in that mixture of law and opinion, which pervades the right honourable gentleman's Resolution. The business of law is with conduct; but when it is put forward to influence opinion, pains and penalties are seldom far behind. I like but little the period of our history, to which my honourable and learned friend, the Attorney-General, was obliged to go back to find a penal statute for settling opinions upon the value of money—that statute upon which the late convictions have taken place, and upon the applicability of which to the present times the Judges are now deliberating. This statute was passed at a period when our coin had been debased, in the course of three years, considerably upwards of £200 per cent. —and when the total debasement, as compared with the original standard, was not less than £355 per cent. The consequence of this debasement, as stated by Lord Liverpool, was, that merchants and tradesmen increased the price of every article which they had to sell. To counteract this effect, Government tried every method to keep up the value of the debased coin; prices were set on all the necessary articles of consumption; laws were passed for regulating the manner of buying and selling; the law against regraters, forestallers, and engrossers, since repealed, was passed on that occasion. Amongst those admirable and judicious efforts of wholesome and enlightened legislation, was enacted the law for inflicting penalties on those who should "exchange any coined gold or coined silver at a greater value than the same was or should be declared, by His

Majesty's proclamation, to be current for within his dominions."

Such is the law which, according to the right honourable gentleman, secures the equivalency of the different sorts of our currency. Such is the shelf from which that law has been taken down and brought into use on the present auspicious occasion: a law passed at a time which the late Lord Liverpool forcibly describes as a "period of convulsion in our monetary system," and in company with laws which have since been repealed as a disgrace to the statute book. Faulty, however, as our legislation appears to have been at the period to which we are referring, it at least did not fall into the absurdity of declaring such laws to be the opinions of the people. If the right honourable gentleman is determined to force opinions to conform to his law, he must come down a few years later in our history. He must pass from the reign of Edward the VIth, to that of Queen Mary, to find the most approved method of applying the operation of law to the reformation of speculative opinions.

Even in times, however, of such ignorance, and such licentious theory, in respect to the value of money, there were not wanting in one part of this island shrewder spirits, who saw the errors into which the English Government were running, and determined to guard against their effects, at least upon themselves. In the year 1529, it is related in a note to Lord Liverpool's Treatise, " Gavin Dunbar, Bishop of Aberdeen, in a contract with William Sutherland, of Duffus, stipulated, that 'if it should happen that the money of Scotland, or of any other kingdom, which passes in Scotland, be raised to a higher price than it is now taken in payment for, whereby the reverend father, his heirs or assigns, be made poorer or in a worse condition, he the said William Sutherland should pay to the possessors (whoever they may be) of the annual rent reserved therein, for every mark of thirty-two pennies, one ounce of pure silver of certain fineness, or else its true value in the usual money of the kingdom of Scotland.' " This contract took place about twenty years before the statute of Edward VI. If that statute shall be revived and acted upon, and if the doctrine of the right honourable gentleman's Resolutions shall be sanctioned by Parliament, it requires no great stretch of apprehension to foresee that men will, ere long, endeavour to guard themselves against the effects of such a system by resorting to contracts of a similar nature.

I have now done with the right honourable gentleman's third Resolution. I will only again say, that if any man had mentioned it to me out of this House, as a proposition which the right honourable gentleman intended to offer for our acceptance, I should have utterly disbelieved him: I should have considered such a rumour as a mere device on the part of his opponents, to place in the strongest light imaginable the absurdity to which, if pushed to all their consequences, the right honourable gentleman's arguments were capable of going.

Passing over the statistical Resolutions, from the fourth to the fourteenth, inclusive, I come now to the fifteenth, which contains the right honourable gentleman's doctrine of exchanges.*

This Resolution partakes, in a very striking degree, of the faults which I had occasion to remark upon in the first of the series to which it belongs. From the vague and imperfect manner in which it is expressed, the proposition intended to be conveyed by it is rather insinuated than affirmed. The right honourable gentleman does not distinctly deny that the state of our currency has any influence on the foreign exchanges, or on the price of bullion; at the same time, he certainly does not admit that it has any such influence. He only asserts that there are other causes "sufficient to account for the unfavourable state of the exchange, and the high price of bullion, without any change in" (what he calls) "the internal value of our currency."

Now it cannot escape so accurate an understanding as that of the right honourable gentleman, that this mode of stating his argument, is

* See Res. 15.

not an answer to the main points in dispute, but an evasion of them. The Bullion Report asserts, that our paper currency is depreciated, and that the depreciation of our currency has raised the price of gold, and turned and kept the foreign exchanges against us. The right honourable gentleman replies, not by denying both these assertions, but by affirming, with respect to the latter, that the imputed consequences may have been produced by other causes, without the existence of the cause specifically assigned for them.

We know, indeed, from the preceding part of the right honourable gentleman's argument, that he does deny the depreciation of our currency. So far he is perfectly intelligible. But as to the second proposition, "that the depreciated currency has occasioned the rise in the price of bullion and the unfavourableness of the foreign exchanges," are we to understand him as saying, that a depreciated currency would not have those effects? or only, that as our currency is not depreciated, such effects cannot in this instance be attributable to that cause?

If he admits that such would be the natural effects of a depreciated currency, admitting at the same time (as he does) that such effects do exist the whole of his argument is destroyed by his own admissions. The utmost advantage that he could then derive even from the undisputed admission of all the facts enumerated in his statistical Resolutions—of his prices of stocks, and prices of corn, his exports and imports, and revenue and expenditure—would be to shew that there are other causes which may enter for something into the degree of the rise in the price of bullion, and into the degree of the unfavourableness of the exchange, which nobody denies.

But to acknowledge the tendency of a depreciated currency to produce certain effects, to acknowledge these effects to have been produced to an extent, and to have continued for a length of time, unexampled in the history of the country, —and then to expect that upon the mere *dictum* of the right honourable gentleman, his adversaries in the argument shall consent to ascribe those effects wholly to other causes, of which they deny the sufficiency, altogether excluding the operation of that one, the efficacy of which he himself admits, is to reckon upon a degree of ductility in those with whom he argues, which even the right honourable gentleman's authority is not entitled to command.

On the other hand, does the right honourable gentleman contend, that the depreciation of our currency, even if it existed, would not affect the exchange? To argue that it would not affect the price of bullion in that currency, is certainly more than he can venture. But it has been contended by others who take the same side with him, that depreciation "of internal value" in the currency of a country has no tendency to alter the foreign exchange. Is this the right honourable gentleman's meaning?

By "internal value," I now understand the right honourable gentleman to signify not "intrinsic value," as I was at first inclined to suppose, but value in internal or domestic currency, as opposed to value abroad. The proposition then of those who push the right honourable gentleman's argument to its extent is, that the currency of a country may be depreciated to an indefinite degree, and yet, if the inhabitants of that country continue, no matter whether voluntarily or by legal compulsion, to receive that depreciated currency at its full nominal value, the foreigner has no business with it, and the foreign exchange would not exhibit any symptom of being affected by it. The very definition of exchange, about which I apprehend there is no dispute, is of itself sufficient to confute this doctrine. The par of exchange between any two countries, being an equal quantity of precious metal in the respective currencies of those countries, how is it possible, that if, by any process, the currency of one of those countries shall cease to contain or to represent that quantity of precious metal which it did represent or contain when the par of exchange with the other country was assigned—the currency of that other country remaining precisely the same—there should not take place a proportionate variation in the rate of the exchange? To say that the rate of exchange will continue unaltered, when one of the currencies between which the comparison is made has lost part of its value, is to say, in other words, that an equation is not destroyed by a change in the value of one of its terms.

We should be sufficiently alive to the fallacy of such a doctrine, if applied to the currency of other countries. In the edict lately published in Austria, which has been referred to more than once in the course of these debates, while a gradual depreciation, amounting in the end to no less than £400 per cent. is acknowledged, and the paper directed to be current henceforth at £400 per cent. below its nominal value; sundry excellent reasons are given why, in Austria, in the particular circumstances of that country, this depreciation ought to occasion no manner of alarm; and especially why foreigners ought not to consider it as vitiating or confounding the transactions of exchange. The foreign creditors of Austria, however, probably entertain a very different opinion: and it is a curious fact, which has been vouched to me on what I believe to be unquestionable authority, that even before the Austrian paper money was depreciated to the present extravagant degree, the monied men on the continent, who were engaged in loans to the

Emperor, were in the habit of stipulating that those loans, if repaid any where else than at Hamburgh or at Amsterdam, should be repaid, not in the currency of Austria, or of any other country, according to its denomination, but in specific quantities of gold or silver. And why this exception in favour of Hamburgh and Amsterdam? For a reason which at once explains the nature of exchange, and the true principles of value in money, namely, that at the Banks of Hamburgh and Amsterdam, all payments are made, not in reference to coins of any country or any denomination, but by the transfer from the debtor to the creditor of a specific quantity of bullion.

Can we really flatter ourselves, then, that the currency of this kingdom might be depreciated with impunity so far as relates to transactions with foreign countries? If a bill upon England for 46*l.* 14*s.* 6*d.* would heretofore have purchased, on the exchange of Hamburgh or Amsterdam, a credit on those Banks for a pound of gold bullion, and if a pound of gold bullion cannot now be purchased in England for less than 58*l.* in English currency, can we imagine that, nevertheless, the bill upon England for 46*l.* 14*s.* 6*d.* will still purchase a pound of gold at Hamburgh or Amsterdam? Yet this is, in fact, the proposition of those who contend that an alteration in the value of the internal currency of a country does not proportionably affect the foreign exchange.

But while this is the argument of many who have taken part in the debate—whilst it is covertly, though not avowedly, the argument of the right honourable gentleman's fifteenth Resolution—it is not the argument of my right honourable friend the Chancellor of the Exchequer, who has admitted the influence of the internal currency of a country upon its foreign exchanges, by admitting that a diminution in the quantity of our paper would tend to turn the exchanges in our favour. Does the right honourable gentleman agree in this admission, or differ from it? If he differs, I refer him for conviction to my right honourable friend: if he agrees, there is no escape from the conclusion to which this admission leads—that the unfavourableness of the exchange, which would be, in part at least, cured by a diminution in the amount, and consequent rise in the value of our paper currency, is, in part at least, occasioned by the excess and consequent depreciation of it.

What then becomes of the assertion in the right honourable gentleman's fifteenth Resolution, whichever sense we assign to it? If it is meant to deny the connection of internal currency with foreign exchange, can the House consent to adopt a vote so directly at variance with the fact? If, admitting that connection, it is meant only to deny its effect now, why, I should be glad to know, is the present time to afford an exception to an universal rule? What is there now to suspend the operation of principles, not dependent upon circumstances, but inherent in the nature of things? There is a great stagnation of commerce it is true, but that stagnation of commerce is not peculiar to this country. The continent shares largely in all the distress which the decrees of the tyrant of the continent produce; and yet it is in comparison with the continent that the exchanges are in our disfavour. True, we are carrying on an expensive and extended war; but the exchanges have been permanently against us in peace as well as in war, when the same cause, a depreciated currency, has operated to produce that effect. In 1696, a period of war, the deterioration of our silver, then our standard coin—in 1773, a time of peace, the deterioration of our gold coin, were indicated alike by the long continued unfavourableness of the foreign exchanges. In both instances the reformation of the coin remedied the evil. What the deterioration of coin occasioned in those instances, the depreciation of paper has occasioned now. The coin had then ceased to contain, as the paper has now ceased to represent, the quantity of precious metal implied by its denomination. Foreign countries estimated the coin then as they do the paper now, not by what it was called, but by what it would exchange for in those commodities—gold and silver—which are, by the consent and practice of mankind, the common measures of all marketable value.

However gentlemen may endeavour to disguise and perplex this simple view of the question, it is, after all, that by which it must be decided. If this be not the test, there is no other. If gold and silver have ceased to be the common measures of the value of other commodities, and weight and fineness combined have ceased to be the standard of value in gold and silver, there is no more to be said: but in that case, instead of these Resolutions, let the right honourable gentleman come forward boldly at once with an assertion, not merely that paper is equivalent to the precious metals, but that it has altogether superseded them.

If, on the other hand, the same standard of value remains, let not the right honourable gentleman attempt to draw a veil over it. In all our departures from it, let us fairly own that we are departing from it—by necessity, if you please, but with a resolution of returning to it again. Let us not, like men who, when hurried down a rapid stream, fancy that the shores are flying from them—

> "terræque urbesque recedunt;"

let us not conceive that, by some strange revolution in the physical world, the precious metals are retreating beyond our reach; when it is, in fact, only by a rapid depreciation that our currency is leaving them behind. Neither let us suppose that we have already gone down so far, that to reascend the stream is impossible—that,

> "Should we wade no more,
> Returning were as tedious as go o'er."

A very little firmness, a very little sacrifice, might at present enable us to retrace our course. The half of the ingenuity which is employed in the right honourable gentleman's Resolutions to gloss over our situation, might suffice to find a remedy for it.

It is asked—shall we attempt this in time of war? Can we attempt it without abandoning our present military system, with all its hopes and all its glories? Undoubtedly, I think, we can. I never can believe of this mighty empire that it has not sufficient energy in itself at once to right whatever may be amiss in its own internal situation, and to maintain its accustomed place and movement in the system of the world.

But, it is said, we are only going on in the course in which greater authorities have led the way; Mr. Pitt had made up his mind to this depreciation of our currency. "He contrived it," says one honourable gentleman. "He could not avoid foreseeing it," says my right honourable friend (the Chancellor of the Exchequer).

First, the inconveniencies which now result from that depreciation, and which constitute the proof of it, were not felt in Mr. Pitt's time. Neither could they possibly be foreseen by Mr. Pitt, if they in fact arise only from the causes to which my right honourable friend and the right honourable gentleman's fifteenth Resolution ascribe them: Mr. Pitt certainly could not foresee the Berlin and Milan decrees. The war, indeed, raged in his life-time with not less violence than since; but yet in the very hottest and most disastrous part of the war, at the moment of the greatest public alarm and calamity, the exchanges were in our favour, and the price of gold did not materially rise. He therefore did not witness any of those symptoms which have awakened anxiety, and led to investigation on the present occasion.

Further, we have the testimony of my honourable friend opposite to me, (Mr. Wilberforce), that in the year 1802, when the probable tendency of unredeemable Bank paper to excessive issue, and consequent depreciation, became a subject of alarm to some men of great ability in financial matters—we have, I say, that most satisfactory testimony, that Mr. Pitt at that time professed his entire agreement in the principles laid down in a very able publication of the honourable gentleman who preceded me in this night's debate (Mr. H. Thornton), which I presume every man who has attended to this question, has read. And what are those principles? —Why, these—

"It is the maintenance of our general exchanges" (says Mr. Thornton), "or, in other words, it is the agreement of the mint price with the bullion price of gold, which seems to be the true proof that the circulating paper is not depreciated."

If these are the principles which Mr. Pitt sanctioned, what pretence is there for saying that he foresaw the present state of things? or that, if he had lived to see it, he would now have asserted our circulating paper to be in an undepreciated state? Are our "general exchanges" now "maintained?" "Does the bullion price of gold" now "agree with the mint price?" Are not, on the contrary, the unfavourable exchanges, and the high price of bullion, the very particulars which are cited as affording the most irrefragable proof of a depreciation? If the absence of these criteria at that time was conclusive one way, must not the presence of them be now admitted to be conclusive the other? If Mr. Pitt was then satisfied that all was right because these symptoms had not appeared, is it fair to infer, that he would have been equally satisfied now, when they are seen in so aggravated a degree? Is not the fair inference directly the contrary?

Nor is it an unimportant evidence of Mr. Pitt's general view of this subject, that the Letter of Lord Liverpool to the King was the result of an investigation commenced in Mr. Pitt's first administration in 1798, and concluded in the year 1805, when he was again minister of the country. In that letter, not only are all the principles of our money system distinctly and ably expounded, according to the authority and the practice of the best times; but, with respect to the system of our paper currency, the danger of its being carried to excess, and the necessity of a parliamentary revision of it, are stated in a manner which shews with how much attention, in the opinion of the Government of those days, that system required to be watched.

But if Mr. Pitt had happily been still alive, what remedy would he have applied to this evil? Far be it from me to presume on this or on any other occasion to usurp the authority of his name, or to employ it for any purpose, which is not warranted by his recorded opinions. But that he would have applied some remedy—that he would not have been contented to let the evil take its course, if there were in human wisdom the means of checking it—that he would not have sought to reconcile delusion with credit, and to palliate a departure from principles by a denial of the principles themselves; every man who remembers his characteristic firmness, who recollects the difficulties which he had to combat, and the manner in which he combated and overcame them, will, I think, be ready to acknowledge.

If I am asked what remedy I would myself apply, I again say, as I have said before, that it must rest with the Executive Government to propose, as they alone can advantageously carry into effect, any measure of practical benefit. But I have no difficulty in offering one suggestion, which has indeed been in some degree anticipated in the course of these debates. The Bank proprietors have made great and unusual gains under the operation of the Bank restriction. I say this without the smallest intention of laying blame upon the Bank, or of exciting any invidious feeling towards them. The Directors of that Institution, I again repeat, have, so far as I can judge, acted for the best in the discharge of a new and most difficult duty. But the fact I believe will not be disputed. Great gains have been made in consequence of the Bank restriction. The issues of Bank paper, whether too large or not in another view, have undeniably been much larger than they could have been, had the obligation to pay in cash upon demand continued, or been renewed. These gains certainly formed no part of the inducement to lay on or to renew the Bank restriction. They form no ground to continue it.

But it is obvious—it is in the principles of human nature—that they must form a temptation to the Bank proprietors to wish for its continuance. It is obvious also, that if the issues are inordinately extended, the difficulty of resuming cash payments must be proportionably augmented. And it is still more obvious, that whether those motives and those causes do in fact so operate or no, from the natural invidiousness attendant on great gains, the world in general will be apt to suspect and impute their operation.

Now the public has no right to complain that the Bank restriction, though not laid or continued in contemplation of advantage to the Bank proprietors, has incidentally been productive of such advantage; but they have a right to expect that no impediment shall on that ground be thrown in the way of the removal of the restriction. A continued increase of profit, and a continued raising of the dividends to the Bank proprietors, if it had not that effect, would have that appearance. The dividend is now, I believe, ten per cent. There surely it might stop. All surplus profit beyond that amount, during the continuance of the restriction, might be strictly appropriated as a fund for the purchase of bullion, at whatever price.

It is not in my contemplation that the public (as has been suggested in several quarters since this question has been in discussion) should enter into any share of the extraordinary profits, or meddle in any degree in the management, of the Bank. No such thing. Let those extraordinary profits remain, in full, undisputed, and unenvied property, to the Bank. But as they are created by the suspension of cash payments, let the public have the assurance that they are so employed by the Bank, as to ensure their ability to resume those payments, without convulsion or distress, at the period which the Legislature has fixed for the resumption of them.

This, I think, is a suggestion, the adoption of which would be no less creditable to the Bank than satisfactory to the public.

For this, or any other measure calculated to remedy the evils acknowledged to exist, we can, after the decision to which this House has already come, rely only on the effect which may be produced by our discussions upon the advised discretion of the Bank, and upon the awakened attention of the public.

But at least, if we will do no good, let us, in the name of common sense, not do any harm. If we will not set right the course of the vessel, let us at least not destroy the chart and compass by which it may steer.

Let us leave the evil, if it must be so, to the chance of a gradual and noiseless correction. But let us not resolve as law, what is an incorrect and imperfect exposition of the law. Let us not resolve as fact, what is contradictory to universal experience. Let us not expose ourselves to ridicule, by resolving, as the opinions of the people, opinions which the people do not, and which it is impossible they should, entertain. This is not the way to settle the public feeling, and to set the subject at rest. It is the way to ensure renewed and interminable discussions. That we may at least not incur this unnecessary mischief, by adopting the Resolutions now before us, I move, Sir, that you do now leave the Chair.

The House divided on Mr. Canning's Amendment, when there appeared—

For Mr. Canning's Amendment	42
Against it	82
Majority against it	40

Mr. VANSITTART'S Resolutions were then agreed to *pro forma*, with an understanding that they should be discussed upon the Report. The discussion on Mr. Vansittart's Resolutions was resumed on the following day; and on the 15th, after some verbal amendments, they were agreed to.

THE CATHOIC CLAIMS.

JUNE 22nd, 1812.

MR. CANNING rose, and said—

MR. SPEAKER,

WHEN you consider the extent and magnitude of the subject which I have undertaken this day to press upon the attention of the House, with the hope, that through their decision I may succeed in recommending it to the serious attention of the Executive Government; when you recollect the various discussions which this subject has undergone, as well within these walls as in other places; when you reflect on the anxiety which it keeps alive in one part of the united kingdom, an anxiety of which I am sorry to say, we have, in the course of this very day, received some strong and painful indications;* you may perhaps be led to apprehend that I shall find myself obliged to trespass on your patience for a considerable length of time. In this apprehension, however, I hope the House will be disappointed: for, however wide the compass, and however complicated the details of this great question may be,

* The Resolutions passed at the Aggregate Meeting of the Roman Catholics, in Dublin, on Thursday, June 18th, which were received in London on the morning of Mr. Canning's motion.

yet the statement which I think it necessary to make of it, for the purpose of my present motion, rests on a few plain and simple principles.

If, Sir, I stood up here this day in the character of a partisan of those whose claims are involved in our decision, I confess I should feel myself under no small difficulty and embarrassment. The intelligence this day received from Ireland, which is probably within the knowledge of most gentlemen who hear me, might well perplex an advocate of the Catholics, and might not unnaturally be expected to disincline the House from listening to him with favour.

But in the view which I have always taken and continue to take of this subject, and which I am sanguine enough to hope that I may induce the House to take of it, the recent proceeding of the Catholic Meeting in Dublin, appears to me only as one symptom of that habitual irritation of the public mind in Ireland, which is produced by the unsettled state of this question; and as one additional motive for recommending the immediate consideration of it, in the only quarters, and in the only mode, by which it can be brought to a final and satisfactory adjustment.

The information of this day, therefore, so far from deterring me from the discussion, will only make me more anxious to treat it in such a manner, as may preclude all invidious topics, and all inflammatory language. It is not as in a struggle of conflicting parties, that I would ask the House to interfere. It is to a great state question, that I wish to direct their attention—a question enveloped, indeed, with many difficulties, and those difficulties certainly not diminished by the circumstances to which I have alluded; but neither ought such circumstances to weigh in any sober mind, as reasons for rejecting the motion which I have to offer to them, much rather should they induce us to lose no time in looking seriously and dispassionately at a question which, in my conscience, I believe must be settled, if we wish to give peace to the united kingdom.

Not only would I endeavour to steer clear of every thing that has reference to the temporary irritation of the moment, but most gladly would I persuade the House, if possible, to lay out of its recollection all former debates and differences on this subject. If we could bring ourselves to consider this subject as if it were now presented to us for the first time—to look at it with a fresh eye—such a view, I really think, might be obtained of it, as would lead, unless I flatter myself unreasonably, to a pretty general acquiescence in the motion which I shall have the honour of proposing.

The principles, Sir, on which I rest that motion, and upon which the whole of this great question appears to me to rest, are these—

First, without subjecting myself to the suspicion of adopting any of those wild theories of abstract right—of rights of man, and rights of citizens—

which have been afloat in the world for the last twenty years, I may assume, as a general rule, that citizens of the same state—subjects living under the same government—are entitled, *primâ facie*, to equal political rights and privileges. This, Sir, I say, is the general rule; exceptions undoubtedly there are: but upon those who maintain the exceptions, lies the *onus probandi*—the shewing that they are necessary, and therefore just. I am far from asserting, at this moment, that necessary, and therefore just exceptions may not have existed; I am not even asserting that they may not still exist, in the case of the Roman Catholics. I am only assuming the general rule to be that which I have stated; and throwing the burthen of the argument in favour of the exceptions where, in truth and in right reason, it ought to lie.

The next principle which I assume is this—That it is at all times desirable to create and to maintain the strictest union, the most perfect identity of interest and of feeling among all the members of the same community. If this be desirable at all times, and in all countries, it will hardly be disputed that it must be more especially so to the British Empire, in the present state of the war, and of the world; when the greatest combination of hostile force of which ancient or modern history affords an example, is arrayed against us under a mighty conqueror, before whom state after state, and kingdom after kingdom, are falling in prostrate subjection; and who considers the subjugation of continental Europe only as the preface and the means of our destruction. To this, as a general rule, it will not be contended that there is, in principle, any exception; it will not be contended that it can ever be wise and salutary to divide and dissipate, instead of uniting the force, the faculties, and the affections of the people; to afford just grounds for dissension and discontent; to leave open some flaw or crevice in the solid body of the state, through which the machinations of the enemy may insinuate principles of disunion. But I am aware that it may be objected, that such an union, though desirable, is impracticable; that there are causes of complaint, inevitable and irremoveable, and differences which, though they ought not to be fomented, yet cannot be healed. This may be so: but here again if the general principle be admitted, the burthen of proof is left with those who maintain that, in a particular case, it cannot be reduced into practice.

The third general principle, and that on which I most confidently anticipate an undivided coincidence of opinion, is—That where there exists, in any community, a great permanent cause of political discontent, which agitates the minds of men, and has agitated them for many years past; and when experience has shewn that, so far from having any tendency to subside and settle itself by mutual forbearance and accommodation, the contest only grows more fierce the longer it is protracted; mingles with all the disquietudes, and allies itself with all the real or imaginary grievances of the country; it becomes the duty of the supreme power of the state, whether residing in one or in many, whether King, or Senate, or Parliament, to take a question of such a nature into its own consideration; to make up its own mind upon it, and finally to determine in what mode it may be most advantageously set at rest. To this general rule, I am not aware of any exception; for I am not aware of any possible circumstances in which it must not be infinitely more dangerous to leave such a question unconsidered and uncontrolled, than to attempt the settlement of it; and I am not prepared to hear that the settlement of any question, however difficult and complicated, lies out of the province, or beyond the competency of the collective wisdom and authority of the state.

These, Sir, are the principles which I take the liberty to assume as the foundation of the motion which I am about to submit to the House. But I am aware that, in examining any proposition, the object or tendency of which is to introduce change of any description in the constitutions of human society, there are two general considerations, clashing very much with each other, which naturally present themselves to every reflecting mind. The one, the most extensive, perhaps the most popular, is the dread of innovation; the other, the expediency of timely reformation or concession. In reconciling these opposite and conflicting principles, and in assigning to each its due weight in human affairs, consists almost the whole art of practical policy.

They, Sir, who argue against any further concession to the Catholics on the ground of a dread of innovation, undertake a task of greater difficulty than, so far as I can judge from any discussion which I have yet heard upon this subject, they seem themselves to be aware. For this argument naturally implies the previous existence of some regular, fixed, and intelligible state of things, formed with deliberate wisdom, or perfected by frequent revision, and established by long consent or beneficial experience—some system, sealed and sanctioned by the acquiescence of successive generations. To innovate upon such a state of things, would indeed bespeak a culpable degree of rashness, and must throw upon the presumptuous innovator the duty of a most difficult justification. But, looking at the code of laws under which the Catholics have lived, and at the remains of that code under which they still live, I should be glad to ask those who stand upon long-established usage; who protest against being led astray from the ancient ways; who will not launch into untried experiments; I should be glad to ask them, at what period of our history they conceive that system upon which they are so fearful of encroaching, to have flourished in full perfection? I ask what was its origin? On what design was it framed? When did it receive the finishing hand, and become incorporated into the institutions of the country, an integral part of a blameless and perfect constitution? Will they look back for this perfection to that period, when the corruptions and disorders of the church first provoked that just inquiry and indignation, and gave rise to those discussions, which convulsed Europe, which split the Christian world into contending sects, and ended in the establishment of the Reformation? Great and manifold as are the blessings which the whole civilized world, and this nation in particular, have derived from the transactions of that time; indebted as we are to them for the substitution of a pure and perfect form of worship, in the place of a system of faith defiled with innumerable corruptions, and incumbered with superstitious usages; yet, can any one be so blind to fact as to contend that the blessings which have been thus derived to us, ought to recommend to our respect and imitation the violences which accompanied their origin? It is the prerogative of Providence to bring good out of evil. The lust and tyranny, the rapine and prodigality, of Henry VIII. were instruments in the hand of Heaven for bringing about the Reformation. But are we therefore to look to the reign of Henry the

Eighth for specimens of civil legislation?—a reign in which the conscience of the subject was made to conform, under bloody penalties, to every varying caprice of the judgment or passion of the sovereign, in which, according to the historians of that period, "those who were for the Pope were hanged, and those against the Pope were burned?" The same Parliament, which, by the sanguinary law of the Six Articles, enabled the Defender of the Faith and Head of the Church to exercise these indiscriminate and impartial severities in matter of religion, did not scruple to bow quite as low in matter of temporal policy; and surrendered into the monarch's hands the liberties of his people, by giving to his proclamation the authority of law. It is not surely to such a reign, or to statutes passed by such Parliaments, that we can be taught to refer for a pure specimen of British legislation, applicable to the times in which we live!

During the succeeding reign, these laws were repealed or suspended, and the Reformation was silently making progress and gaining strength. The horrible butcheries of Queen Mary, while they curdle the blood, and make the soul sick in the contemplation of them, dispose us to look with an eye of peculiar favour upon her successor Elizabeth; and to fancy that the reign of that great and admirable Princess was illustrated by the complete enjoyment of civil freedom, as well as by glory abroad and prosperity at home. Undoubtedly the government of Elizabeth was conducted with a wisdom and success that covered the British Empire with glory and prosperity; but it is surely not to that reign that the opponents of all change will refer us, as to the time at which the system which they wish to uphold was in a state that should have been preserved inviolate. In the latter years of that reign, a spirit of persecution arose, for which even her warmest admirers think it necessary to apologise. Bishop Burnett himself, in his History of the Reformation, quotes the testimony of Walsingham to this effect—not denying the severities to which Elizabeth had recourse; but justifying them as necessary to the security of her crown, against the plots and conspiracies of the Pope and his adherents. Where is now the popish conspiracy against which the Crown has to guard? Or are the enemies of innovation desirous only of adhering to Queen Elizabeth's severities, but careless of her justification?

It is not to the reign of James I., when the gunpowder treason naturally excited a horror of papists, and forbade any relaxation of the laws in force against them—it is not to the turbulent and unfortunate times of Charles I. that we shall be taught to look back for a model for any part of our legislative system. If the troubles of Charles the First's time are to be connected with religious tenets, assuredly the Roman Catholic religion is not that to which we have to attribute the overthrow of the monarchy and of the established church. During the Protectorate, a regular system, not of coercion and penal law, not of confiscation merely, but of extirpation, was acted upon towards the Catholics of Ireland. In the reign of Charles II. we find the establishment of the test, and the exclusion of the Roman Catholics of this country from Parliament; transactions, however, which must be coupled in our recollection with the special grounds of jealousy and alarm, which dictated and justified such precautions.

But the Revolution is the period to which we are desired to refer most particularly, as well for the laws against Roman Catholics as for the spirit in which they were framed, and in which we ought to maintain them. It is undoubtedly true that great restraints were at that period imposed upon the Catholics, both in England and Ireland, as the consequence, and a just and legitimate consequence, of the intimate connection of the Catholic religion, at that time, with political doctrines hostile to the civil and religious establishments of this country, and with the interests of an exiled and abdicated Sovereign. But neither would the policy of those times be necessarily just, when the connection between the religious and political doctrines no longer subsisted; nor is it true that the penal and disabling statutes which were passed in Ireland immediately after the Revolution, statutes which gleaned the refuse of the sword of the conqueror, and which are fairly to be considered rather as means of enforcing and ensuring the obedience of a conquered country, than as sound legislative enactments for the government of a kingdom in loyalty and peace; it is not true, I say, that these statutes did in fact constitute the whole, or near the whole, of that code of penal laws, which we are called upon to preserve as the legacy of our forefathers, as the testament of our civil freedom. That code was not completed until a much later period. We must come down through the reigns of Anne, and of the two first princes of the House of Hanover, before we find the system brought to perfection.

The House will therefore observe, that it was not till the middle of the last century that this system of laws was really matured. In latter times, the character of the enactments became less sanguinary, though hardly less severe. Under the furious and fanatical government of Cromwell, the active principle was that of absolute extermination. At the Revolution, a civil war and a contested crown naturally led to confiscations and proscriptions. Subsequently to the Revolution, and up to the period at which the last penal law was passed, the principle upon which the system has proceeded, has been calculated to stunt the growth; to destroy the moral energies; and to cramp the industry of the Irish Catholic population; to keep the mass of the people of Ireland, for such they may be called, in poverty and ignorance, for the purpose of ensuring their submission. That such a plan of policy should have been acted upon, nay avowed, by statesmen of splendid abilities and comprehensive minds, by ministers who served this their country with zeal and honour, and whose names are held in veneration among us, may be matter of curious and indignant speculation to the philosophical inquirer: but I think we want other arguments than a mere appeal to great names, to reconcile us to the adhering to such a system, or to induce us to regret that it has been abandoned.

Let us look at the state of the Catholic in the year 1760, at the accession of his present Majesty, when the system in Ireland had received the finishing hand, and before any remedial or alleviating measures had been applied to it. We find him cut off from all the relations of social life; we find the law interfering between the parent and child—between the husband and the wife; stimulating the wife to treachery against her husband—and the son to disobedience towards his parent; establishing a line of separation in the nuptial bed, and offering an undivided inheritance as the tempting prize for filial disobedience. I am sure that no man will now venture to say, that this is a state in which, consistently with the spirit of British legislation, any class of His Majesty's subjects ought to be placed: yet this is the state to which those who admire the penal code in its perfection must refer: and it is to this state that we should return, if we were to reject, as innovation, every amelioration that has been made in that code since the period of its maturity.

But it belongs to this system, in a degree beyond other systems of unnatural violence, that no sooner had it arrived at its maturity, than it began to decay. Other systems have had a period during which they grew, a period during which they flourished, and in which they flourished for some time before their vigour began to decline: but in this, ripeness and decay were nearly coincident. After the greater part of two centuries had been spent in bringing it to maturity, this code existed in perfection only about fourteen years. From the beginning of his present Majesty's reign, to the year 1774, when the first relaxing statute was enacted, is the short period during which it was at once complete and stationary. That, therefore, is the period at which those must look who would admire it in all the fulness of its glory. Every step taken in respect to it since 1774, has been in the spirit, so much deprecated, of irreverent innovation.

On what grounds have those several steps been taken? What is the justification of the Parliaments of George III. for having undone, piece by piece, the measures of his royal predecessors? What but this? That in every stage of our preceding history, not religious tenets, but political disaffection, was the cause of the severities against the Catholics; that the penal code was not intended to exclude the believers in transubstantiation, as a sect: but to repress, or disarm, or punish them as traitors or rebels. Such, as I have already said, was the defence which the apologists of Elizabeth thought necessary for the rigour of the latter years of her reign; such is the language of every penal statute since the Revolution; in none of which do we find the imputations against the religious creed of the Papists, dissociated from the charge of treason or treasonable design. The preambles to these statutes recite, not that the Catholics are bigots, but that they are disloyal subjects. On this alone, the best constitutional writers, lawyers, and others, whose opinions are the most entitled to our reverence, have undertaken the defence of these harsh; though, at some time, necessary laws. See how Mr. Justice Blackstone describes the nature and effect of the penal statutes against the Catholics: —"This is a short summary (says he) of the laws against the papists, under three several classes of persons professing the popish religion; Popish recusants, convict, and Popish priests; of which the President Montesquieu observes, that they are so rigorous, though not professedly of the sanguinary kind, that they do all the hurt that can possibly be done in cold blood. But in answer to this, it may be observed (what foreigners who only judge from our statute-book, are not fully apprised of), that these laws are seldom exerted to their utmost rigour: and, indeed if they were, it would be very difficult to excuse them; for they are rather to be accounted for from their history, and the urgency of the times that produced them, than to be approved (upon a cool review), as a standing system of law."

The learned writer proceeds with some historical allusions to the events which gave birth, successively, to the different parts of the penal code affecting Catholics, and then goes on to say—

"But if a time should ever arrive, and perhaps it is not very distant, when all fears of a Pretender shall have vanished, and the power and influence of the Pope shall become feeble, ridiculous and despicable,"—(who but must think that the learned judge anticipated the moment in which I am now speaking?)—"not only in England, but in every kingdom of Europe; it probably would not then be amiss to review and soften these rigorous edicts, at least till the *civil* principles of the Roman Catholics called again upon the legislature to renew them; for it ought not to be left in the breast of every merciless bigot, to drag down the vengeance of these occasional laws upon inoffensive, though mistaken subjects, in opposition to the lenient inclinations of the civil magistrate, and to the destruction of every principle of toleration and religious liberty."

What, Sir, is the fair inference from these sentiments? That not the religious tenets of the Catholics, but their political opinions and attachments, operating upon their civil conduct, were the grounds of the penal statutes against them:—That not their religious differences from the Church of England, but their connection with foreign powers, and with interests politically hostile to the state, constituted the justification of the enactment of that code, and furnished the only apology that could be equitably urged for its continuance.

We have then to ask, if this be so, whether the relaxations which have actually taken place in the latter part of the reign of his present Majesty, have been made in a spirit of just indulgence and political wisdom?—a proposition which, be it remembered, the clamourers against innovation are bound to controvert with all their might.

With a view to the solution of this question, it will be curious to trace the history of the relaxing statutes, and to ascertain how far they have proceeded in conformity to the principle thus laid down by Mr. Justice Blackstone. A short examination of their preambles will be sufficient to shew that the legislature uniformly had that principle in their contemplation; that they uniformly looked at the religious tenets of the Catholics, but as the signs and symbols of their political opinions. The first relaxation was by the Irish Act of 1774, the preamble of which is as follows:—

"Whereas, many of His Majesty's subjects in this kingdom are desirous to testify their loyalty and allegiance to His Majesty, and their abhorrence of certain doctrines imputed to them, and to remove jealousies which hereby have for a length of time subsisted between them and others of His Majesty's loyal subjects; but, upon account of their religious tenets are, by the laws now in being, prevented from giving public assurances of such allegiance, and of their real principles and good will and affection towards their fellow subjects," &c. &c. It then proceeds to describe that test, the taking which is to entitle the Catholics to be considered as good subjects.

Four years afterwards, in the year 1778, another relaxing statute sets out with the following declaration as to the conduct of the Catholics—

"Whereas, from their uniform peaceable behaviour for a long series of years, it appears reasonable and expedient to relax the same," (the laws of Anne); "and it must tend not only to the cultivation and improvement of this kingdom, but to the prosperity and strength of all His

Majesty's dominions, that his subjects of all denominations should enjoy the blessings of a free constitution, and should be bound to each other by mutual interest and mutual affection," &c. &c.

Is not this a distinct legislative recognition of the capacity of a Catholic to become a good subject to a Protestant state, as well as of the principle which I am desirous this day to recommend to the House, of identifying the allegiance, the interests, and the affections of both classes of His Majesty's subjects? Is not this a clear and indisputable acknowledgment on the part of the legislature, that such common interest and mutual affection are necessary, or mainly conducive at least, to the prosperity and strength of His Majesty's dominions?

Pursuing the same course, in four years after, we find another statute, the preamble of which, referring to the statute of 1774, runs in these words:—"Whereas all such of His Majesty's subjects in this kingdom, of whatever persuasion, as have heretofore taken and subscribed, or shall hereafter take and subscribe, the oath of allegiance and declaration prescribed by an act passed in the thirteenth and fourteenth years of his present Majesty's reign, entitled an Act to enable His Majesty's subjects, of whatever persuasion, to testify their allegiance to him, ought to be considered as good and loyal subjects to His Majesty, his Crown, and Government," &c.

Here we have that quality and character assigned to the Catholics, the quality and character of "good and loyal subjects," which alone can be wanting to entitle men to participate in that free constitution which His Majesty's Protestant subjects enjoy; and the absence of which has been imputed, and is imputed still, by the few who still maintain the argument as the single, but unchangeable ground of disability and exclusion.

The most recent of the relaxing statutes is that well-known one of 1793, the preamble of which declares that—

"Various Acts of Parliament have been passed, imposing on His Majesty's subjects professing the Popish or Roman Catholic religion, many restraints and disabilities to which other subjects of this realm are not liable; and that, from the peaceable and loyal demeanour of His Majesty's Popish or Roman Catholic subjects, it is fit that such restraints and disabilities shall be discontinued."

Upon this I need make no further comment, than that the principle plainly laid down is notoriously not followed out by corresponding enactments: that many disabilities do still continue, and that the question which Parliament has now to determine, is not whether these disabilities were originally right, but whether, having been pronounced in principle wrong, the time is yet come when it is safe wholly to "discontinue" them? I beg not to be understood as intending to imply that more could properly have been done than was done in 1793: I merely mean to say, that the principle then laid down was wider than the practical consequences which were then drawn from it; that near twenty years have since elapsed; and that the question is therefore now not upon the principle itself (which was then settled), but upon the extension of its operation.

Again, then, I ask those who rail against innovation; who warn us against departing from the established usage; who tell us that we ought to adhere to the wisdom of our ancestors; who dread that we are now, as if for the first time, in danger of breaking in upon a wise and perfect system: when and where, and for how long that system existed in perfection? What is the prescriptive veneration, what the authority of usage and of opinion, due to a code of laws, which, after a growth of near two centuries, remained only for fourteen years in a state of maturity, and has been for half a century sinking into gradual decay? To what point of time, I again ask them, do they mean to refer, when they exhort us to adhere to the wisdom of our ancestors, and to avoid innovating upon the system which our ancestors had framed?

Let it not be supposed, however, that I mean to disparage our ancestors for the failure of their experiments in legislation upon this subject. Most true it is, that the government of Popish Ireland has been to this Protestant country a problem of infinite difficulty. It is true that the most enlightened statesmen have found—or thought—it impossible to apply to that country the same principles of rule upon which the legislation of this country has been conducted; and it must be confessed that the impediments which stood in their way, have been of no ordinary magnitude. It must be confessed that they had no precedent to guide them; and if, in the absence of such experience, nothing less than the extermination of the Catholic population of Ireland was considered at one time as consistent with the safety of the state; if afterwards it was attempted to grind down that population by statute; the harshness of such expedients must be attributed partly to the necessities, and partly to the temper, of the times in which they were tried. But it is not less true that both these expedients utterly failed. We may surely have become wise from the example of our ancestors, and may adopt or pursue a better course of experiments, after the trial and failure of theirs, without being supposed to cast blame upon them. We ought to make full allowance for the different genius of different ages. I leave to philosophers the problem, whether the human race upon the whole degenerates or improves; but this at least must be admitted to be a fact, whatever be its bearing, that in modern days a spirit of mildness and lenity has pervaded and influenced legislation, unknown to times more remote. An honourable and learned gentleman, who the other night brought under the consideration of the House, a subject of much commercial and national importance—I mean the Orders in Council—in his eloquent and able speech upon that occasion, introduced a remark which is not inapplicable to my present argument. He said, that in the treaty of Utrecht, on many other accounts the subject of violent condemnation (more violent indeed than I think it really deserved), there was this blot, which was sufficient to damn it to all posterity, that the chief commercial advantage which it secured to this country, was the Assiento Contract, or a participation of the African Slave Trade. There cannot be a circumstance which more strikingly marks the progress of opinion, and the improvement of the human mind, within the space of one century. The reign of Queen Anne has been justly styled the Augustan age of England. Nobody can impute to the statesmen of that period a deficiency in knowledge of the science of legislation. Nobody can deny that there were moral writers, at that time, eminently qualified to correct and purify the feelings, as well as the taste of their countrymen; to mark, with the nicest discrimination, the boundaries of right and wrong; to be the guides of their own age, and the instructors of posterity. Yet at that time not a voice was lifted against the immorality, injustice, and inhumanity of the Slave Trade. Let any man suppose the possible case of a minister in the present day, standing up in Parliament, with a treaty in his hand, similar to that of Utrecht, securing to Great Britain a regulated monopoly of the African Slave Trade—and on that, and no other ground, claiming the approbation and congratulations of Parliament. Let him imagine how such a proposition would be this day received, even though supported by an appeal to the practice of our ancestors:—and thence let him be convinced of this plain fact, that, whether for better or for worse, the genius of the times is different; and that we may be permitted to legislate on some subjects in a different spirit.

The question, therefore, is not—whether we shall maintain the system which exists,—for no system exists whole and unbroken: it is not (at least I hope it is not) whether we shall recur to a system which formerly existed, but which we have partially abandoned:—it is—whether, having abandoned that system, as altogether inefficient in politics, and unjustifiable in morals, we ought to be now contented with negative advantage, or whether we should not rather endeavour to give effectual operation and fair play to those other principles of which we have recognized the superior justice, and those other measures we have begun to adopt, but not thoroughly pursued.

We read, Sir, in the history of ancient Rome, that when one of the armies of the republic had fallen into the power of the enemy, and was surrounded by the Samnites at the Caudine Forks, the victorious General, desirous to make the most of the advantage which he had obtained, dispatched a message to his father, a Senator celebrated for his wisdom, to counsel him as to the most expedient mode of disposing of his captives.—" Dismiss them unransomed and unmolested;"—was the answer of the aged Senator. This was a strain of generosity too high for the comprehension of the son. He re-dispatched his messenger to consult his oracle again. The answer then was; "Exterminate them to the last man." This advice was so unlike the former, that it excited a suspicion that the old man's intellects were deranged:—he was brought to the camp to explain the discordancy of his counsel. "By my first advice," said he, "which was the best, I recommended to you to insure the everlasting gratitude of a powerful people; by my second, which was the worst, I pointed out to you the policy of getting rid of a dangerous enemy. There is no third way. *Tertium nullum consilium.*" When asked, what if a middle course should be taken, what if they should be dismissed unhurt, but if at the same time harsh laws should be imposed upon them as a conquered enemy? *Ista quidem sententia,*" said the old man, "*ea est, quæ neque amicos parat neque inimicos tollit.*" The son, however, unhappily for his country, thought himself wiser than his father; the middle course was adopted: he neither liberated the Romans, nor exterminated them; he passed their necks under the yoke, and sent them home.

Sir, in respect to Ireland, the severe, the exterminating counsel has been tried—and it has been found inefficient for its own purposes. We have adopted the principle of the more generous counsel; shall we halt in the pursuit of it, or try it fairly to its end?

I would have recommended the latter policy, even while Ireland was a separate kingdom. How much more safe as well as more desirable must it be, now, when she is inseparably united with this country!—The Protestants of Ireland were heretofore but as a garrison in the midst of a subdued country, obliged for their own safety to keep down the people among whom they were stationed. United now with the mass of the Protestants of England, they form part of the great majority of the inhabitants of the whole empire, instead of being a small minority in a detached fortress surrounded by overwhelming numbers. Formerly justice and prudence might point different ways; at present surely they are united, with the union of the kingdoms.

I imagine, that it will not be denied that such complete identification of Catholic and Protestant interests is desirable: it will be only contended that it is impossible. It is impossible, because, we are told, there is in the genius of the religious profession of the Catholics, something which can never be reconciled to the government of a Protestant state;—there is in it a perfect faithlessness of principle towards other religious persuasions; a spirit of encroachment never at rest; a bigotry and spirit of persecution, which, if once let loose by indulgence, would make us speedily wish to retrace our steps, and to recal even the boons which have already been lavished upon the Catholics. I am no advocate or panegyrist of the Roman Catholic religion: but let these charges be tried by comparison with the history of the two last centuries. If the Catholic religion be of so encroaching a disposition, and so formidable in its encroachments, how happens it that it has lost one-third of Europe, not one inch of which it has ever been able to regain? The spirit of persecution may not be extinct. Nor is there any question, I trust, of arming it with power. But the proof of the continued existence of that spirit in the modern Catholic Church,—that proof at least which has been most frequently adduced in the debates of this House,—is not, I think, so clear as it has been supposed to be. "*Hæreticos persequar et expugnabo*"—is said to be still the doctrine of their Church, and to be incorporated in the solemn oath of their episcopal ordination.

God forbid that I should say a word in palliation of so detestable a clause, if it be really to be construed literally, or as practically influencing their conduct. But they deny that sense, they disclaim and abjure it. They profess their entire abhorrence of it, and give it up to the execration of mankind. Yes, but it is said, we ought to distrust their abjuration. Let us be quite sure that such an example of distrust might not go farther than we might desire. In the oath taken by King William and Queen Mary, on becoming King and Queen of Scotland, is the following clause: "We swear to *root out* all heretics and enemies to the true worship of God, that shall be convicted, by the true kirk of God, of the aforesaid crimes, out of our lands and empire of Scotland, &c." Are we ready to admit that William and Mary were pledged by this oath literally to exterminate all heretics with the sword? Such an imputation, we know, would be most unjust. Yet it might be countenanced by citations from ancient Scottish Acts of Parliament, and from commentators upon the Scottish Law,—in one of whom (Stewart of Purdevan), we find it asserted that, "The severity of the laws against Papists will be further justified, if we consider that by the Law of God Idolaters were *put to death;* and agreeable thereto, Popish idolaters are to be punished with death—by the 104th Act of the 7th Parliament of James VIth." How would such a passage be hailed, if quoted from the decrees of Lateran or Constance!—King William, however, we are told, remonstrated against the obligation to be imposed upon him by this clause of the oath. The Commissioners quieted his conscience by leaving the words to his own construction. With this explanation he took the oath in his own sense of it, which meant we know not exactly what; but certainly no such thing as the words appear to imply. I do not urge this as a justification of the doctrine of the Popish Church: God forbid!—but, if we claim to ourselves the liberty of construing our own doctrines, it is perhaps somewhat hard to refuse the same privilege to others. It is hard to say, that when King William swore to "*root out*" heretics in Scotland, he was to be taken metaphorically; but, that when the Catholics swore *persequi et expugnare* heretics in Ireland, they were to be taken as actually and literally entertaining that precise intention; it is hard to say, that King William did not mean any thing like extermination, but that the Catholics, even at this time of day, are prepared with the sword and the torch to spread their tenets through the world. It is farther to be observed, that though the oath taken by King William was never repealed till the union of the two Crowns, that of the Catholics, so far at least as relates to the Irish Roman Catholic Bishops, was repealed by the Pope, in 1791.

But what trust can be reposed by a Protestant

government in Roman Catholic subjects, considering that it is one acknowledged principle of their religion "never to keep faith with heretics?" The answer to this question is to be found in the whole series of relaxing statutes in their favour; in the oaths which these statutes prescribe to be taken by the Catholics. Oaths to be taken by men whom it is said no oaths can bind! oaths tendered to persons whose profession and creed is perjury! oaths of allegiance to a Protestant government, exacted from those who are previously sworn to overturn it! It must be admitted that our practice is not very consistent with our theory: and if our theory be true, if the oath of a Catholic is really no security, it is vain to deny that we ought at once to repeal all the statutes that have passed in favour of the Catholics. This is the vice or the force, be it which it may, of the whole of the reasoning drawn from the unalterable nature of the Roman Catholic religion. It is generally, and I believe truly, understood, that a right honourable and learned gentleman, whom I do not now see in the House (Dr. Duigenan), was the framer of the last oath imposed upon the Irish Catholics—that of 1793. He, in common with those who contend that, by the tenets of the Catholic Church, oaths with Protestants are not binding upon Catholics, so far forgot the clear and inevitable consequence of this assumption (if true), as to exert his utmost industry and ingenuity in drawing up such a test as must, in his opinion, be binding on the most fugitive and volatile conscience.

Surely all this labour was misapplied. Surely it was futile to forge chains of this sort for minds incapable of being restrained by any obligation. If such be the minds of the Catholics, where is the chance of their refusing, and what is the use of their taking, any oath that could be tendered for their acceptance? I am afraid, Sir, that you must either give up your past policy to maintain your argument; or that, till human wit can devise some other bond for the consciences of men, you must be contented to rest on that very principle of good faith attested and confirmed by those very sanctions, the obligation of which upon the Catholics you are so forward to deny.

In the late debate on this important question, we were told by the right honourable doctor (whose absence on the present occasion I deplore), that the Catholics ought to be quiet and contented; that they should make themselves satisfied with their condition in Ireland, by looking abroad and comparing their own lot with that of the people of the rest of Europe: by which they would see how much happier they are, or may be, under the limited franchise of which they are possessed, than the inhabitants of other countries, of whatever religious persuasions, are under their respective governments. Now, Sir, I have two objections to this advice. In the first place, I should not like to teach the Catholics to look abroad, if I could: secondly, I could not, if I would, prevent them from looking at home, and comparing and contrasting their situation with that of their fellow subjects. It is natural that they should do this: and it is better that they should do it, rather than get a habit of indulging in any foreign speculations. Their feelings, their views, and their wishes should be bounded by the country which gave them birth, and the government under which they live. But, granting that they do look abroad, what do they see there to reconcile them to their own peculiar fate? If they look at the enemy, they will see all nations, and tongues, and creeds, united under the same banner against us and our allies. If they look at those allies, at the Emperor of Russia, for instance (whom I may perhaps, venture to class under that description, as in heart and principle he must be with us), they will see the Emperor of Russia marching to meet the congregated forces of his enemy, at the head of an army composed of different religions, and surrounded by ministers representing that diversity of creeds, by a schismatic arch-chancellor, a Roman Catholic secretary, and a Protestant general. If they look at another great power of Europe, Austria, and if they advert to the circumstances of the late war in which she was engaged with France, they will recollect that, in 1809, Buonaparte issued a proclamation to the Hungarians, inviting them to throw off the Austrian yoke, and offering them, amongst other things, the free exercise of their several forms of worship. To the Hungarians, however, this was no temptation; for in Hungary, a Roman Catholic establishment, co-existing with a Greek hierarchy, amidst a Protestant population, does not prevent all the offices of the state, civil and military, from being open to the ambition of individuals of every class and religion. But the Catholics may perhaps be invited to direct their attention to Spain. In Spain, I am sorry to say, they may find, in a recent public act, something to countenance, though not to justify, the state of degradation in which they are kept at home: an act which, like some others of narrow and illiberal policy, has disappointed the hopes entertained by the friends of religious liberty, has, in my opinion, disgraced the Cortes, from which it emanated. But in what country has this occurrence taken place? In a country notoriously the most bigoted in Europe, and the most blind in religious prejudices. Has this act been approved by us? We know how freely the conduct of Spain in other respects has been discussed in this country. Our Government, we know, has, with all the freedom allowable to an ally, advised the rulers of Spain, in other particulars, to correct and enlarge their system of policy—to ameliorate, for instance, the condition of their colonies, to place their commercial policy on true and sound principles. No doubt we have protested also against their late declaration of intolerance. In truth, Sir, we are pretty lavish in advice to others: and it may be lamented, perhaps, that we have not kept some of our counsel to guide our own policy at home. Perhaps Spain, when we have been recommending to her the practice of liberality and toleration, might have retorted upon us, not wholly without justice, and asked whether Ireland, adult and mature Ireland—Ireland, now a co-ordinate part of the united kingdom, ought still to be governed on those principles, or on the remnant of those principles, which were applied, justly perhaps, in former times, to the population of a conquered state, or to an insignificant and rebellious colony?

Of the cruelties exercised against the first reformers by the ancient church, then struggling for the maintenance of its authority, history speaks with just horror and indignation. But can any man now entertain a serious apprehension that it is necessary to be on our guard against their recurrence? Good God, Sir, what should we say if the early violences of the Reformation itself were to be arrayed against Protestants as a lasting and inexpiable reproach? If the outrages and extravagancies of the Anabaptists of Munster—the tyrannical caprices of Henry VIII.—the severities of the latter part of the reign of Elizabeth—the burning of Servetus, by Calvin, at Geneva—the coarse and sacrilegious fury of

John Knox and his followers in Scotland—nay, and the oath taken by King William himself—were to be alleged as evidence that the several descriptions of reformed religion are necessarily and eternally of a violent and sanguinary character? We should object to such an inference as absurd and unjustifiable; and may not the Catholics of the present day protest in like manner against conclusions being drawn against them, from the crimes and cruelties, the perfidies and atrocities, of those who held the same faith two hundred years ago?

I have been shocked at seeing exposed to sale, in the shop-windows of this metropolis, an address to the worst passions of the vulgar, entitled, "An Awful Warning, or the Massacre of St. Bartholomew." Who the writer is I know not. It is not right to attribute bad motives to any man, but I am at a loss to conceive a good one for such a publication as this which I hold in my hand. Why publish such a narrative at the present moment? What purpose, what legitimate feeling can it be intended to gratify? What have the public now to do with Charles the Ninth and Admiral Coligny? By what sentiment can any one feel himself called upon at this time of day to narrate that the Guises sprinkled themselves with the blood of their unfortunate victim, and that the Duke d'Angouleme viewed his butchered corpse with emotions of delight? Why represent these horrid scenes to the eyes of the populace? What good can it do to recal the memory of them? If the torch of religious animosity could be rekindled at the present moment, what would the effect be but to risk the safety of the British empire? This mischievous publication is illustrated by plates, to heighten the horrors of the narrative. In one is exhibited the assassination of Coligny, in another the Duke d'Angouleme dipping his handkerchief in his blood. Does not this mode of illustration clearly show to what description of readers the publication is peculiarly addressed? upon what class of understandings it is intended to operate?

But neither are there wanting other indications of the same purpose; among these is the dedication. It is dedicated to the memory of that eminent and virtuous man whose loss in this House we are still deploring, and who, had he been alive, warm as he was in his resistance to the question now before the House, would assuredly have disdained and discountenanced such a mode of resisting it. The dedication is as follows:—"Sacred to the memory of the Right Honourable Spencer Perceval, Prime Minister of these realms, whose relative situation in respect of the established religion of the United Kingdom, was similar to that of De Coligny in France." What does this mean? How was Mr. Perceval's situation, with respect to the established religion of this kingdom, similar to that of De Coligny with respect to the established religion of France? So much for the accuracy of the fact. This circumstance is one which also clearly shows for what scale of intellect this writer calculated his publication. On human beings, capable of investigation and discussion, he knew that he should make no impression; he therefore directed his efforts to infuriate the mob, not, I hope, in this day, to be infuriated by such unhallowed means. The dedication proceeds, after this comparison between the situation of Mr. Perceval and that of the Admiral De Coligny, to say that Mr. Perceval "fell *like him*, a martyr to his duty to his King, to his country, and to his God." History, we know, is sufficiently liable to misrepresentation and perversion; but so shameless an attempt as this, within one short month after the transaction to which it refers, I should think is not to be found in the records of historical falsification.

If, Sir, with a deep sense of a dispensation so awful and afflicting as that with which we have recently been visited, it may yet be permitted to us to render thanks to Providence for having intermixed some qualification of mercy in its wrath, that gratitude is justly due, when we image to our minds the mischiefs that might have been occasioned, had the desperate wretch who committed this detested deed been either a Catholic or an Irishman. It is very possible that he might have been either, or both, and yet not have been influenced by any motive of religious fanaticism. But I appeal to the common sense of the House whether, if, by accident, the assassin of Mr. Perceval had been born in the sister island, if by accident he had been a Roman Catholic (as, in the paragraph I have just read to them, it is not asserted indeed, but, with jesuitical ambiguity, is more than insinuated); whether, I say, the same blind zeal which is manifested in this publication, would not in all probability have availed itself of that circumstance to stir up a furious and fanatical spirit, which might have laid both countries in blood?

Sir, when I first gave notice of the motion which I have this day brought forward, many weeks ago, it was my expectation that I should have to contend with my late lamented Friend, as my most formidable antagonist upon it. I really wished for the opportunity of such a contest; I wished to see the side of the question which he espoused, arrayed in its most striking colours; I wished to hear all that could have been said upon it, and from him I should have heard it all; I wished for this contest for the sake of thorough discussion, and of arriving at the truth: but I anticipated it, God knows, with no feelings of hostility; I should have come to it with sentiments the very reverse of personal animosity; I should have argued the question with him in no other spirit, and with no other feelings, than

> "If a brother should a brother dare"

to the proof and exercise of arms. I know not who is to buckle on his armour, and to wield his weapons against me on this day. Would to God that he were here to wield them with his own hand! Would to God that the cause had the advantage of his abilities, so that we had the advantage and delight of his presence!

> "Tuque tuis armis, nos te poteremur, Achille!"

Before I dismiss the publication to which I have alluded, I wish to notice a passage which appears to me conclusive as to the real object of the writer. It is the concluding paragraph of the work, and is couched in the following words: "A slight examination of the principal contemporary and other historians, will readily prove that the massacre must ever remain a blot in the annals of France and of Rome: may it also operate as an awful warning—as the warning of St. Bartholomew, nay, even of Heaven itself—to Protestants of this and every age, to convince posterity, but more especially the supine, we cannot say blind, of 1812, of the great truth that PAPISTS KEEP NO FAITH WITH PROTESTANTS."

Can any man doubt what this means? or at least what feelings it tends to excite, what purposes it is calculated to encourage? This, Sir, is not the first time that the history of the massacre of St. Bartholomew has been so employed, in modern times. The author of this work might imagine that he was performing his duty to his country, by awakening the attention of the Protestant Church to the dangers with which, in his opinion, it was threatened. But example is not in his favour. In the early periods of the French Revolution, a representation of the massacre of St. Bartholomew was brought on the theatre of Paris. Was that done with a view of mitigating the violent spirit of the Catholic Church, of extinguishing religious animosities, of healing the grievances, or of reconciling the differences which distracted the country? Hear what Mr. Burke says upon this subject: "Your citizens of Paris," said Mr. Burke, in his letter to a member of the National Assembly, "your citizens of Paris, formerly had lent themselves as the ready instruments to slaughter the followers of Calvin at the infamous massacre of St. Bartholomew. What should we say to those who could think of retaliating on the Parisians of this day, the abominations and horrors of that time? It was but the other day that they caused this very massacre to be acted on the stage. They introduced the Cardinal of Lorraine, in his robes of function, ordering general slaughter. Was this spectacle intended to make the Parisians abhor persecution and loath the effusion of blood?

No! it was to teach them to persecute!" I will not say, that such must be the intentions of any man who represents such scenes as these at the present moment, and forces the record of such transactions upon the public eye. I will not say, such must be his deliberate intentions: but I must say, that the mistaken zeal and perverse ingenuity which such a publication displays, naturally subject him to observations such as these of Mr. Burke.

Sir, out of the contents of this work which I have brought under your notice, no less than out of the intelligence which has this day arrived from Ireland, I collect additional motives for taking into consideration the situation of the Catholics, and for discussing their claims with that temper which their importance demands.

The mention of the name of Mr. Burke, and of that of my late right honourable friend, naturally suggests the consideration of the authorities by which the view that I take of the great question now before us, has been supported or opposed. No man can deem more highly than I do of the sagacity, the integrity, the force of my late right honourable friend's understanding; of the purity of his mind, the charity of his temper, and the unaffected piety by which he was so eminently distinguished. But, considering this, as I must always do, as a great state question, I hope I may be excused if I cannot put his authority in competition with the united authorities of so many great men who have preceded him; with the authority not of Mr. Burke alone, who, on this as well as on other subjects, outran, with a prophetic celerity the progress of the public sentiment, and had arrived many years ago at that opinion in which I believe it may be said that the generality of the public are now agreed; not only of Mr. Fox, whose general love of liberty, and whose ardent and hardy and uncompromising spirit naturally inclined him to extend to the widest range the limits of freedom and toleration; not only, I say, with the authorities of these great men—men who, being of a warm and sanguine temperament, might be subjected to the accusation of adopting too eagerly every proposition which tended towards the liberty of mankind: but to these are to be added the name of Mr. Windham, whose mind was cast in a different mould, whose disposition, so far from being rash and sanguine, inclined him rather to view every approach to an enlargement of popular privilege with jealousy, and to suspect all general propositions of fallacy and danger. I must add also the great and venerable name of Mr. Pitt, whose generous philanthropy, whose attachment to civil and religious liberty, were as warm and sincere as those of any man that ever lived; but in whom those feelings were tempered and disciplined by early habits of business and long practical experience, which had taught him to examine specious theories with distrust, and to build his plans for the public good on sure and solid foundations. If then the question were to rest upon authority, I could have no apprehension as to the decision.

But to return to the argument: it is the misfortune of all those topics which are derived from the bloody history of earlier times, and from the alleged unchangeable nature of the popish religion; that, if good for any thing, they are good for too much. They are good against what has already been done, as well as against that which it is proposed to do. The practical question now before us is, not—what are the existing dangers from concessions already made? but, whether or not those dangers will be increased, whether they may not even be removed, by further concessions? If I could be made to think that by taking one more step we should destroy our Protestant institutions, and establish in their stead a Roman Catholic hierarchy and Roman Catholic ascendancy in church and state, most undoubtedly I would stop where we are: but I maintain that this is the very point where the necessity of proof lies heaviest on those who contend against further concession. It is for them to show, not the advantage and security which might have been derived from the continuance of the total disqualification of the Catholics; not the absolute incompatibility of any concessions to the Catholics with the safety of the Protestant establishment: what they have to show is this, that the concessions already granted, are at once safe for the Protestant establishment, and calculated to satisfy the cravings which they are unquestionably calculated to excite in the Catholic mind; but, that a single step beyond the point at which we stand, is danger and destruction; that it is safe to fill the ranks of your army with Catholic soldiers and Catholic subalterns, but that a Catholic major-general would bring confusion upon your arms; that the four Courts of Dublin may swarm with popish lawyers in stuff gowns, and law and justice flourish by their labours, but that if one of them had a gown of silk, he would infallibly overturn the whole frame of your legal constitution. They who are for retracing our steps, and recalling what we have, according to them, improvidently granted, are consistent and intelligible. But the present controversy lies between those who would go on with me, and those who see no danger in what we have given, but yet would give no more. This is the point upon which illustration is required; this is the hinge on which the dispute turns. To this I hope that those who are this day to oppose my motion, will have the goodness to address themselves; for it is here that their argument labours, and wants a helping hand.

You say, you will not give to the Catholics

political power; I say, you have given them political power: how wisely, I will not inquire—but you have given them the elective franchise. If the option were now to be argued, it would not be difficult (in my opinion) to show that the introduction of twenty or thirty Catholic gentlemen in this House would by no means operate such powerful political effects, as the letting loose to two or three hundred thousand of the Catholic population of Ireland the right of electing members of Parliament. I do not mean to say, that I therefore impeach the wisdom of the decision which, in 1793, gave the preference to the one mode of concession over the other. I can easily understand the apprehension which might exist in a limited and local Parliament, lest the Protestants should in time have been outnumbered by the admission of Catholic representatives. But, speaking of the Parliament of the united empire as it is now constituted, I have little hesitation in saying, that the admission to seats among us of twenty or thirty Catholic gentlemen would be less dangerous, (if indeed the term dangerous be applicable to the subject, which I do not believe it to be), than the boon, which has been already granted, of the elective franchise to the large body of the Catholics.

What then is it that you have done towards reconciling the Protestants and Catholics? Resolving to introduce the Catholics partially at least into the bosom of the constitution, whom among them have you chosen to associate in the first instance with yourselves? Those of them who were peculiarly distinguished for rank, for property, for talents? those who, from their station and their character, are naturally looked up to as leaders of the body? those with whom you are in the habit of mixing in every other place, and whose admission into this House, you would therefore hardly perceive? those who, from their property and their rank, have a decided interest in the conservation of the present frame and system of society? No such thing. All these you have rejected, and still continue to reject: while, on the principle of universal suffrage, or something very like it, you have admitted to a participation in the constitution, to political power, the great mass of the Catholic population, without distinction or selection. You adopt the peasantry, and reject the gentry.

With this choice, the next danger which is stated, appears to be somewhat inconsistent. The Catholic priesthood possess a great and alarming influence over the Catholic peasantry. True: and when had not a priesthood great influence over the mass of the people? And ought they not to have it, and more especially over a rude and uncultivated people? But what is it that has augmented this influence of the Catholic Priests, if it be augmented, beyond its due proportion?

What but their poverty, and still more, in former times, the persecution which they have undergone? In proportion as these causes are removed, the effects cease. The influence of the Priests will always continue, and it is to be wished that it always should continue, adequate to the performance of their spiritual duties. Its salutary effects will not cease; but the obedience of their flocks will be divested by degrees of that blind and slavish principle from which so much danger is apprehended.

But, it is not the influence of the clergy alone, that is an object of apprehension. The great body of Irish Catholics are, it is said, in the hands of agitators, who wish to keep their discontents alive; who care not for the professed object of Catholic desire, but look to ulterior purposes of mischief, to separation and revolution. If this be so, we can only defeat the evil intentions of such men in two ways: either by correcting their disposition, or by taking away their means. The former is beyond human power. Let us avail ourselves of the latter. Let us remove those circumstances which, operating upon the feelings of the Catholics, render them fit instruments in the hands of agitators, for the promotion of such dangerous designs. I am inclined to believe, that there *are* those who have ulterior views and objects. Of those who are the most clamorous for concession, there are some, I do believe, who would be most disappointed if that concession were granted. And next to the gratification which I should feel in tranquillizing a loyal and high-minded people, by the introduction of that equality of rights, without which there can be no reciprocal liking and confidence, is that of disappointing the guilty hopes of those who delight not in tranquillity and concord, but in grievances and remonstrance; who use their sincere and warmhearted countrymen as screens to their own ambitious purposes; and who consider a state of turbulence and discontent, as best suited to the ends which they have in view. That state it may be their wish to prolong, but so much the rather is it our interest and our duty to terminate it as speedily as possible.

But, what are the securities to be taken against the dangers of further concession? (for be it always remembered, that the question is *further* concession; it is not the introduction of a new principle, but the following up of one already established.) It has been lately stated in another place, that when the Catholics are called upon to show their securities, their answer is, "Show us your dangers;" and this has been complained of, as a saucy way of begging the question. Sir, it is a fair answer. I do not mean that it is absolutely and abstractedly an answer to the question proposed: but I say it is a fair answer on the part of the Catholics. The Catholics see no danger; they deny the existence of any danger; and they therefore are the last persons who can be expected to devise securities. It is certainly the duty of the Catholic to submit to any provisions that the Legislature may think necessary for that purpose: but it is not his business, nor can he be competent to suggest those securities himself. How can he provide against dangers of which he is not aware? How is he to fit that which he has no means of measuring?—It is the province of the Legislature to say to the Catholic—"These are the dangers which we apprehend; and these the securities which we deem to be requisite for guarding against them." Let the boon be accompanied with the condition that is to make it safe to the giver: and I feel confident, notwithstanding the delusion and irritation of the moment, that the Catholic will joyfully accept, and thankfully acknowledge it.

What may be the plan of securities to be annexed to concession, this is not the time to discuss. I know that we have to guard not against real dangers only, but against the imagination of dangers that perhaps may not exist. Of this imagination much, I hope and believe, is to be done away by previous discussion. I hope also that discussion may soften the temper of the Catholics, and prepare them to receive as they ought whatever may be tendered to them. But I am sure that to bring forward any specific plan at this moment, would be only to throw it wide for misapprehension and misrepresentation; for the fears of the timid, and the cavils of the disaffected; to be held up to obloquy and suspicion by those, whose object is not settlement but continued irritation. It is not at a moment of violence and clamour, that the voice of reason can be heard. But such violence and clamour, however they may disgust or dishearten us; however much they may increase the difficulties of the discussion, by increasing or creating distrust and indignation among the people of this country; or, however much they may damp one's hopes of an arrangement of mutual satisfaction and concord, yet ought they not for a moment to interrupt the sober and straight-forward course of Parliament.

Parliament would not legislate wisely, if it suffered itself to be swayed by clamour either way, by appeals to their fear on the one hand, or to their pride on the other. Nothing can be more erroneous for a government, than to erect a disputed question into a point of honour. This may be necessary to the character of individuals, but it would be mischievous in administering the affairs of a great state. It is to the indulgence, during the American war, of such feelings as those which I now deprecate, that the disastrous result of that contest may in great measure be attributed. How much wiser would it have been in the Parliament of that day, if they had not permitted any thing like pique and ill-humour to mix in their proceedings; if they had not treated the speeches of a few obnoxious individuals in America, or the clamours of a few popular meetings, as the deliberate voice of regular defiance, or grounded upon them acts of premature and decisive severity!

Let us be cautious how we permit the sayings and writings of unauthorised individuals, or the exaggerated declarations of tumultuous assemblies, to generate a feeling of impatience in this House, and to turn us from the grave consideration of a subject, involving the welfare and happiness of the kingdom. A few angry demagogues may declare that they will hear of no arrangement—will consent to no securities. And there are not wanting those on this side of the water, who will be glad to lay hold of this declaration, as a clear and authentic exposition of the general and deliberate feeling of the Catholics; and as a sufficient ground for putting an end, at once, to every attempt at considering a question, the result of which, they say, must be hopeless. I agree with neither the one nor the other of these parties. I cannot think the existence, if it were proved, of an irritated, and unruly, and unreasonable spirit on the part of the Catholics, a sufficient ground for our leaving this question loose, to float upon the breath of popular opinion, and to be mixed with every ebullition of public discontent. Neither can I do the Catholics, on the other hand, so much injustice as to believe that they entertain and avow the design of disobedience to the law. Whatever is done in their favour, will be done by the enactment of Parliament. By the same act which confers the boon, will be imposed the corresponding obligation, whatever it may be. To accept the one, and reject the other, will not be in the power of the Catholics. Be assured they will not attempt it. Be assured they have no such serious intention. They will accept your benefit: and they will obey your law. Listen, therefore, with dignified coolness and indulgence, equally unmoved either by anger or by fear, to the language of temporary disappointment and vexation: but do not set down the ungoverned effusions of the tongue as the settled purpose of the heart.

At all events let us put ourselves in the right. If this question is unhappily to be a source of eternal disquiet to these nations, let it not be through our fault. Let us do our part to settle it in a manner conformable at once to justice and to policy: and if, after all our endeavours, such a settlement cannot be made, on their heads be the blame who shall reject the good work, and disappoint the good intentions of the Legislature! But I hope for better things.

A refusal by the Catholics to come into such arrangements as the fears, even of the liberal, of the wise, and of the just among their Protestant fellow subjects might require, would put them decidedly in the wrong. The very arguments that are now most strong in their behalf, would in that case be turned against themselves. The examples of other countries would then be used, not to show how much is unnecessarily withholden from the Catholics here, but to show how unreasonable they are in their exactions. If in the great empire of Russia we see Catholics in office, if we see there a Catholic Church, and even an acknowledged Catholic Episcopacy;—be it remembered that this establishment exists without any dependence upon the Pope, except in matters of a merely spiritual nature. Even in France we see the Gallican Church secured at this moment, by the late concordat, from undue subjection to the papal power. Consider then, how impossible it is that the Pope, under the present circumstances of Europe, even if restored to his dignity and independence, should recover his ancient authority, be looked to with that awe, or possess that influence, in other countries, which he formerly enjoyed. Consider how much the progress of public opinion has mitigated the violence of religious dissensions. Surely these are favourable circumstances for enabling us to unite with concession to the Catholics the indispensable condition of security to the Protestant Church; and it will be hard, indeed, if, in proportion as the obstacles diminish on the side of those who are to grant, they shall rise up and multiply on the side of those who solicit concession. I hope better things.

But, Sir, upon this part of the subject, I am unwilling to detain the House. It has already been ably and amply discussed in former debates, particularly by an honourable baronet (Sir J. C. Hippisley), from whose speeches and publications on these topics, I confess I have derived no small share of whatever information I have upon them. This only I beg the House to believe, that it certainly is not from any doubt as to the practicability of framing adequate arrangements for combining the security of our Protestant establishments with the concession of what remains to be conceded to the Catholics, that I abstain from any detail at the present moment. I think it, in the present instance, sufficient for the House of Commons to declare their determination to take the whole question into their consideration, early in the next session of Parliament; defining only the great object we have thereby in view, namely, conciliation; and leaving the measure to be deliberated upon in the interval between the sessions, in order that it may be so modified, when it comes to be proposed next year, as to secure the attainment of all the objects which we have in contemplation. I have in my own mind a tolerably clear conception of what, as it appears to me, might be the fit course to be taken; but my conception may be just or incorrect. It is a work upon which the wisdom of Parliament and the prudence of Government must be exercised.

Sir, in framing the specific motion which I am about to submit to the House, I have followed and endeavoured to unite two precedents: The first, a precedent of the most auspicious nature—that of the message brought down to the House by Mr. Fox, in 1782, which led to the "final adjustment," as it was called, that gave to Ireland her political constitution: the other—no less auspicious—the Resolution of the year 1806, which produced the ultimate settlement of the so long agitated question of the Slave Trade. For eighteen years had my honourable friend (Mr. Wilberforce), the able and indefatigable advocate for the abolition of the Slave Trade, laboured, to his own immortal honour, but in vain. In 1806, Mr. Fox, then a Minister, moved a Resolution, that the House of Commons would, early in the next Session of Parliament, take the subject into consideration. This Resolution was agreed to; it was communicated to the House of Lords; and early in the next session of Parliament (although a dissolution had intervened), a Bill founded on that Resolution was brought in, and happily carried almost without opposition. I indulge a sanguine and earnest hope that the motion with which I shall conclude will be equally fortunate with the precedents on which it is framed.

It is true, as I have said, that when Mr. Fox moved the Resolution to which I have alluded, he was in power; and it was therefore to be inferred that the Executive Government of that day were through him made a party to the decision of the House of Commons. To supply in the present case that advantage, it will be necessary that, if my Resolution should be successful (as I trust it will), it should be laid before the Throne, in order that the Executive Government may be formally apprised of the intention of the House, and prepared to co-operate for its due execution. Upon the two precedents then which I have quoted—of which the one gave to Ireland her political constitution, and the other removed from the character of this country the foulest blot with which it was ever stained—I have framed a Resolution which I now offer to the House—a Resolution which, if carried, will be equally conducive to the happiness, to the honour, and to the mutual good will of Great Britain and Ireland. I conjure the House to consider that if they do not take this question into their own hands, it will not be, it cannot be, set at rest. Even if it were not altogether vain to suppose that it can be put aside, and kept quiet till we have more leisure upon our hands—nay, if it could be put out of sight or out of memory by a wish—still I should not hesitate (although others perhaps might) to bring a proposition, which I am convinced is just and beneficial, under consideration. But to imagine that a question of this sort, affecting the interests and feelings of so large a population, can remain unagitated, is to indulge a visionary hope, a hope unauthorised either by the particular circumstances of the case, or by the general course of human conduct. The difference is simply this :—if we leave it to be discussed out of doors, we know to what tongues and to what pens we commit the discussion; we know in what tone and with what temper it will be treated; we abdicate the functions of Parliament and of Government, and incur a deep and awful responsibility for consequences which it is better to imagine than to describe. On the other hand, the deliberate consideration of the question by this and the other House of Parliament, may lead—I trust will lead—to a result satisfactory to all parties interested in it, a result which will command their acquiescence, and tranquillize their agitation. The interference of Parliament may be often wisely withholden in cases where the ferment of the people arises from temporary causes, and is therefore likely to subside of its own accord: but where the causes are permanent and deep-seated, the time of interfering and the mode are the only points admitting of doubt. I trust the moment is not past at which our interference may be effectual; but most sincerely do I think that it ought not to be much longer delayed. We have already decided that no practical step is to be taken in this House this session. The knowledge of our intention to enter upon the subject early in the next will, I hope, have the effect of procuring an interval of quiet and confidence; and I trust that interval may be well employed.

I conclude then, Sir, with moving—

"That this House will, early in the next session of Parliament, take into its most serious consideration the state of the laws affecting His Majesty's Roman Catholic subjects in Great Britain and Ireland, with a view to such a final and conciliatory adjustment as may be conducive to the peace and strength of the United Kingdom, to the stability of the Protestant establishment, and to the general satisfaction and concord of all classes of His Majesty's subjects."

One word, Sir, before you read the motion from the chair, on a point which I should be sorry to have left unexplained. I have not in the course of my argument adverted specifically to the condition of the Roman Catholics of England, as distinct from that of the Roman Catholics of Ireland. Their situation is, however, in many respects different; and the difference is greatly to the disadvantage of the English Catholics; while their exemplary conduct and distinguished loyalty entitle them to the most kind, partial consideration. But they have themselves waived this year any separate application to Parliament: they have been contented to abide the result of a general consideration of the question, and it is hardly necessary to say, that they must in justice be comprehended in any general measure of relief which Parliament may hereafter think fit to sanction.

The House divided—

For the original Resolution	235
Noes	106
Majority in favour of the Resolution	129

NEGOCIATIONS FOR A CHANGE IN THE ADMINISTRATION.

MAY 21st, 1812.

Mr. S. Wortley this day moved, "That an humble Address be presented to His Royal Highness the Prince Regent, humbly praying that he will be pleased to take such measures as will enable him, under the present circumstances of the country, to form a strong and efficient Administration.

The House divided:—

For the Motion	174
Against it	170
Majority	4

JUNE 11th, 1812.

THE Address agreed to on the 21st of May, was presented to the Prince Regent, who returned an answer, "That he would take into his serious and immediate consideration the Address which he had received from the House of Commons."

Negociations for forming a new Administration were carried on immediately subsequent to his answer; but without success.

MR. STUART WORTLEY on the 11th of June, moved the following Address, respecting the failure of the negociations:—"That an humble Address be presented to His Royal Highness the Prince Regent, to express our regret that the expectations held out in His Royal Highness's most gracious answer to our Address of the 21st of May, have not yet been realized; to assure His Royal Highness of our determination to support, with undiminished zeal, such measures as may appear calculated to ensure prosperity at home, and respect abroad; but, at the same time, humbly to represent, that (consistently with the duty we owe our Sovereign and our constituents) we can no longer defer the expression of our earnest entreaties that His Royal Highness would, without delay, form such an Administration, as may be entitled to the support of Parliament, and the confidence of the Nation."

Two amendments were moved upon this Address by Lord Folkstone and Lord Milton.

Mr. Canning* observed, that the manner in which the right honourable gentleman (Mr. Ponsonby), had done him the honour to allude to him, and the share which it had been his lot, humble as he was, to take in the recent negociations, induced him to trespass for a short time on the attention of the House. The part which he had acted under a noble lord, (Marquis of Wellesley), in the course of these transactions, left him no option but to come to the defence of the noble persons, who were the immediate friends of the right honourable gentleman, against any charge of want of candour and liberality on their part; and he now entered on this discussion with the same temper and moderation which his noble friend had displayed throughout the whole negociation, for the purpose of stating the colour and nature of those transactions in which he was personally engaged, abstaining cautiously from any comment, and from any mention of himself beyond what might be inevitably forced upon him by the circumstances of the case. The right honourable gentleman had truly stated the wish which prevailed on both sides, to have been to provide a strong and efficient Administration. He had also justly characterised and defined wherein such an Administration might be supposed to consist, at least in point of principle and public confidence. But there was one error under which it appeared to him the right honourable gentleman and his friends laboured, and that was, that such an Administration could only be understood in one way; which was, in fact, leaving all others who might join them nothing to do but to surrender the pre-eminence into the hands of him who could count the most numerous supporters in that House. Now obviously Lord Wellesley did not stand in that situation; he had not the numerical followers who could give this sort of strength to an Administration. Undoubtedly then, they differed in their views on this point. It was not Lord

Wellesley's opinion, that, because his force was not the larger of the two, therefore he was to pursue all the measures of the larger party with which he might connect himself, and into whose power his power must merge, but rather that mutual consideration, and weighing of those measures, should be the consequence. True it was, that an Administration might then be pronounced most strong when it contained no conflicting principles, and no contradictory opinions; when it came forward with long concerted plans on public subjects, and when its members had been connected for a series of years past, in political agreement. But still when such a description of men came into power, it could not be said to be an union of parties on an extended basis, but a transfer of power from one party in the state to another. When the commission was first offered to Lord Wellesley, he was aware, that to lay the foundation of an extended and efficient Administration, though differences of opinion might exist as to points of inferior importance, yet an understanding should be come to with regard to the two great points of our external and internal policy—the conduct of the war, and the claims of the Catholics. Besides these, there were others which might become matters of mutual discussion. He now referred to the orders in council, which involved much matter of serious deliberation, and about which there might be some difficulty in coming to a practical conclusion. This then was a point which Lord Wellesley conceived might remain fairly open in all its bearings to mature consideration. But he did imagine that an union on the two great points of external and internal policy to which he had alluded, might form a basis sufficiently strong and extended for the superstructure of an efficient ministry to be erected upon it. He did not deny that the American question was extremely important, but still it was so complicated in its details, and so many recent negociations had taken place upon it, that it at least required the most serious and dispassionate attention. Were he called upon to yield any of the great principles of maritime law on which this country had acted, he had no hesitation in refusing his assent to any such proposition. With regard to the conduct of the war in the Peninsula, no man could mean to offer the proposition that it should be persisted in at all events, or that the blood and treasure of the country should be drained in a contest evidently hopeless. In the proposition which his noble friend made to Lords Grey and Grenville, it was perfectly understood that they might retain their opinions on the origin of that war; all that was wished was, that they should be prepared to agree to its maintenance in the mean time, and that they should reserve to themselves the right of examining the means, the extent, and the mode of carrying it on. The difficulty of complete concurrence of opinion on these and other points, his noble friend and himself did not disguise from themselves; nor did they disguise, that if they required conciliation upon all points, it would be impossible to form any administration. They thought it better, therefore, to limit themselves to two great objects—the one a leading feature of internal policy—the other embracing almost our whole external system. Upon these it was necessary to ascertain an union of sentiment; and that union, if complete, would, they thought, be sufficiently strong to bear the superstructure of a combined administration, though differing upon other questions, not perhaps of inferior importance, but not so immediately affecting the leading features of our present policy.

With these impressions, his noble friend made a communication to Lords Grey and Grenville; of which the following was a minute:

Minute of a Communication made by Lord Wellesley to Lords Grey and Grenville, at Lord Grey's house, dated May 23d, 1812.

" Lord Wellesley stated, that he had received the commands of His Royal Highness the Prince Regent, to lay before His Royal Highness the plan of such an Administration as he (Lord Wellesley) might deem adapted to the present crisis of affairs.

" That he had apprised His Royal Highness of the necessity of ascertaining the views and dispositions of all parties with regard to certain general principles, previously to the formation of any such plan.

" That he considered himself merely as the instrument of executing His Royal Highness's commands on this occasion; and that he neither claimed nor desired for himself any station in the Administration which it was in His Royal Highness's contemplation to form.

" Under these circumstances, he requested to know whether any obstacle existed to the concurrence of Lords Grey and Grenville, or their friends, in the following general principles, as the basis upon which an Administration might be formed :—

" 1st. That the state of the laws affecting the Roman Catholics, and the claims of that body of His Majesty's subjects should be taken into immediate consideration, with a view to a conciliatory adjustment of those claims.

" 2nd. That the war in the Peninsula should be prosecuted on a scale of adequate vigour.

" Lord Wellesley stated, that as Mr. Canning and he agreed in these principles, he had requested Mr. Canning to communicate them to Lord Liverpool.

" Lord Wellesley has reduced the substance of this

communication to writing, and now submits it to Lord Grey and Lord Grenville. (Signed) "WELLESLEY."

To this communication the noble lords made the following reply:

Memorandum from Lords Grey and Grenville, dated May 24th, 1812.

"In such a moment as the present, we feel it to be the duty of all public men, both by frank and conciliatory explanations of principle, and by the total abandonment of every personal objection, to facilitate as far as may be in their power, the means of giving effect to the late vote of the House of Commons, and of averting the imminent and unparalleled dangers of the country.

"Lord Wellesley has selected two, among the many important subjects which must engage the attention of any men, who could, in such circumstances, be called upon to consider of the acceptance of stations of public trust.

"On those two points our explanation shall be as distinct as it is in our power to make it.

"On the first, indeed, our opinion is too well known, and has been too recently expressed, to need repetition.

"We have derived a very high gratification from Lord Wellesley's powerful exertions in support of the claims of the Roman Catholics; as well as from the manner in which that subject is adverted to in his minute; and we do not hesitate to assure him, that we will warmly support any proposal made by any Ministers, for the immediate consideration of those claims with a view to their conciliatory adjustment; a measure, without which, we have already declared, that we can entertain no hope in any case of rendering our own services useful.

"As to the second point, no person feels more strongly than we do the advantages which would result from a successful termination of the present contest in Spain. But we are of opinion, that the direction of military operations in an extensive war, and the more or less vigorous prosecution of those operations, are questions not of principle but of policy; to be regulated by circumstances, in their nature temporary and fluctuating, and in many cases known only to persons in official stations, by the engagements of the country, the prospects of ultimate success, the extent of the exertions necessary for its attainment, and the means of supporting those efforts without too great a pressure on the finances and internal prosperity of the country.

"On such questions, therefore, no public men, whether in or out of office, can undertake for more than a deliberate and dispassionate consideration, according to the circumstances of the case as it may appear, and to such means of information as may then be within their reach. But we cannot in sincerity conceal from Lord Wellesley, that, in the present state of the finances, we entertain the strongest doubts of the practicability of an increase in any branch of the public expenditure."

Lord Wellesley's declared object being to form a comprehensive administration, which should unite, if possible, all the great parties of the state, it was necessary that a proposition should also be made to the members of the suspended Government.

At the same moment, therefore, at which his noble friend made the communication which he had read to Lords Grey and Grenville, he (Mr. Canning) made a proposition to Lord Liverpool, of which the following was a minute:

Minute of Mr. Canning's Proposition to Lord Liverpool, dated Fife-house, May 23d, 1812.

"The Prince Regent having laid his commands upon Lord Wellesley to form a plan of an administration, to be submitted for his Royal Highness's approbation, Mr. Canning was requested by Lord Wellesley (as the channel of communication thought likely to be most agreeable to Lord Liverpool) to inquire of Lord Liverpool, whether there would be a disposition on the part of Lord Liverpool, and of his colleagues, or of any of them, to entertain any proposal which should be made to them for forming part of that administration.

"The principles upon which the administration was intended to be formed were stated to be, first, the taking into the early and serious consideration of the Executive Government the state of the laws affecting the Roman Catholics, with a sincere and earnest desire to bring that important question to a final and satisfactory settlement: secondly, the prosecution of the war in the Peninsula with the best means of the country.

"It was stated, that there would be the strongest wish to comprehend in the arrangement, without any individual or party exclusion whatever, as many as possible of such persons as might be able to agree in giving their public services to the country on these two principles.

"With respect to the distribution of offices, it was stated, that nothing of any sort was decided or stipulated; but that every thing would be open to be arranged to the honour and satisfaction of all parties."

To this proposition the noble earl answered as follows:

Letter from Lord Liverpool to Mr. Canning, dated Fife-house, May 23d, 1812.

"My dear Canning.—I have communicated to my colleagues the memorandum which I received from you this afternoon.

"They do not think it necessary to enter into any discussion of the principles stated in that memorandum; because they all feel themselves bound, particularly after what has recently passed, to decline the proposal of becoming members of an administration to be formed by Lord Wellesley.—Believe me to be, with sincere personal regard, my dear Canning, very faithfully your's,

(Signed) "LIVERPOOL."

With regard to the proposals made by his noble friend to Lords Grey and Grenville, he was willing to admit that they were met in a fair, frank, and conciliatory manner. He would willingly admit also, the force of the objection made by the noble lords to the second proposition, that it was a matter of policy rather than of principle, and that its adoption was to be regulated by considerations that could arise only from knowledge of official details. At the same time, however, the right honourable gentleman would concede to him, that to form an Administration, without knowing, generally, what were the opinions of its members, upon certain great leading questions, would be to risk dissension and discord in the very outset. It was no part of his noble friend's desire to dictate to the noble lords, that they should carry on the war in the Peninsula, under all circumstances, that they should drain the country of its resources to prosecute a hopeless contest, and they should disclaim all considerations of expediency; but he was justified in asking, if they would come to the question with the disposition to continue the war, if they found its continuance a matter justified by every circumstance they should learn? and if they replied, that their disposition was to continue the war, provided they should be convinced, from official details, that it would be a measure of sound policy, then their demand to know those details before they gave any pledge, would be considered only as the demand of men acting from the dictates of just discrimination and good sense.

The right honourable gentleman had stated, that there was some difference in the terms of Lord Wellesley's communication to Lords Grey and Grenville, and in those of his (Mr. Canning's) communication to Lord Liverpool; but he had not distinctly described the extent of that difference, or the mode in which it was subsequently explained. Lord Grey required an explanation in the following letter:

Letter of Lord Grey to Lord Wellesley, dated Portman-square, May 27th, 1812.

"My Lord,—I have the honour of returning the papers which your lordship was so good as to put into my hands this morning.

"I observe a material difference between the terms in which the two principles, proposed as the basis of a new administration, are stated in Mr. Canning's minute, and in that sent to Lord Grenville and me by your lordship. I think it necessary to call your lordship's attention to this circumstance, because if these discussions should proceed further, it may become of the utmost importance. I am, with the highest regard, my lord, your lordship's very faithful humble servant,

(Signed) "Grey."

To this letter Lord Wellesley replied as follows:

Letter of Lord Wellesley, to Lord Grey, dated Apsley-house, May 28th, 1812.

"My Lord,—I should have returned an earlier acknowledgment of the honour of your lordship's letter of yesterday, had I not thought it necessary to see Mr. Canning before I troubled your lordship with any answer to your observations on our respective minutes.

"Having carefully examined those papers, and compared them with our view of the points to which they refer, we have drawn the enclosed paper for your lordship's informa-

tion, and have authenticated it by our respective signatures.
—I have the honour to be, &c.

(Signed) "WELLESLEY."

Paper signed by Lord Wellesley and Mr. Canning.

"The variance in point of phrase in the two propositions as stated by Lord Wellesley and Mr. Canning in their minutes of conference, arises from this circumstance, that Lord Wellesley and Mr. Canning went to their respective conferences without having thought it necessary previously to reduce into a written form the communications which they were to make, being in full possession of each other's sentiments upon the subject of them.

"The two minutes were written by them as containing the substance of their respective communications; that of Mr. Canning in Lord Liverpool's presence; that of Lord Wellesley immediately after his return from Lord Grey.

"There does not appear to Lord Wellesley and Mr. Canning to be any substantial variance in the first proposition.

"The word 'early' in Mr. Canning's minute might be exchanged for the word 'immediate,' used by Lord Wellesley, without in any degree altering the sense: as with a motion actually pending in the House of Commons, which, (but for the events that have recently taken place) would have come on this very day, the object of which was to compel the Executive Government to take the subject of the Catholic question into consideration, it cannot be necessary to say that Mr. Canning has no wish to defer that consideration. On the other hand, consideration by the Executive Government is the object which it is Lord Wellesley's intention to recommend: nor does he conceive any farther parliamentary proceeding to be necessary or practicable this session than such as might be sufficient to insure, either by compulsion upon a hostile Administration, or by pledge from a friendly one, the consideration of the question during the recess, with a view to its being brought before Parliament by the recommendation of the Crown, early in the ensuing session.

"A committee to inquire into the state of the laws has been already negatived in both Houses this session.

"A 'conciliatory adjustment' of the claims of the Irish Catholics is the object which Lord Wellesley and Mr. Canning have equally at heart; and it enters equally into both their views that to be 'conciliatory' that adjustment must be so framed as to embrace the interests and opinions of the English Catholics, also to obtain the enlightened and deliberate consent of the Protestants of both countries. They would think any adjustment very imperfect, which instead of extinguishing discontent, only transferred it from the Catholic to the Protestant.

"But they concur in entertaining a confident belief, that the great purpose of securing the peace of the empire may be best answered, not by giving a triumph to any one party, but by reconciling all.

"In the substance of the second proposition, there is no variance as to any practical and prospective purpose, though undoubtedly there is, and it is natural there should be, some as to the past, arising from the difference of Mr. Canning's and Lord Wellesley's respective situations.

"When Mr. Canning says, that the Peninsular War is to be carried on 'with the best means of the country,' he intends the greatest scale of exertion which the means of the country may be found capable of sustaining.

"If Lord Wellesley's expression, 'a scale of adequate vigour,' may be construed to imply the proposition, that the late exertions of this country have not been proportioned to the great object of the war, or have not been duly distributed or apportioned, this prosposition Mr. Canning certainly does not intend either to affirm, or to deny; simply because, not having been in the Government during the last two years, he has not sufficient information to be able to pronounce an opinion, whether the exertions of those two years have or have not been below the proper scale, or have been well or ill administered; nor how far they may now admit of being extended or more judiciously applied.

" He concurs, however, entirely with Lord Wellesley, in wishing to extend thom to the utmost power of the country; and to apply them in the manner best calculated to answer their end.

(Signed) " WELLESLEY.
" GEORGE CANNING."

To this communication Lord Grey made the following rejoinder:

Letter from Lord Grey to Lord Wellesley, dated Portman-square, May 29th, 1812.

" MY LORD,—I had last night the honour of receiving your lordship's letter, enclosing a paper explanatory of the difference which I had remarked between your lordship's minute and Mr. Canning's, together with a copy of the latter.

" I beg your lordship to be assured that in the observation to which I had thought it necessary to call your lordship's attention, I could have no object but that of preventing the possibility of any future misunderstanding. We had not entered into any explanation, which, under the circumstances of the moment, would perhaps have been premature, of the details of conduct necessary to give effect to the first of the propositions, offered by your lordship as the basis of a new Administration. From the difference of the time used by Mr. Canning in stating that proposition, I was apprehensive that it might be his opinion, in concurrence with your lordship's, that no parliamentary proceedings with reference to the claims of the Catholics, should take place during the present session. To such an opinion I could not have assented; and I felt it to be due both to your lordship and to Mr. Canning, immediately to draw your attention to a point on which it was so desirable that there should be a clear understanding between us.

"I hope it is unnecessary for me to state, that I can look at the situations of the Catholics (both Irish and English) with no other view than that of the public interest; and that nothing can be further from my disposition, or my intention, in a matter of such pre-eminent importance, than to give to any one party a triumph at the expence of another. But I do not conceive, that the repeal of the disabilities of which the Catholics complain, can give any just cause for discontent to their Protestant fellow subjects; and I am strongly of opinion, that the efficacy of that measure must in a great degree depend on its being carried into effect with the least possible delay, and with the clearest demonstrations of a conciliatory and confiding spirit. Under this impression I should very reluctantly abandon the hope of passing a Bill for such repeal, even during the present session; but if this cannot be done, I hold it to be indispensable, that the most distinct and authentic pledge should be given of the intention, both of the Executive Government and of Parliament, to take this matter up as one of the first measures of the next. To a proceeding of this nature, from the paper signed by your lordship and Mr. Canning, I am led to hope that you would not be averse.

"As to the second proposition, the difference which I had observed was much less important. It is impossible to reduce a question of this nature to any fixed principle. Whatever we can say with our present means of information must necessarily be general and inconclusive, the whole subject being left open to future consideration and decision. I can have no hesitation in subscribing to the proposition, that, if it shall be found expedient to continue the exertions we are now making in the Peninsula, they should be conducted in the manner best calculated to answer their end.

"I have, I fear, troubled your lordship much more than is necessary under the circumstances of our present situation; and I will only add, that if we should be called upon to pursue these considerations in their practical details, it will be my most anxious wish, that no difference of opinion may be found to exist between us, respecting the conduct to be adopted by a government equally solicitous for the internal peace and harmony of the empire, and for the prosecution of military operations in such a mode as may appear most conducive to our ultimate security. Lord Grenville, to whom I have communicated your lordship's letter, and its enclosures, desires me to express his cordial concurrence in this wish. I have the honour to be, with the highest regard, my lord, your lordship's very faithful humble servant,

(Signed) "GREY."

In consequence of the declaration on the part of Lord Liverpool and his colleagues, that they must decline becoming members of any administration to be formed by Lord Wellesley, he (Mr. Canning) had thought it his duty to write the following private letter to Lord Liverpool:

Letter from Mr. Canning to Lord Liverpool, dated Gloucester Lodge, May 24th, 1812; half-past eight, A.M.

"MY DEAR LIVERPOOL,—I have received your letter of last night, which I will immediately transmit to Lord Wellesley.

"Before I do so, however, and of course, therefore, without Lord Wellesley's consent or privity, I cannot forbear suggesting to you to consider, whether the sort of personal objection which your letter evidently and exclusively implies, will stand fairly before the country, at such a moment, as a justification for refusing to act in an Administration, to the public principles of which you do not feel, or at least do not state, any insurmountable repugnance.

"I would suggest to you further to consider, whether, resting your refusal on an objection merely personal, you do quite justly either by yourselves or by the individual concerned, in leaving the precise nature of that objection wholly unexplained.

"In offering these suggestions, I perhaps exceed the limits of a correspondence such as ours is, upon this occasion: but they strike me so forcibly, that I think I owe it to you, not to withhold them. Whether to communicate them to your colleagues or not, I leave entirely to your discretion; but you at least will not resent, so far as you are yourself concerned, a freedom which may be justified by that regard with which I am, ever, &c.

(Signed) "GEORGE CANNING."

To this private letter Lord Liverpool sent the following reply:

Letter from Lord Liverpool to Mr. Canning, dated Fife-house, May 24th, 1812.

"MY DEAR CANNING,—I have this moment received your answer to my letter of last night.

"As that letter was not written without all due consideration, I do not feel that it can be necessary for me to call my colleagues again together upon the subject of it.

"I can answer, however, for myself (and I am confident equally for them), that I am not actuated, in declining the proposal made to us, by any objection of a nature purely personal. But when I advert to the opinions and statements recently sent forth to the world respecting public men with whom I have been connected, and public measures in which I have been engaged, I do not feel that I should have acted consistently with my own honour and character, or with the respect which I must ever owe, and shall ever feel, to my departed friend, if under such circumstances, I could have consented to have entertained the proposal which you were authorised to submit to me.

"As these considerations afforded an insuperable obstacle to my becoming a party to the proposed arrangements, I thought it wholly unnecessary to enter into any explanation on the two principles on which the Administration is stated as intended to be formed, or on other points of the greatest public imporance; and I must protest against any inference whatever being drawn from my silence in this respect.

"I can assure you that I am most willing to render you every degree of justice for the motives which have dictated your answer to my letter.

"And I remain, with sincere regard, &c.

"LIVERPOOL."

He had entered into these details, because he thought it due to both parties to do so; and because he wished to render exact justice to all. Lord Wellesley had had the opportunity of such complete and ample justification in another place, that it would be quite unnecessary for him to travel over the same grounds. He would content himself with observing, that the whole of the noble lord's negociation discovered the most marked characteristics of a magnanimous spirit and an innocent heart. The right honourable gentleman had justly stated, that there was here an interval, during which nothing appeared to be done. It was his duty to account for that interval; and he could assure the House, that it was not unemployed,—that the commission of his noble friend was not suspended, but that attempts had been making to induce the late colleagues of Lord Wellesley to form part of the intended Administration. It was true that these attempts had not been successful; but surely upon their own principles, the gentlemen opposite could not censure the effort. Upon the principle of numerical strength, on which they acted, they had no right to quarrel with what was not a very unusual thing,—a stipulation of numbers in, or a balancing of the cabinet. It ought, however, at the same time to be remembered, that however balanced, or however dissected, the cabinet might be, there was a majority of one offered to the noble lords. This concession of his noble friend, might, on the principle of a balanced cabinet, be considered even rash; but under the present circumstances of the state,—in the present divisions of public men, he did not know how a cabinet could be got together, between no two of whom there should be a difference of opinion. All hope of such a cabinet was now gone; and it was not too much to assume, that they who had put an end to that hope, thought that they ought to have, and to continue to possess, exclusively the power of the Government. He did not say that that might not be very fit, but it was not certainly the principle on which the negociation was founded; and on the whole he could not help again declaring, that the offer made by his noble friend to the noble lords was generous, was liberal, was even rash: that offer was rejected, and it was not for him to say one word on the motives which dictated that rejection. He did not by any means impeach their conduct,—but they withheld their services; and it was in his opinion a just conclusion, that unless the whole power of the Government was put into their hands, their pretensions could not be satisfied. Again he begged leave to observe that he did not attach blame to the noble lords. He did not say that they rated their political consequence too high, but he only wanted to show the principle on which they acted. The right honourable gentleman complained, that the noble lords were not honoured by the Prince with a personal interview; his answer to that complaint was, that somebody was sent for. And here again, what could those complaints mean, but that the right honourable gentleman thought, that the whole Government should be yielded to the disposal of his noble friends? He did not blame the noble lords, nor the right honourable gentleman, for thinking they had a right to such disposal: he was only explaining the principle on which Lord Wellesley's offer was rejected. That offer being, however, thus rejected, Lord Wellesley surrendered his authority, and it was then consigned to Lord Moira. As to Lord Moira's negociation with the noble lords, he of his own knowledge could say nothing, nor indeed should he advert to it at all, except that he wished to do justice to the noble lord, whose efforts had been rendered unsuccessful by the condition made so peremptorily and entirely by the noble lords. He had before stated, that he could say nothing of his own knowledge of the steps taken by Lord Moira subsequent to the failure of Lord Wellesley's negociation. The reason that he was thus ignorant was, that as he had been one of those mentioned as a Cabinet Minister in the first proposition, he had a motive of delicacy in wishing not to be mentioned by Lord Moira in his transactions with Lords Grey and Grenville, until he saw what progress would be made in the arrangement between them. He wished to watch their proceedings; reserving to himself, after what had passed, the right of acceding or not to any proposal which might be made to him. He at the same time told Lord Moira, that if this new negociation should happen to be broken off, then his services would be at his lordship's command. This was, perhaps, all that he was called upon to say concerning the late negociations, as far as they regarded himself; but he thought it was due to Lord Moira, to give all that evidence of the sincerity with which he acted, by alluding to the letters which passed between him and the noble lords. On the 4th or 5th of June he sent his compliments to the noble lords, "begging them to advert to his communication of the 3d of June, and stating how happy he should be to obtain permission from the Prince Regent to address them formally, with respect to the very objects they all had in view." This letter was written by Lord Moira, under a notion that his former communication was some way or other considered disrespectful, and that the noble lords did not conceive themselves approached in a manner consistent with their dignity. The answer of the noble lords to this communication declared, "how desirable any personal communication of the noble lord could be always to them, but that they did not conceive how any unauthorised discussion could be useful." It stated also, "that they would ever receive, with feelings of the highest respect, every communication from His Royal Highness, and that they yielded in zeal for his interests to none others whosoever." To this Lord Moira replied, "that he would leave no efforts untried in the pursuit of the object he had in view, and that he was authorised to communicate with them from the Prince, but that he wished Lord Erskine to be present with him, at his interview with the noble lords." This brought down the transactions to the minute read by the right honourable gentleman, which was commented upon in a manner that to him appeared the most unfair. It was said by the right honourable gentleman, that Lord Moira insisted on a denial of power which the noble lords considered inseparable constitutionally from the Government. In the right honourable gentleman's view, it would appear that Lord Moira thought as if some "hedge or sanctity" had been thrown over the household which protected no other political department: but Lord Moira thought no such thing. With that candour and frankness which ever distinguished Lord Moira, and which, to say the truth, were called for by the equal candour and frankness of the noble lords, that noble lord said, it was not to the existence of the power of displacing the household, but to the application of that power, now, under all the circumstances of the case, that he objected: and he himself would contend, that in thus acting, Lord Moira was swayed as well by public principle as by private feeling; and that if he had acted otherwise, he would have betrayed both. Lord Moira did not hold that in ordinary cases this power should not be exercised; but what he protested against was, the making the exercise of it, in the present instance, the very first act of the new Administration. The noble lord was of opinion, that the present exercise of that power would be fastening on a quarter which it was most desirable should be free from imputation, those calumnies which were so much in the mouths of men. He did not object to the right of the new Administration to displace the great officers of the household, but it was the policy of doing so which he condemned. Such policy, he knew would tend to fix a stain indelibly, where no spot ought to be allowed to remain.

Now in this conduct of the noble lord, he would ask the right honourable gentleman, could he be accused of any partiality or predilection for the persons whose interests seemed to be declining? Could it be thought, that he wished to stand in the way of realizing that efficient Government of the formation of which he himself was to have had the credit and the honour? The fact was, that Lord Moira acted solely on public grounds. He saw that a construction would be given to the displacing of the officers of the household far beyond the opinion of the noble lords, and that great public mischief would be the direct consequence. He, in one word, resisted the application of a power which he acknowledged to exist. There was one point connected with this part of Lord Moira's conduct which he was authorised to state particularly. Fearing that he was not entirely understood by the Prince when he received his unrestricted commands to form an Administration, when he returned to the royal presence, he put this question directly: "Is your Royal Highness prepared, if I should so advise it, to part with all the officers of your household?" The answer was, "I am;" "Then," said Lord Moira, "your Highness shall not part with one of them." In this conduct of Lord Moira, he (Mr. C.) saw nothing but what was most honourable, and it was quite unfair to say with the right honourable gentleman, that this was an attempt to put persons holding high offices beyond the controul of government. But supposing, as a preliminary step, that Lord Moira had agreed to the exercise of the power alluded to, and that afterwards some other point of difference should arise which would be fatal to Lord Moira's patriotic efforts, what would the country say of the failure? The country, panting with the expectation of an Administration, would have said, "You have come out of a five hours' negociation, and what have you done? You have disjointed a household, but you have not formed a government." Whatever others might think of Lord Moira's conduct, he thought him right; and he, therefore, upon the failure of the negociation with the noble lords, placed his humble services at his disposal. What happened afterwards it was unnecessary for him to state; but on Monday morning the noble lord surrendered his commission. As to any further mention or defence of the noble lord, he had now only to correct a misapprehension which had gone abroad, that on surrendering that commission he advised the revival of the present Administration. It was not for him to say what passed between the noble lord and his Prince; but of this he was assured, that five minutes after the interview between them, the noble lord related to him every thing that had passed, and in the whole of what he said, there was not one tittle as to any such advice. He stated this with no particular view, but merely for truth's sake; wishing to correct an erroneous impression, and not caring how that correction might be felt. As he was on the subject of correcting erroneous impressions, he thought it right to advert to a misapprehension of the right honourable gentleman, in an allusion to the speech of a noble lord (Yarmouth). In speaking of the household, that noble lord did not say that there would be, if Lords Grey and Grenville were in power, more removals than are usual on ordinary changes of Administration, but that there would be more voluntary resignations. He had now gone through the course of those transactions which afforded an opportunity of confiding the affairs of the country to that powerful phalanx, so splendid in great names, and so brilliant in ability. On public grounds alone he believed they most sincerely acted, and from him they should ever have the credit of having withheld their services from public views alone. He lamented that such an opportunity was not likely soon to occur again. (Here Mr. Whitbread smiled.) The honourable gentleman might smile, because he, perhaps, thought that the talents and character of his friends would yet force their way into power; but notwithstanding, he should continue to lament, that such an opportunity had been lost for realizing what had been long considered by many a mere creature of imagination, namely, an honest coalition of public men sacrificing some of their opposite doctrines to the general good of their country. He could not help thinking that such an opportunity would not speedily recur, whatever the honourable gentleman opposite might hope for. To those who looked on such a coalition as that to which he alluded as a mere chimerical experiment in politics, the present failure would be a matter of rejoicing; but to him, who had always held a contrary opinion, it was matter of sincere regret. He should now allude to one point more, and then sit down. The right honourable gentleman, and those on his side of the House, seemed to consider, that the great families and connections of this country had a kind of right to interfere in the nomination of Ministers. He himself, who was so very humble an individual, who could not boast of any of those high connections, and who, perhaps, though unknown to himself, was influenced by those circumstances of his humble rank, did not certainly believe in the existence of any such right or pretension in the aristocracy. He thought that in the very best spirit of the constitution, the Crown had exclusively the appointment of Ministers, subject, of course, to the controul or advice of a free Parliament. He did not, however, blame many of the gentlemen opposite for holding such an opinion. It was one that did not want the sanction of exalted authority; for even that great man, whose genius, infinitely more than that of all his cotemporaries, would mark our time with posterity, Mr. Burke himself, held that opinion. He concluded his speech by saying, that he did not feel himself called upon to vote for any of the amendments; and advised his honourable friend, in the peculiar circumstances of the present Government, to withdraw his motion.

The original address moved by Mr. S. Wortley, as well as the two amendments, were negatived.

ADDRESS RESPECTING THE WAR WITH AMERICA.

FEBRUARY 18th, 1813.

Lord Castlereagh moved the following Address:

"That an humble Address be presented to His Royal Highness the Prince Regent, to acquaint His Royal Highness that we have taken into our consideration the papers laid before us, by His Royal Highness's commands, relative to the late discussions with the Government of the United States of America. That, whilst we deeply regret the failure of the endeavours of His Royal Highness to preserve the relations of peace and amity between this country and the United States, we entirely approve of the resistance which has been opposed by His Royal Highness to the unjustifiable pretensions of the American Government; being satisfied that those pretensions could not be admitted without surrendering some of the most ancient, undoubted, and important rights of the British empire. That, impressed as we are with these sentiments, and fully convinced of the justice of the war in which His Majesty has been compelled to engage, His Royal Highness may rely on our most zealous and cordial support in every measure which may be necessary for prosecuting the war with vigour, and for bringing it to a safe and honourable termination."

Mr. Canning and Mr. Stephen rose together; a general wish being expressed by the House, that the former should proceed, the latter gave way, and Mr. CANNING addressed the House nearly as follows:

I should not have persisted, Sir, in claiming the attention of the House, in opposition to the learned gentleman to whom personal allusions have just been made, had not my opinions also been called in question in more than one sense, at an earlier period of the debate. I have been asked, from two different, indeed opposite quarters, whether I still persist in the opinions which I formerly stated on the subject of America. Those opinions were of two descriptions; the one relating to the justice of the war into which the United States have thought proper to plunge us, the other to the management of that war on our part. I retain both. But the noble lord has very properly said, that the main question, indeed the only question for deliberation and decision to-night, is, whether we will uphold, by our votes, the justice of the cause of our country, laying aside all dispute upon the less important point of the practical management of the war. And agreeing with the noble lord in this view of our present and most pressing duty; agreeing that our first object must be to inform our new enemy that we, the Parliament of the British Empire, think our country in the right, and that we are determined to stand by the Executive Government in maintaining that right against any power that may venture to dispute it, and thinking, at the same time, that any very anxious or angry discussion, as to the vigour and effect with which the cause of the country has hitherto been maintained by the Executive Government, might, if it impaired the unanimity of this vote, detract from its weight and consideration with the Government and people of the United States of America, I confess that I am glad to postpone all such details, however important they may be in other views of the subject, or however fit for separate discussion hereafter; and I shall be much less solicitous to examine this night the conduct of Administration, since the war has began, than to vindicate the principles on which this and preceding Administrations have acted, in the transactions from which the war has sprung, and to establish those upon which it must be maintained, and upon which alone it can be concluded with safety and with honour.

The honourable gentleman (Mr. Baring) who spoke last, observed at the outset of his speech, with regret, mingled with some consolation, that the differences with the United States, were now reduced to a single point, and he recommended that the negociations should be revived, with a view to an amicable conclusion on that point. I agree with the honourable gentleman that the grounds of dispute are ostensibly so much narrowed, that if a negociation could be set on foot, which should have regard merely to the true interests of the republic of the United States, and should not be disturbed and diverted from its course by the influence of those passions by which its Government has been agitated, then, indeed, we might hope for conciliation and tranquillity; but I cannot concur with him, either that the point in dispute is of such easy settlement, complicated as it has been in the course of the negociations with national feelings and animosities. Still less do I think that so prompt a solution of the difficulty, as he seems to reckon upon, is afforded by his construction of the English Act of Parliament to which he has referred. If, indeed, the true meaning and intent of the statute of Anne, were to give to foreign sailors, entering and serving on board the British navy, not only all those privileges here, but all that protection against their natural sovereigns and native governments, which the United States both claim the right of conferring, and in practice attempt to confer upon British sailors, seduced or deserting into their service, then I admit that this country would have to make to America an equal concession for an equal infringement of national rights; and that as there would have been a parity in the infringement, there could be no difficulty in a parity of concession. Neither Government could in that case have had any thing to reproach to the other: and instead of a question of violation of the law of nations, on the one side, and of forcible and summary self-redress on the other, the whole matter would be one of mutual acknowledgment, as to the past, and of conventional arrangement for the future. There would be no difference of principle, and the point in dispute would be settled only on grounds of reciprocal convenience. But I acknowledge that my construction of the act of Anne, was altogether different. I understood that by it this country professed to give that only which it is competent to bestow, without interfering in any degree with the rights or claims of other powers—that it imparted to foreigners, on certain conditions, certain municipal privileges, but leaves untouched and unimpaired their native allegiance. The operation of this act, as I understood it, before the honourable gentleman's commentary, was not to hold out to foreign seamen, that at the same time that they may become entitled to possess or to inherit property, and to participate in all the blessings of the British constitution, all the ties which bind them to their native country, are loosened; not to assert that by any service to a foreign state, he can relieve himself from that indelible allegiance which he owes to the Government under which he was born. The enactments of this statute are a testimony of national gratitude to brave men, of whatever country, who may lend their aid in fighting the battles of Great Britain; but not an invitation to them to abandon the cause of their own country when it may want their aid; not an encouragement to them to deny or to undervalue the sacred and indestructible duty which they owe to their own Sovereign, and to their native soil. Such being the real intention of the act, what similitude, what analogy can be drawn between it and the pretensions of America? In the papers upon the table of the House, it is asserted by our enemies, that British seamen once enrolled in the American service, become the seamen of the United States of America: and the Government of that country declares that it must protect them against the claims of their undoubted Sovereign, even when he on their allegiance demands their service in war; in the present war, for instance, which he is unwillingly compelled to wage. Taking the converse of the honourable gentleman's proposition, then, I should say, that if the American Government would adopt such a provision as that quoted by the honourable gentleman, from the act of Queen Anne, in that case, if all differences were not instantly and altogether removed, at least the question in dispute would be greatly and advantageously narrowed.

But, coupled with the inordinate and unheard-of rights of citizenship which the United States pretend to confer, to the annihilation of the claims of nativity and allegiance, the practical abuses of which we have also a right to complain, in seducing or harbouring our seamen, even independently of the principles and pretensions by which they are defended, would be of themselves matter of serious grievance. Were these principles and pretensions, once fairly given up, indeed, the road would be opened to the discussion of the practice. It would be open to consider whether any adequate security could be provided by diplomatic arrangement, and municipal regulation, against a grievance which it is impossible that we should tolerate; such as should supersede the necessity of that summary and effectual method of doing ourselves justice, which we cannot relinquish till some satisfactory substitute is found for it: but the exercise of which, it must be admitted, may be liable to some abuse or irregularity. Now, on a fair perusal of the documents, I find nothing which proves any disposition, in the English Ministry, to shut the door against a consideration of that important question. The fact is, that different modes of entering upon the subject have been suggested, but there is one preliminary demand on the part of America, which it is absurd to suppose that we could comply with. We are, by ancient and unquestioned usage, and by the law of nations, as they are now understood, in the possession of the right of search. It has been, and is, of ancient and uninterrupted usage. It is proposed by both parties, that a discussion should be commenced, as to the more unexceptionable mode of exercising this right; but what does the American Executive insist upon? That we should first abandon it, and trust for its restoration to the result of the negociation. We are required to trust to an act to be hereafter passed by the American Legislature, for the restoration of this right, or for the provision of an equivalent. Can any thing be more manifestly absurd and unjust? Is not the natural course, not by the law of nations only, but by the rules of common sense, that we should retain that which we rightfully possess, until the equivalent for which it is to be exchanged shall be fully discussed, and satisfactorily ascertained? The honourable gentleman says, that it will cost us a war to maintain the possession of it. I wish to ask him what wars would it not cost us to regain possession, if it were once resigned? At least, maintaining our right, we are safe until force compel us to resign it.

I am sure that gentlemen, upon reflection, must see the proposed compromise is at least attended with difficulties which, if not absolutely insuperable, are extremely hard to be surmounted. The appointment of a tribunal similar to a prize court, as suggested by an honourable gentleman (Mr. Baring) in this debate, approaches nearest to my ideas of possibility; but is this likely to be found practicable or palatable to America, if the proposal of it should come from this country? Were it suggested by America, it might perhaps produce some beneficial result; but if proposed by Great Britain, would it not be repelled with indignation? Would America bear to see her citizens made subjects of judicature, like bales of contraband goods? Would she endure that a judge of our appointment should settle the fate of her natives, as we assign chattels to the right owner? Or would not such a proposal, instead of tending to the settlement of differences, and the extinction of animosities, be employed by the demagogues on the other side of the Atlantic to inflame the public mind, to exasperate the jealousies and hatreds of the enemies of Great Britain, and to make all amicable arrangement utterly hopeless?

I have, however, as I have said, no objection, and the British Government has not shown any, throughout the correspondence now under our consideration, to any attempt to make the exercise of this right the subject of diplomatic arrangement, provided the principle of the right itself be unequivocally acknowledged; provided the suspension, or tacit abandonment of it be not expected to precede the substitution of some other effectual mode of securing the objects to which it applies; and provided it be distinctly understood that, failing the attempt to effect that substitution, our right, and the practice of it, are to continue not only unimpaired, but thenceforth unquestioned. The dispute relating to the impressment (as it is termed) or rather the recal of our own seamen, is not, however, as the honourable gentleman admits, the only point to be adjusted, before we can return to a good understanding with the United States. The American Government also requires the renunciation of the system and principle of what they call paper blockades; that is to say, of the right which we claim and have exercised under the orders in council of 1807, and should, I trust, exercise again, if again occasion arose for it, of retorting upon the enemy any attempt which he may make to wound us through the sides, or by the instrumentality of neutrals. With respect to blockades, the honourable gentleman has appealed to my recollection, whether the blockade of 1806 did not stand on different principles from those of 1807? The honourable gentleman is perfectly correct. The order of 1806 established, or professed to establish a blockade upon the old principles, by the application of a specific and competent force to particular ports. In January 1807, an order was issued professedly of a retaliatory character. The order of 1806 merged in it. What had intervened between the order of May 1806, and that of January 1807? The French Berlin Decree. In retaliation, and avowedly in retaliation for that decree, the order of January 1807 was issued; doing away the strict legal blockade, and instituting what has been and may justly be described as a constructive blockade, not supported by an adequate specific force, but excluding neutrals from the coasting trade of the enemy by a prohibition retaliatory of that sweeping prohibition of the Berlin Decree by which they were precluded from all trade with Great Britain. The orders of November, 1807, extended the operation of the order of January: but did not vary its principle. I have no wish to revive the differences which the honourable gentleman and I have so often discussed upon that subject, but I am equally prepared to contend now, as four years ago, that though there was some difference in degree between the orders of November, and that of January 1807, there was no difference in the principle; and certainly the honourable gentleman must own that the Americans have made no such distinction in their remonstrances.

The orders in council, however, both of January and, November were abandoned: wisely or not, there is now no advantage in enquiring; with little chance of satisfying America, as I thought at the time, and as must now be manifest to all mankind: and for this plain reason that the American Government was not to be satisfied. They had an itch for war with this country, and they were determined to have it. Although, therefore, these are the only two points on which any practical discussion is pending, I cannot agree that they only entered the minds of the American Executive when they declared war (for be it always remembered, that the war originated in *their* declaration). The spirit of animosity to this country, indeed, was not confined to the persons forming the cabinet of the United States; the gall of bitterness not only overflowed in Washington, but at the very court of London. The notes of the republican Chargé d'Affaires, Mr. Russell, contain abundant evidence not only of the predetermination to war, but of the real motives of that policy. In the month of August, he, with warning voice, pointed out to Ministers the consequences of hostility; he told them "if concessions are not speedily made, the passions of the inhabitants of the United States will be roused, and conquests may be gained on terms that forbid restoration." When this sentence was penned, had not Mr. Russell Canada before his eyes? Was he not in the transport of his visions of success betraying incautiously the secrets of his employers, which were not to be divulged till the promulgation of the declaration? Low as he was in the rank of diplomacy, he was intrusted with this grand and favourite design; and it is impossible for any man not to see from the commencement to the termination of all the proceedings of the Government of the United States an eager desire to gain possession of our North American territories: a plan long cherished, and not wholly, I fear, repugnant to the sentiments even of that party in the United States whom it is usual to designate as our friends. Even when their whole military establishment was 1,000 men, the American Government and its partizans loudly proclaimed their sanguine hopes of victory in an expedition against British America, and delighted their fancies by imaginary conquests. I say, that even those who are called our friends in the United States, are not averse from this enterprise, and would be won by the acquisition of Canada to the support and approbation of the war. But I use the expression "friends of this country,"—as I do that of friends of France,—not as implying on the one hand a British influence, nor on the other hand, imputing an actual conscious subserviency to Buonaparte: (though it must be owned that for the latter imputation there are appearances of but too probable grounds): but simply as designating the two parties in the United States who respectively think the interests of their country best consulted, the one by a British, the other by a French connection.

And here I must confess that the censure of the honourable gentleman (Mr. Whitbread) upon that part of the noble lord's (Lord Castlereagh's) speech which referred to the period chosen by the American Government for declaring war, appears to me exceedingly ill-founded. The noble lord's remarks upon that subject did not appear to me unjust or unnecessary. Looking at the present state of the world, who shall say what America might not have achieved? Not by mixing in the contest, and involving herself in the complicated relations of European politics; (for I have never wished to see America involved in the war,) but merely by abstaining from the course which she has unfortunately taken, by refusing to administer to the passions, to flatter the hatred of the tyrant, to afford him that new hope of victory, and that consolation in defeat, which he boasts of deriving, from the diversion of our means, and the distraction of our efforts by the American war? What assistance might she not have rendered to the late glorious struggle in the north, not by active concert, but merely in forbearing to aid Buonaparte's arms by partly occupying ours? Who would have expected to have seen this favourite child of freedom leagued with the oppressor of the world? She who, twenty years ago, shed her blood for independence—She that, ever since that time, has boasted of the superiority of her citizens above all the nations of the globe—She that, watched over in her infancy by Great Britain, with parental tenderness and anxiety, nursed in the very lap of liberty, and educated in the school of republicanism, is now seen truckling to France, and condescending to become the tool of an ambition which threatens to lay prostrate at its feet the independence of every government, and of every people! Is this the same nation that we once remember to have heard shouting for emancipation? Is this the people that was to set an example of magnanimity to the world? I can scarcely believe it: I would willingly persuade myself that I am deceived; but facts cannot be discredited, and I behold the free republic of America lending her aid to crush those principles to which she owes her own existence, and to support the most desolating tyranny that ever afflicted the race of man. It is impossible not to lament the loss to such a nation, of such an opportunity, which no combination of circumstances can ever restore. I do not say, that America should have been induced to assist us against France. I would not have asked her to risk her tender and unconfirmed existence in a war, and to endure all the dangers, or to incur all the expences that must have ensued from her taking part in such an enterprize. She might have maintained a just and noble neutrality. But were it put to me indeed as matter of opinion, supposing (what I do not suppose) that she could not avoid deciding one way or other, and that the risk of war on one side must be run, which would best become her history, her character, and her constitution, to unite with England or to league with France;—I should not have hesitated in my determination. There was a time when I hoped that her choice, under such an alternative, would have required little deliberation; but though I should have applauded her option in such a case, I would not have forced nor even have solicited it. She was welcome to be neuter, could she but have persuaded herself to be impartial.—There is still something imposing in the name of a republic. The veneration for that form of government is, even in this monarchical country, interwoven with our earliest impressions of honour, of liberty, and of virtue. But, I fear, that in the republic of America we look for the realization of our visions of republican virtue in vain. The sacred love of freedom, displayed in the annals of Greece and Rome, "made ambition virtue," and consecrated even the weapons of the conqueror. The modern republics of Europe polished mankind by their industry, and their arts. But I am afraid that neither the hardy valour, the ardent patriotism and the lofty magnanimity of ancient Greece and Rome, nor the gentle manners and artificial refinements of Genoa or Florence, are to be traced in the hard features of transatlantic democracy. Would it were otherwise! The heartless and selfish policy pursued by America will lead her far astray from her real interest. The first consequence of it will be, the loss of much internal prosperity, and I am much deceived if she will compensate this loss by the acquisition of much military glory. The honourable gentleman (Mr. Foster,) describes a thousand soldiers, four or five frigates, to guard an extent of coast of fifteen hundred miles, and a revenue of only two millions and a half of dollars, I think, or thereabouts, as the means, physical and pecuniary, of which the United States were in possession, when they declared war against this country. Undoubtedly no man could hear the statement without exclaiming—"And could a nation so circumstanced venture upon a war with the mighty empire of Great Britain, with the most distant prospect of success?" Unluckily it did. The unwelcome truth cannot be concealed. Two out of these four or five frigates have captured two frigates from the British navy. I advert with unwillingness to this part of the subject, because in my opinion, (an opinion before expressed and still retained) vigorous measures becoming this great nation might have averted disasters which may have the effect of prolonging hostilities. It is no answer to say, that our navy is immense, but that it is proportionably extended on the different stations. I complain not of the naval department, but of the policy which controuled its operations. I complain that the arm which should have launched the thunderbolt, was occupied in guiding the pen: that Admiral Warren was busied in negociating, when he ought to have been sinking, burning, and destroying. Admiral Warren sails from this country in the middle of August, and on the 27th of September he reaches Halifax with his squadron, where he employs himself in writing despatches to the American Government; while Commodore Rogers on the 10th of October, sails unmolested from Boston. But we waited, it seems, to be quite sure that we were actually at war? Granted for argument's sake (for no other purpose could I consent to grant it) that in the first instance there might be not full conviction of the certainty of war; but even after the American declaration was received in the end of July, no hostile measure was resorted to by this country till the 14th of October, when letters of marque were issued, upon the receipt here of the intelligence (and as might be not unfairly suspected, in consequence of that intelligence) that the Guerriere frigate had been captured by the Americans.—What is the next advance towards actual war? The blockade of the Chesapeake; and the order in council announcing that blockade, was issued, when?—the day after the arrival of the intelligence that the Macedonian, another of our frigates, had fallen into the power of the Republic. The loss of these two fine ships of war, produced a sensation in the country scarcely to be equalled by the most violent convulsion of nature. I do not attribute the slightest blame to our gallant sailors, they always do their duty; but neither can I agree with those who complain of the shock of consternation throughout Great Britain, as having been greater than the occasion justified. Who would represent the loss as insignificant, and the feelings of shame and indignation occasioned by it as exaggerated and extravagant? That indignation was a wholesome feeling, which ought to be cherished and maintained. It cannot be too deeply felt that the sacred spell of the invincibility of the British navy was broken by those unfortunate captures; and however speedily we must all wish the war to terminate, I hope I shall not be considered as sanguinary and unfeeling, when I express my devout wish that it may not be concluded before we have re-established the character of our naval superiority, and smothered in victories the disasters which we have now to lament, and to which we are so little habituated.—Sir, I entered on these points reluctantly on the present occasion. Other occasions will arise for their discussion. I hasten to quit them. But having been expressly called upon to declare if I retained the sentiments which I before expressed upon the conduct of the war, I felt bound in fairness not to decline the avowal that my opinion not only remains unaltered, but has received additional confirmation from subsequent events. If it be true (as I believe it to be) in general, that indecision and delay are the parents of failure; that they take every possible chance of detriment to the cause in which they are employed, and afford every advantage and encouragement to the adversary; it was peculiarly true in the present instance, that promptitude and vigour afforded at once the surest pledge of success in the war, and the only hope of averting it altogether, if while the elections were pending, the result of which was to place Mr. Madison, the arch enemy of this country, in the president's chair, a decisive blow had been struck by this country, the tide of popular opinion in America might have been turned, and the consequences of a long and ruinous war might have been avoided. I lament, for the general happiness of mankind, that no such vigorous exertion was attempted; and though I am not disposed to unnecessary cruelties, nor would countenance the wanton effusion of human blood, yet I cannot help thinking that if some signal act of vengeance had been inflicted on any part of the United States exposed to maritime attack, but particularly on any portion of their territory where there prevailed the greatest attachment to the interests of France, it would have at least been a useful warning, and might have prevented the continuance of the contest, if they had not prevented its commencement. I protest against the doctrine of half measures, and forbearance in war; for where vigour has a tendency to decide the contest, hesitation is cruelty. But with these topics I have done. Whatever may be the result of the contest, after the declaration issued by the United States, this country will stand right in the eyes of the world and of posterity. Nay, it is not paradoxical to say that we shall stand right, at no distant time, in the eyes even of our enemies in the United States; for by a singular anomaly, upon the issue of this struggle in which America is attempting to cripple our resources, depends not only the independence of Europe, but perhaps ultimately, the freedom of America herself.

The question was put and carried *nem. con.*

COMMITTEE ON THE LAWS AFFECTING ROMAN CATHOLICS.

MARCH, 11th, 1813.

Sir J. C. Hippesley moved, "That a Select Committee be appointed, to examine and report the state of the laws affecting His Majesty's Roman Catholic subjects within the Realm: the state and number of the Roman Catholic clergy, their religious institutions and their intercourse with the See of Rome, or other foreign jurisdictions: the state of the laws and regulations affecting His Majesty's Roman Catholic subjects in the several Colonies of the United Kingdom: the regulations of foreign states (as far as they can be substantiated by evidence), respecting the nomination, collation, or institution of the Episcopal order of the Roman Catholic clergy, and the regulations of their intercourse with the See of Rome."

Mr. Canning rose, and before he proceeded desired that the motion might be read; he desired also that the resolution moved by Mr. Grattan in April last, and then negatived, might be read also. These documents were accordingly read, the former by the Speaker, and the latter by the Clerk at the table.

And (said Mr. Canning) it is after this (Mr. Grattan's) resolution for referring the Roman Catholic petition to a Committee, has been negatived by a majority, of which my right honourable friend (Mr. Ryder) was one, that he comes forward this night to support the motion of the honourable baronet; and to accuse those of inconsistency who disapprove of that motion! I really do wonder at the versatility displayed upon this occasion by my right honourable friend, a versatility not at all belonging to his general character; but entirely owing, I must presume, to the helplessness of his cause. Nothing in my recollection of parliamentary tactics ever surprised me so much as the tactics of this evening. When I heard the honourable baronet express a doubt, whether his motion would be seconded, I confess that I felt some surprise: but when that doubt was removed by his finding a seconder in my right honourable friend, my surprise was indeed of a different description, but much greater in degree. The nature of the honourable baronet's motion; the manner in which it has been supported; the attempt made to impute inconsistency to those who dissent from that motion, because they see plainly that it can mean nothing but delay, after the House has, by no equivocal majorities, determined in favour of the principle of the Bill brought forward by my right honourable friend; the still bolder attempt to arraign the determinations of the House itself; and the aspersions thrown on the proceedings of those members to whom the House was pleased to entrust the difficult and sacred duty of framing this Bill; all these things present an appearance in this evening's debate, to which my memory cannot furnish a parallel; and show how flexibly extremes can be made to meet, and how harmoniously contradictions can be reconciled, to answer a particular purpose.

The House and the country cannot fail to see the tendency of the honourable baronet's motion. It is visible to the world. It calls upon the House to retrace its steps. It proposes by ambiguous words, to effect an object which cannot but be plainly understood. There is one language proper to be used within the doors of this House, and another without; but it cannot but be plain to the lowest intellect, that this motion, however innocent its author, or disguised its character, can have no other effect than to defeat the Bill to which it refers, and to disappoint the recorded intentions of the House of Commons. Is it possible that the honourable baronet himself should not see his motion in this light? The honourable baronet has been loudly cheered by those who, should his motion succeed, will no doubt indemnify themselves out of doors for their acclamations within, by unconstrained laughter and exultation at the honourable baronet's unintentional defeat of his own (I really believe) sincere intentions, in favour of the cause which he has so long espoused. It is we (the supporters of the Bill,) and not those who flatter the honourable baronet into this motion, that are his true friends: they will triumph in his success (if unhappily he should succeed) this night, not from participation in his immediate views, but from enmity to his ultimate objects. The honourable baronet professes to desire a pause for inquiry: they well know that a pause to-night will be a pause of which this session will not see the end.

The honourable baronet tells you that you ought to have all the information connected with the Catholic religion, before you agree to a Bill, upon the principle of which you have already decided. He says, that he has thought so for eight years. To attain the information desired by the honourable baronet, a circuit of the world must be taken—every quarter where the Catholic religion is known, must be explored. How such an inquiry is to be prosecuted—by what process this House or its Committee can reach the information sought for—has not been explained. But if the progress of the Bill is to be suspended until returns can be had from Africa; until the practice and effect of the Catholic religion in Canada shall be ascertained; until commissioners sent out for these purposes (and I should recommend the honourable baronet himself, as one of the commissioners to be selected, if by such appointment I should not have to deplore his absence from this House) shall have returned; if the Committee must continue its office, until the archbishop of Mohilow is brought before it for examination, with his patent in his hand, to explain the degree of his dependence upon the see of Rome; it requires no great sagacity to foresee that the Bill must stand still for more sessions than one; and that this House and the Catholics must lay in a good stock of patience, if they are to look to no end of their anxiety, till this incalculable labour shall be completed.—Looking indeed at the honourable baronet's motion, as it has been announced, it is impossible to say where his proposed inquiry is to terminate—for it is not only all the learned lore which the honourable baronet has treasured up in his own mind that is to be laid before the Committee; it is not only (let not the House be deluded into the hope that it is only) the contents of that bursting box which is placed beside your table; but all the theological controversy in existence must be thoroughly sifted and understood before this inquiry can close, if the honourable baronet's motion, such as I hold it in my hand, be indeed, to be fully complied with. Nay, and after all the various branches of his motion shall have been disposed of, the labours of the Committee will not be at an end—for at the end of the motion I find a saving clause, as follows,—" Sir J. H. proposes to move for various *other* papers to refer to the Committee." I am not so wholly unlearned in those branches of study, in which the honourable baronet peculiarly delights, as to be ignorant from what original author the honourable baronet derived this style; for I find its archetype in the great Smalgruenus, who first published a treatise " *De omnibus rebus,*" and then added a supplemental discourse, " *De quibusdam aliis.*"

To take the motion in its most restricted shape, does it not call for information respecting the nomination, collation, and institution of the Catholic clergy, in all Roman Catholic, as well as other countries in Europe? The honourable baronet may smile, but will the House be so ready to smile with him, when they learn that this would require at least one hundred folio volumes to be laid before the Committee? Can they look forward without dismay, to the wading through such a mass of learning—however interesting in itself, or however lightened their toil might be, by the able comments of the learned chairman (such I am sure the honourable baronet would be), addressed to a listening Committee, or to a despairing *quorum?* One hundred volumes in folio, did I say? One hundred would not comprise even the elementary books. They would be but a specimen—a mere scantling. In the first place, there are the works of Saint Augustine, in eleven folio volumes, who was called by Erasmus, "*Doctor ecclesiæ incomparabilis.*" Then there is an author familiar to the honourable baronet; Thomas Aquinas, who was called, "*Doctor Angelicus sive Theologiæ Aquila.*" His works are in nineteen volumes folio. Of him it was said, "*animam Augustini migrasse in Thomam,*" that the soul of Augustine had migrated into Aquinas. Into whom the soul of Aquinas has migrated this is not the place to inquire. Next comes Duns Scotus, who was called, "*Doctor Subtilis,*" and he was opposed to Aquinas tooth and nail: not with less violence, hitherto, have been opposed the honourable baronet and my right honourable friend, (Mr. Ryder). Duns Scotus only wrote twelve volumes folio in his controversy with Aquinas. But following these writers, who must be consulted, before, as the honourable baronet expressed himself, any one could step over the threshold to the proposed investigation, we must resort to Bellarmine, a name more familiar to us, a great luminary of the church, who wrote "*Circa potestatem Pontificum in secularibus,*" and whose works are comprised in four quarto volumes, which may be read through in a short sitting of the Committee. Bellarmine again is opposed by Dr. Milner, and that reverend doctor is opposed by the honourable baronet on this very point *de potestate Pontificum.* I say nothing of the difficulty and perplexity occasioned to this unhappy Committee by such opposition and contradiction of equiponderant opinions.—But in addition to the works I have mentioned, I have another, which must be particularly inspected, which is indeed the very grammar—the accidence—of theological policy—which every member of the Committee must have at his finger's ends. I mean the "*Oceanus juris civilis sive Tractatus Tractatuum de Ecclesiâ,*" in twenty-nine volumes, folio.

After reading these few books, the Committee, to attain all the honourable baronet's objects, would be under the necessity of resorting to the examination of numerous individuals, in order to ascertain the universal practice of the Catholic Church. Nay, the Pope himself should be forthcoming; his examination would be very material, to show not only the existing practice of the church, and also what new regulations his holiness would be willing to make with a view to the conclusion of a concordat with this country for the future government of our Catholic fellow subjects.

On some points, however, particularly on one which appears to occasion great alarm to the honourable baronet, it was not necessary to resort to distant parts of the world for information. I refer to his apprehension that the Lord Mayor and Aldermen of London might, after the passing of this bill, go in procession to a Catholic chapel. Now, by a law of the 5th of George I. any corporate officers who should proceed with their official paraphernalia to any other place of worship than that of the Church of England, would be subject to certain penalties, and be for ever disabled from holding such office, and this statute is left untouched by the bill. Therefore the honourable baronet's apprehension is wholly unfounded in this particular; and for ascertaining the necessity of a provision on this head, his Committee is wholly unnecessary.

Another part of the honourable baronet's speech, which appeared to deserve great attention, and to which my right honourable friend (Mr. Ryder) has very naturally been eager to attach more weight than it deserves, related to the establishment of a society of Jesuits* in this

* Some members of this excellent Society (to which the civilized world owes more for its substantial services in the diffusion of useful knowledge of every kind than to any body of men that ever existed), have founded a College for the education of youth in England, and a most able and learned divine,—the Rev. Mr. Kenny,—has formed a similar establishment in Ireland. In the latter I was educated: it contains some of the best men I ever met; and it is with the utmost satisfaction, I avail myself of the opportunity which the present publication

country. Undoubtedly, that such a society should be established in this country, after having been abolished in every Popish country in Europe, is a fact of a very alarming nature; but still more alarming is it, that the fact of such an establishment should be communicated, for the first time, to the Executive Government of the country by a private individual, for the sake of pointing an argument in a debate! But more alarming still to my mind (if it were not so ludicrous as almost to preclude the more serious feeling of alarm) would be the inference which a person of my right honourable friend's wisdom and gravity draws from such a fact, viz.—that the system of laws under which this takes place, is one which must not be touched till you have made a tour of the globe.

Other visions of danger arise to the eyes of the honourable baronet, and are magnified to those of my right honourable friend. The honourable baronet has, with infinite assiduity and industry, collected information that not more than 5,000 Catholics had taken the oath prescribed by the last Act passed for the relief of the Roman Catholic body. The fact, admitting its correctness, furnishes no valid objection. The statute containing those oaths presents nothing imperative. It is a law granting certain immunities upon cer-

affords, of bearing my willing and grateful testimony to the principles of obedience to the laws, and of loyalty to the King and constituted authorities of the land, which they inculcate with a zeal and earnestness not inferior to any Protestant seminary throughout the British Empire.—EDITOR.

tain conditions, among which conditions were these oaths; and those who do not seek the immunities, do not comply with the conditions. But would any considerate man seriously maintain that the neglect to take certain oaths of a public nature furnished any evidence against the loyalty of any man, or body of men? If indeed such a criterion of loyalty were established, how many persons would unjustly suffer. Suppose in the case of Protestants that a return was ordered of the number, who in the several districts had taken the oath of allegiance, and that in any particular district none, or but few, were found to have taken that oath, would any rational being propose, that such district should be placed under a separate system of coercive law? Certainly not. Then upon what principle could any portion of the Catholics be doomed to censure for omitting some oaths which were in fact not oaths of infliction, but of qualification? The bill now under consideration, providing, as it does, a general oath to be taken by all the Roman Catholic clergy, containing an imperative provision with respect to oaths; without any reference to immunity, or any object of advantage to the individual to whom the provision applies.

Such are the only novelties in argument which the honourable baronet has carried with him to the side of the question which he espouses to-night. I give the honourable baronet full credit for having persuaded himself, though I know not by what process of reasoning, that he is not, by his present conduct, essentially prejudicing the cause of which he has so long been one of the most eminent supporters. I am willing to go as far as I can in believing that he has persuaded himself that he is doing that cause a service. But, in the name of common sense, I conjure those who wish well to that cause, to beware how they suffer the honourable baronet to persuade them of that, of which he must, no doubt, have persuaded himself. Let them not imagine for a moment, that the adoption of this motion (with whatever good intentions it may have been brought forward) is any thing but hostile to the ultimate success of the bill. To pause now—to retrograde now—to descend from the pinnacle on which we are now placed, and which commands a view of the affection, the harmony, and the gratitude of our Roman Catholic fellow subjects, would be to lose all the ground that we have gained. That ground once lost, will not be easily recovered. "There is a tide in the affairs of men," on the height of which we are now riding towards the accomplishment of our object. The hands of Protestant and Catholic are outstretched to meet each other, and nearly touching. The interposition of this motion, if unfortunately it should be carried, may drive us as far asunder as ever.

And why? for what reason is this mighty mischief to be incurred? An intemperate paragraph, it seems, has appeared in the most intemperate publication in Ireland. Be it so: but have we no more safe rule and guidance for our own conduct than the intemperance of an Irish journalist? Let the House recollect that last year they pledged themselves to take the Catholic claims into their consideration early in the next session. Very soon after the close of that session Parliament was dissolved, and the pledge so recently given was in great hazard of being done away. It happened fortunately, however, that the merits of the question had, from repeated discussions, made so deep an impression on the minds of men, that the new Parliament had sat but a very little time before they renewed the pledge given by their predecessors; and by a very considerable majority, gave leave to my right honourable friend to bring in the bill which is now the subject of discussion. We are come to the second reading of that bill. Is it proposed that the second reading shall be negatived, and the bill thrown out, because an Irish newspaper has been absurd and impertinent? That would be foolish and illogical enough; but that, it seems, is not what is proposed to-night. Oh, no! the bill is to go on. The motion of to-night is all for the good of the bill. But somehow or other it so happens that all the sworn enemies of the bill are highly in good humour with this motion, which is so eminently calculated to promote it; and their reasoning upon it, I suppose, must be this, "because an Irish newspaper is very absurd, let us match it in absurdity by going into the honourable baronet's committee." I really see not in what other way the argument from the Irish newspaper bears upon this question.

But, Sir, the plain truth is, that the enemies of the bill see they have no chance of throwing it out by a direct opposition, and therefore they would endeavour to get rid of it by a side wind. Accordingly, no mode of attack upon the bill, independent of the substance and merits of it, comes amiss to its opponents. One gentleman complains of hurry and precipitation—another of delay in bringing it forward. It has been stated that my honourable friend had given notice that he should bring his bill forward before the recess. No such thing: he had said, indeed, that if he could hope to get it through the second reading before the recess, he should be glad to have it printed and circulated, that gentlemen might be in possession of the contents. But in consequence of the press of business, and particularly of the inquiry into East India affairs, it was found that it would be impossible to get it farther than to the first reading, and nothing would have been more improper than to send it out to the world in that imperfect and immature state. My right honourable friend, the seconder of the honourable baronet's motion, himself fixed the second reading of the bill, by fixing this day for the call of the House; my right honourable friend (Mr. Grattan), having declared that he would not move the second reading till the day of the call. Had he done otherwise, what triumphant sarcasms should we not have heard against him for taking the House by surprise, and flying from the test of a full attendance! But after all, how is it possible that the enemies of the bill should still flatter themselves with the hope of being able entirely to prevent a measure which the House has so unequivocally declared to be necessary? In fact, they do not entertain that hope. Delay is all that they now venture to contend for. The language which we heard last session from the learned and right honourable member for the University of Oxford, the venerable magistrate (Sir William Scott), whom I see on the bench above me, sufficiently shewed that in the opinion even of the persons most adverse to unnecessary change, the laws respecting the Catholics could not remain in their present state; that it was necessary to adopt some measure; and this opinion the House adopted, in giving leave to bring in the bill of my right honourable friend. In the first instance, my right honourable friend had been divided in his opinion, whether, having obtained his Committee, he should proceed by way of resolutions, or should bring in a bill at once. His adversaries said, "take the manly course, and bring in a bill." He adopted their advice; but as soon as he has done so, they immediately turn round on him and say, "we will have another Committee."

What may be the fate of the bill in this or in the other House of Parliament, I certainly do not presume to predict; but of one thing I am certain, that if it should happily find its way through this House to the other, it will not there be combated in the miserable manner in which it is attacked by this night's motion. My noble friend in the other House (Lord Liverpool), said fairly on this question, "Let the House decide upon the principle, and I won't be shabby enough to dispute with you the details." And still less, I am sure, would he stoop to attempt defeating such a measure, by interposing vexatious propositions for delay.

The principle, Sir, which has been agreed upon in the Committee, and which the House has confirmed, is, that the disabilities of the Catholics should be removed, taking security that their admission into the franchises of the state shall be in no way dangerous to the Protestant establishments. So far as we have gone, difficulties have vanished, not before vague inquiries into Africa and America, but before discussion. Pursuing the same course, difficulties will gradually disappear, and the public mind will become calm and satisfied. Not that it may not still be possible to hire a corner in some venal newspaper, to undo the work of legislation, and restore the empire to disorder; if with most unaccountable and unexampled folly we determine that this question, unlike all others, and of all others the most unfit to be left to the mercy of popular discussion, shall in fact be liable to be turned round by every breath of prejudice or disaffection. Such is not the policy which this House ought to pursue: such is not the duty which this House has to perform. Our duty as well as our policy in the state to which the question has now been brought is, to proceed without further delay to those stages of the bill, in which it can, consistently with the forms of the House, be moulded into that shape, and receive those additions and improvements by which its principle is to be carried into most effectual and most beneficent operation. Thinking every moment that is wasted before we proceed to this great work, an interval of unnecessary inconvenience, disquietude, and danger, I certainly shall give my vote against the honourable baronet's motion for delay, and for immediately reading the bill a second time.

[Mr. Canning proceeded to say that he could have wished to avoid troubling the House further on this occasion, especially as other occasions would occur more proper for entering into the detail of the provisions which he thought necessary to be introduced into the bill; but as it might be expected of him that he should not omit to explain generally the nature and object of those provisions, he would do so as shortly as possible. The principle which the Resolution of the House and the Committee had sanctioned, was this, that it was expedient to afford substantial relief to the Catholics, with certain exceptions, and under certain regulations. Now, if the right honourable framer of the bill had dealt altogether in abstract rights and universal propositions, it might have justly been objected that he had outgone the principle on which the measure professed to be founded. But he had not gone into any extreme of that kind, he had professed his readiness to receive into his bill exceptions and restrictions which he himself should not have ventured to propose. The amendments which he (Mr. Canning) wished to introduce into the bill, he had given into the hands of the right honourable member, (Mr. Grattan). If he (Mr. Grattan), had thought proper to adopt them, he should have given his most cordial support to the whole measure, without indulging the poor ambition of vindicating any part of it as peculiarly his own.——There were three points to which it was necessary to look. The first was, the ascertaining the loyalty of the Catholic hierarchy; the second was the prevention of foreign interference; the third was the finding some security that our concessions to the Catholic body should not be thrown away, but should be met by a corresponding spirit of conciliation on their part. On the first point—of the veto, he had given no opinion, nor was it now before the House; in his judgment, testimony and not nomination, testimony that the person chosen (no matter by whom) was a peaceful and well-disposed subject, was all that was requisite. The next question was, how this testimony was to be obtained? The difference between his plan and that of the veto would be, that upon the one, this information would be collected privately and anonymously, and upon the other from acknowledged and regular sources. It was his intention to fill up the blanks in his clause with the names of the five oldest Catholic peers, whom he proposed to constitute a commission for this purpose. Their responsibility would ensure to their testimony to the character of the person to be made a bishop, the highest possible authority. ——On the second point all parties were so far agreed as to concur in admitting the necessity of preventing foreign interference. It appeared from the honourable baronet's information that night, if indeed it were not before sufficiently notorious, that the existing laws were insufficient for this purpose; and it was a consideration well worthy the attention of those who are against making any changes whatever, and who are at the same time in alarm at the power of the See of Rome in this country, that by rejecting the present bill, they would leave the correspondence between the Catholics and Rome unrestrained. There was, it is true, a law in this country which made the receiving of bulls and other instruments from the court of Rome high treason; yet bulls and instruments were continually received, without any notice being taken of them; and this was the state of things which the tremblers at foreign interference would continue! Would the House accept of some such plan, or by rejecting the bill render the illicit correspondence between the Catholics and the court of Rome immortal? The opposers of the bill were driven to this dilemma, unless indeed they avowed that they had some measure of unmitigated severity in contemplation; and then the question would be, whether the severity would be more effectual without the boon, or whether we should take advantage of the boon to make the severity palatable? He was not so bigotted to his own particular opinions as not to change them if good reasons were offered against them; the Committee would, however, be the place to inquire into the details. At any rate, the security allowed on all hands to be necessary to the state, ought no longer to slumber in obsolete black letter——The third point to which he should now come, was but a short one; it was the obtaining some pledge that our concessions to the Catholics should not be thrown away—that they should be received in the same spirit in which they were granted. "You may pass your bill—you may enact and concede what you please, but the Roman Catholics will give you nothing in return. How do you know that your proffered boon will be acceptable to those whom you profess to relieve by it? Have you ascertained the sense of the Roman Catholics on this question?" To such interrogatories he should answer, that it was nonsense to talk of obtaining the opinion of four millions of people individually; and it must be remembered that we had laws (he was bound to believe wise and provident laws), which prevented the expression of it by delegation. The sense of the Catholics therefore could only be collected by the measure of a parliamentary enactment, and their consequent reception or rejection of the opportunities which such an enactment would open to them. So far, however, as it was possible to obtain a previous signification of their concurrence, he thought that purpose answered by the last clause of his proposed amendments, which enacted that the Roman Catholic lay commissioners should meet, within a given time after the passing of the Act, and that all the other enactments of the bill should take effect from the date of the day on which the commission should be constituted. By this clause the *onus* of putting the statute in force was, in fact, thrown upon the Roman Catholics: if they refused to constitute the commission, the whole of the provisions in their favour would, *ipso facto*, fall to the ground. He should not hesitate to say, that so far as his communications with English Roman Catholics had extended, he had found no reason whatever but to believe in, and to hope for a cheerful and ready acquiescence in the provisions of his clauses as they now stood—some alterations might probably render them still more acceptable; but he believed that no changes in them, made in an amicable spirit, would be seriously objectionable. His knowledge, with respect to the Catholics of Ireland, did not enable him to speak of their sentiments with confidence; but he had grounds for believing that, though some alterations might be wished for, there was no contumacious or unthankful spirit prevailing among the Catholics of that country: and that, more especially among those whose opinions were the most to be valued, there existed a disposition to acquiesce in whatever the wisdom and benevolence of Parliament might ultimately decide. He hoped and trusted that no turbulent spirit would step in between the good will and beneficent intentions of Parliament, and the acquiescence and gratitude of the Catholics, to prevent a settlement so desirable to the whole empire. This, however, was more than he could be expected to undertake for, or to promise. But he most anxiously hoped, that those who sought to overthrow the Bill, that night, would not find themselves able, in the event of their success, to cast the blame upon the misconduct of the Catholics. Mr. Canning concluded by exhorting the opposers of the Bill, who aimed at defeating it through the honourable baronet's motion, rather to come forward manfully, and defeat it in the face of day; not to shelter themselves in the cloud which the honourable baronet's learned dust raised around them—in that misty obscurity which Homer described as

" better than night for evil deeds." If they really thought that we could best maintain the domestic security and tranquillity of the empire upon the anomalies of a tattered legislation, let them avow it boldly; if they admitted measures of conciliation to be necessary, let them not put off those measures till messengers had been sent to the north, and to the south, to the east, and to the west, and till the honourable baronet, like another Sinbad, should return from a series of voyages of discovery, with an abstract of the manners and customs, the religion and polity, of half mankind! For the peace and safety of the country, for their own honour and reputation, he conjured them, if they felt themselves strong enough openly to oppose the Bill, to cast away the armour which they had borrowed from another, and to display their force, effectually and finally, by putting an end to the Bill that night. He conjured the honourable baronet, from whom he said that he had learned all that he knew, and all he wished to know, on abstruse points of theological controversy, and to whose extraordinary erudition, indefatigable industry, and meritorious exertions, he bore the most ample testimony, to pause ere he frustrated all the important services which he had formerly rendered to the cause, by now throwing his great weight into the scale of the enemy. He conjured him to remember his past deeds, and, like another repentant Coriolanus, to quit the camp of his Volscian allies, and return to Rome again.

The Motion was negatived on a division :—

For the Motion	187
Against it	235
Majority against it	48

VOTE OF THANKS TO THE MARQUIS OF WELLINGTON.

JULY 7th, 1813.

Lord Castlereagh moved, "That the thanks of the House be given to Field Marshal the Marquis of Wellington, Knight of the Most Noble Order of the Garter, for the energy and distinguished ability with which he had conducted the late operations of the allied forces in Spain, and particularly for the splendid and decisive victory obtained upon the 21st of June last, near Vittoria, when the French army was completely routed, with the loss of all its artillery, stores, and baggage!"

Mr. Freemantle seconded the motion.

Mr. Canning * said, he felt in common with the honourable gentleman who had seconded the motion, and with the gallant general (Sir Eyre Coote), who had just addressed them, the difficulty (a difficulty in which no man had more frequently placed his friends, the House, and the country, than Lord Wellington) of expressing, in adequate terms, the feelings which filled the mind of every man in the country. And he was persuaded, that the strongest language he could use would be but a faint echo of the public sentiment on this glorious occasion. If the honourable gentleman (Mr. Freemantle,) from his private feelings on this occasion, and if the gallant general, from his feelings as a soldier, could not refrain from trespassing on the House, however unnecessary their apology for doing so; he trusted the interest which he had ever taken in the cause of Spain would excuse him for offering a few words on the same subject. It was now five years since this country, involved as it was in difficulties, and engaged in a contest the end of which it was impossible to foresee, had the glorious prospect opened to it of what this splendid achievement led to the hope of having brought to a happy consummation. At that particular period, amidst the pressure of events, and all the troubles peculiarly her own, she had not hesitated one moment in becoming the friend of those whose only claim to her friendship was their being the victims of tyranny and oppression. This choice was crowned with success; but it was a choice which they would not have had cause to regret, even had the struggle ended in hopelessness and disappointment. Thank Heaven, the result was of another character, and proved that generosity and justice, while they were the most liberal, were also the wisest system of policy, and that honourable feeling for others was nearly connected with our own national safety. At the period to which he had alluded, there were many who despaired of the success of the cause, and who, though forced into the current, had expressed their disapprobation of it. That enterprize, which many thought rash and hazardous, which many believed almost hopeless, had ended in a blaze of glory, that will live recorded on the glowing page of history, even if glory should be its only result; but he did not despair to see added to it other pages of political arrangement and final settlement, calculated to promote the happiness and secure the liberties of mankind. With regard to the honours to be bestowed upon Lord Wellington and his companions in arms, they could not be too lavish of them—but to this subject the word 'lavish' could not be applied—but, while they expressed their sentiments on this subject, they ought also to pay the tribute merited by those whose pains, care, anxiety, solicitude, and attention, had been unceasingly cherished to prepare at home the mighty means for the accomplishment of this mighty achievement. Not only his Majesty's Ministers, but this House and the country had also to congratulate themselves, as well on the generosity and wisdom of their first determination, as on the firmness with which, under every variety of circumstance, and vicissitude of fortune, in the course of a long contest, sometimes unpromising, sometimes leading to despondency, (though never those who felt that confidence in the commanding genius of the great leader of our armies, which this day would render universal,) and amid every difficulty under which the country laboured, they had continued the contest in a way which demonstrated that it never had been the prevailing sentiment of the nation, that they ought to shrink from the task they had undertaken, to be guilty of a dereliction of principle, or give up the glorious cause in despair. The confidence with which he and many others had set out in this contest, the present victory had now made general. It was now that the fruits of their exertions began to appear. It was now that they had to look for the reward of their policy in engaging in, and their constancy in persevering in this arduous conflict. The revolution (as it had been called) of 1808, seemed as if given by Providence in contrast to that mighty and dreadful revolution, whose tremendous successes had almost led mankind to believe that success was inseparably linked to the car of those, who assailed with insatiable fury every established institution. But the Spanish revolution, exhibiting the same splendid successes as those which marked the early career of that of France, had proved, that triumph is not unachievable by those who are attached to the sovereignty, and whose principle is to conserve rather than to destroy. It was not to Spain alone that the effects of the late victory will be confined. Spain had been the theatre of Lord Wellington's glory, but it would not be the boundary of the beneficial result of his triumph. The same blow which has broken the talisman of the French power in Spain, had disenchanted the North. How was their prospect changed! In those countries, where at most a short struggle had been terminated by a result disastrous to their wishes, if not altogether closing in despair, they had now to contemplate a very different aspect of affairs. Germany crouched no longer, trembling, at the feet of the tyrant, but maintained a balanced contest. The mighty deluge by which the Continent had been overwhelmed began to subside. The limits of nations were again visible, and the spires and turrets of ancient establishments began to re-appear above the subsiding wave.* It was this victory which had defined these objects,

* Mr. Canning delivered this passage with great animation; the effect which it produced upon the House was quite electrical. The idea of illustrating the political aspect which the nations of Europe at this time presented, by the sublime image of the earth on its first and gradual reappearance above the subsiding wave of the great deluge, is new, both in its conception and application; and in both it is as beautiful as original. It possesses a Burke-like elevation of style and sentiment, and displays a kindred glow and vigour of imagination to those of that illustrious statesman, which Pitt and Fox never—and Sheridan seldom—reached. Many passages of corresponding excellence are profusely scattered throughout the Speeches in the present collection.

Sir Walter Scott, in his Life of Napoleon, makes the same

so lately involved in overwhelming confusion. To whom, under God, were they indebted for this? To the man to whom they were this day voting their thanks. As the noble lord had justly said, it would be presumptuous to anticipate the result of this heroic achievement. But they knew that it must be good. If war continued, in war it would furnish means and heart for the maintenance of the struggle; for peace, it would furnish the best of means, the association of peace and victory, without which, he would not say that peace ought never to be attempted, but without which, he would say, it could never be secure with the enemy against whom they had to contend. It was the illustrious Wellington who furnished them with these means so to be applied. His admirable conception of what ought to be done; his rapidity in executing the designs he formed; his wonderful comprehension of measures directed to one end; the completeness of his plans, and the thunderbolt of war which he launched at last upon the foe, enabled this country to furnish the most ample data ever given as the basis of a secure and lasting peace. One topic more, and he would intrude upon the House no longer. The honourable seconder, from the warmth of his feelings, had intimated a wish, that a

simile as Mr. Canning uses here, and introduces it in illustration of the same sentiment. It is not however so beautiful as Mr. Canning's, and, besides, it has not the merit of originality.—Editor.

"The retreat of the French armies, or their relics, across the land which they had so long overrun, and where they had levelled and confounded all national distinctions, might be compared to the abatement of the great deluge, when land marks, which had been long hid from the eye, began to be once more visible and distinguished. The reconstruction of the ancient sovereignties was the instant occupation of the allies."—*Scott's Napoleon*, Vol. VII. page 606.

special mode of transmitting their thanks should be adopted, in order to mark their high sense of this glorious victory: greatly as he felt the transcendent merits of Lord Wellington, he also felt for the dignity of that House; and he considered that there was nothing within the power of a subject to execute which would not be adequately rewarded by their thanks, conveyed in the ordinary forms. He trusted therefore that the honourable gentleman would not press any proposition which might cause a difference of opinion, while on the main question there could be but one unanimous and cordial feeling. He apologised to the House for having occupied so much of their time, and sat down amid loud cheering.

The Resolution was put, and carried, *nem. con.*

FOREIGN TREATIES.

NOVEMBER 17th, 1813.

Lord Castlereagh moved, "That the sum of three millions be granted to enable His Majesty to carry into effect certain engagements with foreign powers."

The motion being put—

Mr. Canning rose, and spoke nearly in the following terms:—Having been unfortunately absent when the general assurances of support on the part of the House were given in answer to the speech from the throne, of which the vote of this day is a partial performance, I am anxious to take this opportunity of expressing, as strongly and as warmly as I am able, both my concurrence in those assurances, and my disposition to make them good, by the way and in the proportion recommended by the noble lord. If in the present state of this country, and of the world, those who, during the course of the tremendous and protracted struggle, on various occasions called upon Parliament to pause, to retard its too rapid and too rash advance, and to draw back from the task it had unwisely undertaken to perform, have manfully and honourably stepped forward to join their congratulations to the joyful acclamations of the nation, and to admit the present to be the period favourable to a mighty and decided effort; how much more grateful must it be to those, who at no time during the struggle have lifted up their voices in this place, excepting to recommend and to urge new exertions; to those who, when the prospects were most dreary and melancholy, insisted that there was but one course becoming the character and honour of Great Britain; a persevering, an undaunted resistance to the overwhelming power of France. To an individual who, under the most discouraging circumstances, still maintained that the deliverance of Europe (often a derided term) was an object not only worthy of our arms, but possible to be achieved, it must be doubly welcome to come forward to acknowledge his transports, and to vindicate his share in the national exultation. If too, on the other hand, there have been those who, having recommended pacification when the opportunity was less favourable, are now warranted, as undoubtedly they are, in uttering the same sentiments, in the confidence that the country will sympathize with them; it is natural for those who, under other circumstances, have discouraged the expectation of peace, and have warned the nation against precipitate overtures, now to be anxious to embrace this occasion of stating their sincere conviction and their joy, as strongly felt by them as by others, that by the happy course of events during the last year, and by the wise policy we shall now pursue, peace may not, perhaps, be within our grasp, but is at least within our view.

The vote we are this night called upon to make is in part prospective, and in part retrospective for services actually performed. Of that portion which is prospective, the lord noble has properly deferred the discussion; but of that portion which is retrospective, we are enabled to judge; and, large as the expenditure now proposed may seem, I think no man, who compares the station we now hold with that which we occupied at any former period of the contest, can doubt that the expenditure has been wisely incurred, and that the services actually performed have fully merited the disbursement. I agree with those who are of opinion, that the time is now arrived when we may look forward to the attainment of peace; but I am far from disguising from myself, and I deem it of infinite importance that the country should not disguise from itself, the difficulties with which we may have still to struggle. We must not deceive ourselves by supposing that the game is actually won; that the problem is mathematically solved; that we have done all that is necessary to insure a lasting tranquillity. What we have accomplished is, establishing the foundation upon which the temple of peace may be erected; and imagination may now picture the completion of that structure, which, with hopes less sanguine, and hearts less high, it would have been folly to have attempted to raise. We may now confidently hope to arrive at the termination of labour, and the attainment of repose. It is impossible to look back to those periods when the enemy vaunted, and we, perhaps, feared that we should have been compelled to sue for peace, amid all the ebullitions of joy, without returning thanks to that Providence, which gave us courage and heart still to bear up against accumulating calamity. Peace is safe now, because it is not dictated; peace is safe now, for it is the fruit of exertion, the child of victory: peace is safe now, because it will not be purchased at the expense of the interest and of the honour of the empire: it is not the ransom to buy off danger; but the lovely fruit of the mighty means we have employed to drive danger from our shores. I must with heartfelt delight congratulate my country, that, groaning as she has done at former periods under the heavy pressure of adverse war, still "peace was despaired of; for who could think of submission?" Her strength, her endurance, have been tried and proved, by every mode of assault, that the most refined system of hostility could invent, not only by open military attacks, but by low attempts to destroy her commercial prosperity: the experiment has been made; the experiment has failed; and we are now triumphantly, but not arrogantly, to consider, what measures of security should be adopted —on what terms a peace should be concluded. But, as I before remarked, peace is only within our view, not within our grasp; we must still look forward to an arduous struggle with an enemy, whose energies have grown with his misfortunes, and who will leave no efforts untried to remove us from the lofty pinnacle that we have attained. We are not yet in a situation in which we have a right to discuss the terms of pacification; but so far I agree with the noble lord, that the happy changes which have taken place, must not alter the principle on which a treaty should be founded: they do not vary with circumstances; we must secure and guard our own honour and interest; but we must not expect from our enemy that to which we ourselves should not submit, that he should sacrifice to us his own honour and interest, to him equally dear. All will agree, however, that this is not precisely the time for these discussions; we must expect from him a renewed and vehement struggle; he will not tamely submit to degradation, but will continue his efforts; and if we arrive at the desired goal, it can only be by the road we are now pursuing.

With reference, however, to the vote of this night, as far as it may be considered prospective, as to the exertions we are called upon in future to make, I must observe, that even if our hopes of peace should be postponed, or even disappointed, is it nothing to reflect upon the posture we are enabled to assume, by the achievements we have already performed? Is it nothing, to look back upon the fallen, the crouching attitude of enslaved Europe, at a period not long distant, and compare it with the upright, free, undaunted posture in which she now stands? Living memory can recal no period when she was entitled to hold her head so high, and to bid such bold defiance to her enemy. What, let me ask, is the first and brightest fruit of the late successful conflict? First, that continuity of system, that instrument of not wholly ineffectual hostility against Great Britain, which, until lately, was supposed to be growing in strength and perfection, has been destroyed; that complex machine directed against our trade, has received a blow which has shivered it to atoms! The enemy is doubly defeated; his arms and his artifices have failed: burdened as it was, still there is something in the incompressible nature of commerce which rises under the weight of the most powerful tyranny: his efforts have been exhausted; his monarchy was reduced, to sink our commerce; but, rising with tenfold vigour, it has defied his puny efforts, never to be repeated. The next point that we have attained is, the destruction of his own darling system of confederation? I mean, that system by which he had formed all the states of continental Europe into satellites of the French empire, that moved only as it moved, and acted only by its influence. They are now emancipated; the yoke has been removed from their shoulders; the nations rise superior to themselves,

> "Free, and to none accountable, preferring
> Hard liberty, before the easy yoke
> Of servile pomp."

But, since all the events of war are precarious, is it impossible, that, after retiring awhile, the tyrant of Europe (now no longer its tyrant) may again burst forward, and again, with desolation in his train, awhile victorious, attempt to collect the fragments of that system, and to reconstruct that mighty engine which we have shattered, but which once, guided by his hand, hurled destruction on his foes? It is impossible. After the defeats that he has sustained, all confidence between him and his vassal states must be annihilated. Admitting that they may be compelled again to act, can he rely upon their exertions, or can they depend upon his support? He may go forth like that foul idol, of which we heard so much in the last year, crushing his helpless victims beneath his chariot wheels; but he never again can yoke them to his car as willing instruments of destruction. Even if Austria, by base submission to the sacrifice of her honour, were to add the sacrifice of another daughter, and of another army of 30,000 men, that mutual confidence which existed at the commencement of the last campaign can never be restored.

So much for the present state of Europe: but has this country gained nothing by the glorious contest, even supposing peace should be far distant? Is it nothing to Great Britain, even purchased at the high price stated by the noble lord, that under all the severity of her sufferings, while her trade declined, her military character has been exalted? Is it no satisfaction, no compensation to her, to reflect that the splendid scenes displayed on the Continent are owing to her efforts? that the victories of Germany are to be attributed to our victories in the Peninsula? That spark, often feeble, sometimes so nearly extinguished as to excite despair in all hearts that were not above it, which we lighted in Portugal, which was fed and nourished there, has at length burst into a flame that has dazzled and illuminated Europe. Shall it then be said, that this struggle has had no effect upon the military character of Great Britain? At the commencement of this war, our empire rested upon one majestic column, our naval power. In the prosecution of the war, a hero has raised another stupendous pillar of strength to support our monarchy—our military pre-eminence. It is now that we may boast, not only of superiority at sea, but on shore: the same energy and heroism exist in both the arms of Great Britain; they are rivals in strength, but inseparable in glory. If, at a future period, by successes which we cannot foresee, and by aggressions which we cannot resist, war should again be threatened upon our own shores, what consolation will the reflection afford, that out of the calamities and the privations of war has arisen a principle of safety, that, superior to all attacks, shall survive through ages, to which even our posterity shall look forward! Compare the situation of England with her condition even at the beginning of the last campaign, much more with her condition at the renewal of the war. Were we not then threatened by the aggressions of an enemy even upon our own shores: were we not then trembling for the safety and sanctity even of our homes? Now contemplate Wellington encamped on the Bidassoa! I know that a sickly sensibility prevails abroad, which leads some to doubt whether the advance of Lord Wellington was not rash and precipitate. Of the political expediency of that advance I can entertain but one opinion: I cannot enter into that refinement which induces those who affect to know much, to hesitate upon the subject: I cannot look with regret at a British army encamped upon the fertile plains of France: I cannot believe that any new grounds for apprehension are raised by an additional excitement being afforded to the irritability of the French people: I foresee no disadvantage resulting from entering the territories of our enemy, not as the conquered but the conquerors: I cannot believe that there are any so weak as to imagine that England wishes to maintain a position within the heart of the enemy's country, or that Spain will attempt to extend her dominion beyond that vast chain of impregnable mountains that seem to form her natural boundary. What is the fact? The Portuguese are now looking upon the walls of Bayonne, "that circles in those wolves" which would have devastated their capital; the Portuguese now behold, planted on the towers of Bayonne, that standard which their enemy would have made to float upon the walls of Lisbon. I cannot think it a matter of regret that Spaniards are now recovering, from the grasp of an enemy on his own shores, that diadem which was stripped from the brow of the Bourbons, to be pocketed by an usurper. I cannot think it a matter of regret that England, formerly threatened with invasion, is now the invader—that France, instead of England, is the scene of conflict:

> "—— Ultrò Inachias venisset ad urbes
> Dardanus, et versis lugeret Græcia fatis."

I cannot think all this matter of regret; and of those who believe that the nation or myself are blinded by our successes, I entreat that they will leave me to my delusion, and keep their philosophy to themselves. There are other observations, growing not only out of the proceedings of the last year, but since the commencement of the war, that to my mind are highly consoling. It is a fact acknowledged by all, that our enemy, who has enslaved the press, and made it contribute so importantly to his own purposes of ambition, at various periods, during the hostilities, has endeavoured to impress upon all those who are likely to be our allies, a notion, that Great Britain only fought to secure her own interest—that her views were completely selfish. That illusion is now destroyed, and the designs of this country are vindicated by recent events. We call on all the powers with whom we are at war, to do us justice in this respect: above all, we claim it of America, with which, as much as any man, I wish for reconciliation. If she were now hesitating and wavering, which of the two great contending parties she should join, would not the conduct of England now decide the doubt? I ask her to review her own, and the policy of this country, and to acknowledge that we are deserving, not only of her confidence, but of the support of mankind. Now, she can behold Buonaparte in his naked deformity, stripped of the false glory which success had cast around him—the spell of his invincibility is now dissolved—she can now look at him without that awe which an uninterrupted series of victories had created. Were she now to survey him as he is, what would be the result? She would trace him by the desolation of empires, and the dismemberment of states; she would see him pursuing his course over the ruins of men and of things: slavery to the people, and destruction to commerce—hostility to literature, to light, and life, were the principles on which he acted. His object was, to extinguish patriotism, and to confound allegiance—to darken as well as to enslave—to roll back the tide of civilization—to barbarize, as well as to desolate mankind. Then let America turn from this disgusting picture, these scenes of bloodshed and horror, and compare with them the effect of British interference! She will see that wherever this country has exerted herself, it has been to raise the fallen, and to support the falling—to raise, not to degrade the national character—to rouse the sentiments of patriotism which tyranny had silenced—to enlighten, to reanimate, to liberate. Great Britain has resuscitated Spain, and re-created Portugal. Germany is now a nation as well as a name, and all these glorious effects have been produced by the efforts and by the example of our country. If to be the deliverers of Europe; if to have raised our own national character, not upon the ruins of other kingdoms; if to meet dangers without shrinking, and to possess courage rising with difficulties, be admirable, surely we may not unreasonably hope for the applause of the world. If we have founded our strength upon a rock, and possess the implicit confidence of those allies we have succoured when they seemed beyond relief, then, I say, that our exertions during the last year, all our efforts during the war, are cheaply purchased. If we have burdened ourselves, we have relieved others, and we have the inward, the soul-felt, the proud satisfaction of knowing that a selfish charge is that which, with the faintest shadow of justice, cannot be brought against us.

[Mr. Canning then proceeded to applaud the system of affording aid by bills of credit, which, without danger to ourselves, mixed the credit of this country with that of our allies. He also stated his concurrence in the treaty with Sweden;

to which last year he had objected, in consequence of the provision regarding Norway. A majority of both Houses had determined in its favour, and he was satisfied with that vote. He also approved of the continuance of the aid to that power. He congratulated the House upon the accession of Austria to the confederacy, whose aid was so necessary to its success. Next to his joy in voting these supplies, would be the indignation he should feel, if either of the three great powers were to forsake the league, and make a separate treaty to secure its own peculiar interests. He did not believe that there was the least reason to apprehend such a defection; for he was convinced that all were now sensible, that the fate of each depended upon the firm union of all, at the present crisis, when the liberty of the world was the prize for which they were contending.]—He concluded in the following words:—

It has been often said, that the language of true poetry is the language of universal nature; but I believe, that the Empress of France was little conscious when she made her speech to the senate respecting her husband, that she was employing almost the very words of our great epic poet, who put them in the mouth of the first rebel and usurper on record, who is speaking of the disappointment of the followers whom he had seduced—

———"Ah me! They little know
How dearly I abide that boast I made;
Under what torments inwardly I groan,
While they adore me on the throne of hell!"

Thus have I stated a few of the remarks which press upon me in the present posture of affairs. I ardently hope that the result will be a general pacification, in which the interests of the civilized world will be duly consulted: if it should be necessary to continue hostilities, may we contend, as we have fought, during the last campaign, with matchless strength, arising from the firmness of the indissoluble union of the allies, whose cause is, and whose exertions ought to be one. May Great Britain still maintain that dignity of station, and support that grandeur and liberality of design, upon which she has hitherto acted! May she continue the unoppressive guardian of the liberties that she has vindicated, and the disinterested protectress of the blessings that she has bestowed!

The motion was agreed to.

SEDITIOUS MEETINGS BILL.

FEBRUARY 24th, 1817.

The order of the day having been read for taking into consideration the Report of the Committee of Secrecy;

Lord Castlereagh moved, "That leave be given to bring in a Bill for the more effectually preventing Seditious Meetings and Assemblies."

Mr. Canning rose and said:

It has often been remarked, Sir, that no creed is so extravagant as the creed of unbelief; that those who are the most incredulous themselves are apt to draw most largely on the credulity of others: but never in my life have I seen this so strongly exemplified as in the present debate, by the argument of some of the honourable gentlemen opposite. They utterly disbelieve all that has been reported to the House, by the Secret Committee—a Committee comprehending friends of their own, who were unanimous in giving their sanction to that Report; and they call upon the House, instead of placing credit in the Report so framed, and so sanctioned, to adopt the extravagant fiction—that all the matter of the Report was a plot invented by Ministers.

The object of this ingenious and diabolical invention, it seems, was to defeat the efforts of the mighty phalanx which is combined to investigate our conduct, and drive us from our seats. And for this purpose we have, it is supposed, gone through the following elaborate but compendious system of operations. We have first devised or resuscitated a set of extravagant and pernicious principles, hostile alike to the peace of nations, and to the welfare of mankind, which we have caused to be circulated throughout the country, and particularly throughout the distressed and suffering parts of it. We have next selected a certain number of desperate, but trustworthy incendiaries to act upon these principles, to the full extent of direct physical resistance and rebellion —risking their own lives, but keeping our counsel all the time. Next, so secure have we felt in the framing and jointing of our conspiracy against ourselves—so confident that nothing would appear that should betray the secret of its fabrication—that we have ventured to submit it to the inspection of a Secret Committee, composed, as I have stated, and as we all know that Committee to have been: and so entirely has the event justified our confidence, that we have been enabled to procure a Report—an unanimous Report from that Committee, affirming the existence of the plot, but without a hint at the suspiciousness of its origin. Why, Sir, all this sounds very foolish: and it is so. But it is the creed, real or pretended, of those who say that the plot is the plot of Ministers: and it is, as I have said, the ordinary course of those who hardly deny what, according to all fair rules of evidence, they cannot avoid believing, to take refuge in some extravagant hypothesis, by which the most implicit credulity would be staggered.

But there is another sense in which the Government are held responsible for the plot, and another charge which we are required to answer. It is said to be very extraordinary that, as appears from the Report of the Committee, Government had information of some of the proceedings which are the subject of it, in the month of November—and that yet, notwithstanding this information, they advised the Prince Regent to prorogue the Parliament till January. What is there extraordinary in this? Though certain circumstances connected with the subject of the Report, had come to the knowledge of Ministers in the month of November, yet does it appear that at that period, the designs of the conspirators wore that alarming aspect which they assumed in subsequent stages? Does it appear on the face of the Report, that up to the first, or even the second meeting at Spa-fields, Ministers had reason to believe that those who took the most prominent part at those meetings, were engaged in a plan for the subversion of the state? For aught that was *then* brought to the knowledge of Government, the real plotters and leaders of the conspiracy might then have been as little prepared to attempt an insurrection, as that unhappy man whose petition has this day been laid on the table (Mr. Hunt), and who, it should seem, mounted the temporary rostrum prepared for him, in the innocence and vanity of his heart; and, only intending to make *a splash*, unconsciously forwarded the views of rebellion.

The members of the Government, like every other individual in the nation, could not but know that a very strong and alarming inquietude and agitation had been excited in the metropolis and throughout the country. They knew that in a time of public distress certain classes of the people were liable to be operated upon by designing men, in a way likely to lead to much practical mischief, and to the misery and ruin of those who were led astray. They knew these things; but with such knowledge, would it have been wise to call the members of this and the other House of Parliament (composing so considerable a part of the resident gentry of the country), from their homes, where it might reasonably be hoped that their presence would tend most effectually to check the practices of the disaffected, and to watch over and alleviate the distresses of the suffering and honest classes of the community?

Undoubtedly, even after affairs began to assume a more serious aspect—after information had been received by the Government, which cast back upon the meetings in Spa-fields a deeper shade of criminality than had been originally supposed to belong to them—there was a great reluctance on the part of Ministers to bring the matter under the cognizance of Parliament; at least until it had been ascertained whether the existing laws were strong enough to meet the mischief. I am indeed surprised that there should be a disposition to attribute to us as a crime this reluctance to come to Parliament for extraordinary powers. When it was seen that bad men were labouring to graft sedition on distress, to stimulate want to rebellion, and to make public calamity subservient to proceedings dangerous to the state—to come to Parliament for extraordinary powers was our duty—a painful duty, though an indispensable one; but we take no blame to ourselves for having waited, in the first instance, a reasonable time, till other means for averting the evil had been tried and found insufficient.

The honourable gentlemen, indeed, object even now to our taking into consideration the propositions which are brought before us, till it shall have been first solemnly decided by the House that the laws already in force are not equal to the circumstances of the times. Surely, Sir, this would be to interpose unnecessary delay in our proceedings. The House will practically decide on that question this night, in deciding on my noble friend's (Lord Castlereagh) motion. If the House are of opinion that the present laws are sufficient, of course they will reject the motion, and thus declare new ones to be unnecessary. I see no advantage in submitting to the House an abstract Resolution that the laws now in force are inadequate to the suppression of the present mischief. The proposal of new laws shows this to be the opinion of the Government—the Report upon your table pronounces it as the opinion of your Committee. Those who hold the opposite opinion, will of course mark their dissent from the Committee, and their distrust of the Government, by voting against the present motion.

One honourable gentleman, while he objects to the measures proposed for meeting the danger, does not go so far as some others have done—to deny the existence of the danger itself; but he is very angry with the Report for not defining the extent of it. But the honourable gentleman has fallen into a similar error: for, admitting, as he does, the danger to be great, I watched in vain through the whole course of his speech, to hear him set limits to its magnitude, and define that line of demarcation which separates his own opinions from those of his friends in the Committee.—What is the nature of this danger? Why, Sir, the danger to be apprehended is not to be defined in one word. It is rebellion; but not rebellion only: it is treason; but not treason merely: it is confiscation; but not confiscation within such bounds as have been usually applied to it in the changes of dynasties, or the revolutions of states;—it is an aggregate of all these evils; it is all that dreadful variety of sorrow and of suffering which must follow the extinction of loyalty, morality, and religion; which must follow upon the accomplishment of designs, tending not only to subvert the Constitution of England, but to overthrow the whole frame of society. Such is the nature and extent of the danger which would attend the success of the projects developed in the Report of the Committee.

But these projects are said to be visionary; they would never have been of importance, it is affirmed, had they not been brought into notice by persecution. Persecution!—Does this character belong to the proceedings instituted against those who had set out on their career in opposition to all law; and who, in their secret cabals, and midnight counsels, and mid-day harangues, have been noting for destruction every individual, and every class of individuals, which may stand in their way? But the schemes of these persons are visionary. I admit it. They have lain by these twenty years, without being found to produce mischief. Be it so. The doctrines, when dormant, may be harmless enough, and their intrinsic absurdity may make it appear incredible that they should ever be called up into action. But when this incredible resurrection actually takes place, when the votaries of these doctrines actually go forth armed, to exert physical strength in furtherance of them, then it is that I think it time to be on my guard, not against the accomplishment of their plans (that is, I am willing to believe, impracticable), but against the mischiefs which must attend the attempt to accomplish them by force.

I do not impute to the Spenceans that they really wish to partition the whole property of the kingdom; that they would carry into effect their scheme for an agrarian division of land. No, but I sincerely believe (and all history teaches that the opinion is not unfounded), that they would labour hard to accomplish the spoliation of its present possessors. In Rome, schemes of agrarian division were often brought forward, and always found partisans. No man ever apprehended from them an actual division of all landed estates; but every man knew and saw that they furnished matter for seditions, which shook the security of the state and the liberties of the people to their foundation.

As to the wild theories of Parliamentary Reform, propagated with so much industry throughout the country, I am relieved from the necessity of any laborious argument by the unexpected and almost unqualified concurrence of some of those who are opposed to me in this debate. They have declared their opinion, that if those plans were carried into effect, they must lead to confusion and ruin. I need only ask, therefore, is there nothing alarming in plans which gentlemen, who make it their boast to be so exclusively friendly to the liberties of the people, think likely to be as ruinous if they are reduced to practice, as they are absurd in theory? Does such a danger require no vigilance—justify no apprehension—call for no exertion on the part of the legislative authorities of the state—to meet and put down, not the opinions themselves (an old and idle fallacy), but the practical assertion of those opinions. It is to check evils so alarming—it is in mercy to those who are engaged in such designs, that the measures now called for are required—in the hope that they may cut short the mischief in its career, recall the wavering, restrain the half-resolved, and avert, even in the case of the guilty deluders themselves, the necessity of having recourse to the last extremity of punishment.

It is not desired of the House that it should enable Ministers to wield at their pleasure an unconstitutional authority—an authority with which any man who could wish wantonly to possess it, must be utterly unworthy to be entrusted. The Executive Government do not ask for these additional powers as a boon (God knows they are no object of desire); but for the due discharge of an embarrassing and distressing duty, we feel bound to receive them as a trust—to support them as a burthen, which we shall most unwillingly carry, and shall most gladly lay down. We ask them—we will accept them—only for the conservation of the public safety. At our own suggestion the duration of the most onerous and delicate part of this trust, is to be limited to a period during which it will be exercised under the immediate observation of Parliament. Does this look as if our application had in view any object which we fear to describe?

It has been asserted, however, that Ministers call for these powers, the better to enable them to make war against the people. We repel the accusation with disdain. We ask them *for* the people—for the protection of that sound and sober majority of the nation, for that bulk and body of the community, which are truly and legitimately *the people*. How few, how very few, among the millions that make up that aggregate, will ever be subject to the operation of these laws! But these laws are nevertheless necessary (in our consciences we believe them to be so), to protect the many against the few, who fail not to make up in violence what they want in numbers.

For let us not be imposed upon, Sir, by the trite and futile argument that our would-be reformers and revolutionists are but few in number. This may be, and it will be, a consolation when the attempt shall have been suppressed; but it is no security against its success, if we omit to take vigorous measures for its suppression. Experience is all the other way. When was a revolution effected in any state but by an active and enterprising minority? If ancient times were barren of examples, has not the history of the last five and twenty years sufficiently proved that the disaffected are not to be despised because their number is not preponderating? Can it be forgotten how frequently, in the course of the French Revolution, the world has seen sanguinary minorities riding in blood over the necks of their prostrate countrymen?

As little should we lay to our souls the flattering hope that the bare absurdity—the monstrousness of any doctrine is a sufficient security against the attempt to reduce it into practice. The same French Revolution, in which the blood-stained few were seen triumphant over the subdued and trembling many, exhibits abundant instances of absurd and incredible theories, reduced into tremendous practice. When Atheism was professed in France as a faith, when it was declared by the

National Assembly that "death was an eternal sleep," who believed that such impious absurdity could flourish? Who would not have held up his hands in astonishment at the folly which feared that the professors of such opinions could make proselytes? But what followed? Proselytes *were* made, and a great nation, robbed of its religion and its morality, was thus stripped of the armour and of the shield which might have protected her from anarchy and desolation. The "sovereignty of the people" was preached up not as a doctrine of abstract theory only, but as a principle and ground of practical political experiment. Wise and experienced men smiled at the gross delusion. They apprehended little from the attempt to act upon it. But again, what followed? On behalf of the "sovereign people," and in their name, France saw the whole of the upper orders of society swept from the face of the earth; that earth deluged with the best blood of the nation, and crimes followed by crimes, in a long train of horrors, which ended at last in an overwhelming but comparatively salutary despotism.

But still, it seems, there is no great danger in *our* case; for our philosophers want influence, and our desperate revolutionists want leaders: nothing has yet appeared among them but what is insignificant and obscure. Let us not rely too confidently on this ground of security. First of all, names *will* be used—names *are* used—without the consent of their owners, to give to the mass of the disaffected the confidence which arises from believing themselves to be highly countenanced and ably led. Next, although we do not know that any man now exists who has deliberately taken the resolution, to come forward and place himself at the head of the conspirators, we must remember that circumstances make men. Is it to be believed that Robespierre had from infancy contemplated the bad eminence to which he attained? Assuredly, no. A disposition so fiend-like never came from the hands of nature; or if the principle of it were implanted in the heart, the circumstances of the time alone could have fostered and stimulated it into action. Robespierre grew from crime to crime, and became gradually familiarized with blood. He learned lessons of atrocity from companions over whom his superior energy enabled him to gain ascendancy and controul. And thus it always is, that bad men reciprocally corrupt each other, till the aggregate of wickedness to which their minds are finally made up, is such as would, at the first moment of their outset, have startled the fiercest spirit and the hardiest imagination among them.

I do not say, therefore, that any man now exists, formed, and trained, and disciplined, to take the lead in the mischievous and malignant plans which are in agitation; but I do say that the training by which such men are to be formed, is in progress, and is well adapted to its end. The first object is to eradicate all sense of religion. Respect for religion once eradicated,—the name of God once erased from the human heart,—it is easy to pour into a heart so void, a spirit of hatred towards its fellow creatures. That this operation is diligently carrying on, will not be doubted by any man who has read but a tenth part of the publications circulated in all parts of the country with a devilish zeal, for the destruction of that religious belief which is the best guard of all human virtue, the best consolation of all human misery. These publications meet the eye in all quarters, wherever there is distress to be aggravated, or discontent to be inflamed. In the nightly councils of the disaffected the discussions upon political subjects are interspersed with digressions into impiety; the overthrow of the state being settled, that of the religious establishments of the country is next taken into consideration; and the sportive relaxation of rebellion is in blasphemy.

If then, the Government demands extraordinary powers, I ask, on the other hand, are these or are they not, extraordinary times? Have we, has England, ever seen the like before? We have had our share, in this country, of every species of political dissension; disputed titles to the crown; disputed rights in the people; invasions; rebellions; the struggles of rival dynasties; and civil wars both of politics and of religion. But in all our varieties of agitation and convulsion, were we ever exposed to such pests as these of the present day? In our civil wars, there was enough of violence and of blood. But principle was opposed to principle, and honest and upright men might be found on either side. Republicanism was opposed to monarchy, and monarchy was overthrown. But the overthrow of monarchy was not effected for the sake of throwing all government into confusion: they destroyed not in those days for the sake of destruction alone. In religion, independency was opposed to episcopacy, and independency triumphed. But it was still for some form of religion that the contest was carried on: it was not for the destruction of all religious principle; it was not the opposition of mere negation, to God. It was left for the reformers of modern times to endeavour to strip the mind of all reverence for the Deity, in order to prepare the man to become a mere instrument of ruin, a remorseless agent of evil.

The discipline I have said, is well suited to its purposes; it is our business to take care that the purposes themselves shall not be fulfilled.

Sir, the same sense of duty which has now caused Ministers to apply for these bills, would cause them to apply to Parliament for still greater powers, if they should become necessary; but those which we have asked, we are satisfied will prove sufficient, because we are satisfied that it is only necessary to check the progress of the disaffected for a season, in order that the sound part of the nation may have opportunity to recover and to array themselves, that the first passive impressions of alarm may be converted into determined confidence, and zealous action. The nation is sound at heart: and when once apprized of the nature of the danger, and secure in the vigilance of the Government, we can have no doubt but they will co-operate with the Government, and that such co-operation will be effectual for the safety of the state, and for the preservation of all that they hold dear.

Two of the four proposed laws are almost generally approved. The third is not wholly objected to, though gentlemen reserve to themselves the right of criticising it in its passage through the House. It is only the fourth—the suspension of the *Habeas Corpus*—that incurs the unqualified disapprobation of some of the honourable gentlemen on the other side of the House.

The Committee has declared, that the ordinary powers given to the Executive Government by the constitution, are not sufficient for the crisis. If new powers are denied to them, Ministers will be left to combat with comparatively less effect, the growing boldness of sedition, encouraged and inflamed by the rejection of these propositions. It is the joint obligation of Ministers and of Parliament to preserve the constitution. Ministers have done all that it was for them to do: what remains is in the hands of this House; and it is for the House to say, whether or not the constitution shall be guarded by those new outworks which the perils of the times have rendered necessary, against the assaults of furious and desperate men; whether that system of law and liberty, under which England has so long flourished in happiness and glory, in internal tranquillity, and external grandeur, shall be sacrificed or saved.

The House divided—

Ayes - - - -	190
Noes - - - - - -	14
Majority for it - -	176

MR. HORNER.

MARCH 3rd, 1817.

Lord Morpeth moved for a new Writ for St. Mawes, in the room of Mr. Horner.

Mr. Canning.—Of all the instances, wherein the same course has been adopted as that which my noble friend (Lord Morpeth) has pursued with so much feeling and good taste on this occasion,

I do not remember one more likely than the present, to conciliate the general approbation and sympathy of this House. I, Sir, had not the happiness (a happiness now counterbalanced by a proportionate excess of sorrow and regret) to be acquainted personally, in private life, with the distinguished and amiable individual whose loss we have to deplore. I knew him only within the walls of the House of Commons. And even here, from the circumstances of my absence during the last two sessions, I had not the good fortune to witness the later and more matured exhibition of his talents; which (as I am informed, and can well believe) at once kept the promise of his earlier years, and opened still wider expectations of future excellence. But I had seen enough of him to share in those expectations; and to be sensible of what this House and the country have lost by his being so prematurely taken from us. He had, indeed, qualifications eminently calculated to obtain and to deserve success. His sound principles, his enlarged views, his various and accurate knowledge, the even tenour of his manly and temperate eloquence, the genuineness of his warmth, when into warmth he was betrayed, and, above all, the singular modesty with which he bore his faculties, and which shed a grace and lustre over them all; these qualifications, added to the known blamelessness and purity of his private character, did not more endear him to his friends, than they commanded the respect of those to whom he was opposed in adverse politics; they ensured to every effort of his abilities an attentive and favouring audience; and secured for him, as the result of all, a solid and unenvied reputation.—I cannot conclude, Sir, without adverting to a topic in the latter part of the speech of my noble friend, upon which I most entirely concur with him. It would not be seemly to mix with the mournful subject of our present contemplation any thing of a controversial nature. But when, for the second time within a short course of years, the name of an obscure borough is brought before us, as vacated by the loss of conspicuous talents and character,* it may be permitted to me, with my avowed and notorious opinions on the subject of our parliamentary constitution, to state, without offence, that it is at least some consolation for the imputed theoretical defects of that constitution, that in practice it works so well. A system of representation cannot be wholly vicious, and altogether inadequate to its purposes, which sends to this House a succession of such men as those whom we have now in our remembrance, here to develope the talents with which God has endowed them, and to attain that eminence in the view of their country, from which they may be one day called to aid her counsels, and to sustain her greatness and her glory.

* Mr. Windham, who represented St. Mawes in 1806, died member for Higham Ferrers, in 1810.

MR. CANNING'S EMBASSY TO LISBON.

MAY 6th, 1817.

MR. LAMBTON this day brought forward the motion of which he had given notice, respecting Mr. Canning's Embassy to Lisbon. In bringing forward this motion, he disclaimed any intention of attack upon the right honourable gentleman (Mr. Canning), whose name was prominently connected with the transactions to which it referred. It was not the conduct of an individual that he arraigned; but the charge which he had to prefer was against His Majesty's Ministers of delinquency, by which, in his opinion, they had subjected themselves to an impeachment (if that was not an obsolete proceeding), on a charge of a criminal misapplication of the public money for the most corrupt private purposes. This was not the first time when this transaction had been made the subject of discussion. Both within and without those walls it had been regarded as a measure resorted to, purely for the purpose of supplying the weakness of the members of Government, by calling to their assistance the talents of the right honourable gentleman (Mr. C.), talents too useful indeed to languish in obscurity. It had every where been asserted, that there were no public grounds for sending an Ambassador to Lisbon after the conclusion of the Peninsular War; that it was a disgraceful waste of public money, and solely to be attributed to the lowest species of political barter and intrigue. The papers which had been laid upon the table of the House fully proved that the mission to Lisbon was undertaken with no prospect of advantage to the interests of this country in its political or commercial relations, but with a view solely to the political, and he might almost say, commercial, advantages of the Ministers themselves; and that for these sinister objects they consented to add to the burthens of the people, already groaning under the weight of an insupportable taxation.

The statement of the case was this:—In July, 1814, a negociation was entered into by the Ministers for the purpose of obtaining the co-operation of the right honourable gentleman opposite (Mr. Canning) and his friends in both Houses. On the 29th of June that negociation was brought to a successful issue, Mr. Canning being appointed Ambassador to Lisbon, Mr. Huskisson Surveyor-General of Woods and Forests, and Mr. Wellesley Pole Master of the Mint. On the 30th of July, the member for Liverpool moved for a new writ in the room of his friend, Mr. Huskisson, on the appointment of that gentleman. The motives assigned for the appointment of an Ambassador to Lisbon had been two despatches from Lord Strangford, the Minister at the court of Brazil to Viscount Castlereagh, respecting the intention of the Prince Regent of Portugal to return to Europe. The first of these despatches had been received on the 24th of April, 1814, the second on the 26th of August. As these were the only authorities on which the measure rested, he should read them. The first was in these words:—

"I should fail in my duty, did I not earnestly recommend to the consideration of His Royal Highness's Government, the speedy return to Europe of the Portuguese Royal Family. The Prince's own feelings, and those of every member of his family, are earnestly in favour of this measure. Some degree of apprehension may, perhaps, operate upon the mind of the Prince himself, to prevent him from coming forward as eagerly as the other individuals of the royal family would wish; but this sentiment would be easily removed, and His Royal Highness has explicitly stated to me, that as soon as ever Great Britain declares that his return to Portugal is necessary, he will accede to any intimation to that effect."

This, it would be observed, contained merely a declaration of the line of policy which Lord Strangford had thought fit to adopt. The next despatch was received on the 26th of August, and was in these words:—

"The glorious events which have given peace and independence to Europe, have revived in the mind of the Prince of Brazil those eager desires to revisit his native country, which had been for a time suppressed. His Royal Highness has lately done me the honour to state his anxious hope that Great Britain will facilitate the completion of his wishes upon this subject, and that he may return to Portugal under the same protection as that under which he left it. And His Royal Highness has, during the last week, intimated to me four or five times, as well publicly as privately, that in case Great Britain should send a squadron of ships of war to this place, for the purpose of escorting His Royal Highness to Europe, it would be particularly and personally gratifying to His Royal Highness that ———————— should be selected for this service."

The blank, he believed, had been filled up by the name of Sir Sidney Smith. Now, on one or other of the despatches which he had read, the appointment of the Lisbon Ambassador must have been founded, if it had any foundation but the desire to find an appointment for the right honourable gentleman. It was ascertained that, in the interval between the 24th of April and the 26th of August, no communication had been made from the Portuguese Ambassador to our Government. An Address had been voted for all the communications from the Portuguese Ambassador respecting the return of the Prince Regent of Portugal, and the answer was, that no written communication had been made. Indeed, he could prove at the bar that not only had the Portuguese Minister made no communication of the probability of the return of the Prince of Brazil, but he had asserted that the Government had quite misunderstood the intention of his master. The appointment could not have been in consequence of the despatch received in April, for it was on the 6th of June that Mr. Sydenham was appointed; and on the 18th of July, when the noble lord opposite had written to Mr. Sydenham, telling him that he could not anticipate any public grounds why he (Mr. S.) should not confine himself within his ordinary allowances, he of course could have had no contemplation of any such appointment. It was still more impossible that the appointment could have been occasioned by the despatch received on the 26th of August, for that was a month after the appointment of the right honourable gentleman had been announced to the public in the newspapers. He supposed it would not be contended that the appointment did not take place until it was formerly announced in the Gazette—the *evidentia rei*, the previous notoriety of the transaction, was a sufficient contradiction of any such idea, and he did not think any of the Ministers would stand forward in their places and assert, that the appointment did not take place in July. But if the right honourable gentleman had really been appointed for the purpose of welcoming the Prince Regent on his return, by what pretence could the appointment be justified in August, when the fleet intended to convey the Prince of Brazil to Europe did not sail till the 29th of October? It was morally impossible, therefore, that His Royal Highness could have reached Europe till the month of May following.

He should now call the attention of the House to the expenses of the missions:—On the 18th of July, 1814, Lord Castlereagh had written a letter to Mr. Sydenham, then the Minister at Lisbon, in which he stated that it was the Prince Regent's pleasure that the expenses of the mission should be reduced to the lowest scale, and stating, that he could not contemplate any reasons for continuing the scale of expenditure which had been adopted during the Peninsular War. He had been rather surprised to find this economical disposition in any production of the noble lord's; but his surprise was of short duration, for only ten days after Mr. Sydenham had been reduced to a salary of £5,200 a year, the right honourable gentleman was appointed Ambassador Extraordinary with a salary of nearly treble that amount. On the 31st of October, in the absence of the noble lord (Castlereagh) at the Congress, Lord Bathurst wrote to Mr. Canning, then in England, to inform him that he was to be allowed £14,200 a year, on the same grounds on which Mr. Sydenham had been limited to £5,200. Why such a change had taken place in the allowance to the Minister, while no change had taken place in the circumstances of the embassy, and when no chance existed of the immediate return of the Prince of Brazil to Europe, yet remained to be explained. The expense of Sir Charles Stuart had been referred to, but that could form no precedent for the expenditure of tne right honourable gentleman. The whole of Sir Charles Stuart's expenses were occasioned by the Peninsular War. He actually held the reins of the Portuguese Government. He was a member, he believed the sole efficient member, of the Regency, and was forced to incur the whole of his large expenditure, to discharge the high official duties of his situation. But the case was very different when the war had ceased, and when the Ambassador was no longer a member of the Portuguese Government. On the 30th of May, 1815, the right honourable gentleman had found out a reason for this increased scale of allowance. In a letter to the noble lord (Castlereagh) of that date, he stated, that "the rank of ambassador, which could make no practical difference in expenses, of which the salary (whether as ambassador or as envoy) supplied only a part, was politically important, as counterbalancing the positive loss of rank and influence, which would otherwise have been occasioned by the British Minister's being no longer a member of the Regency." The right honourable gentleman had by that time forgotten the letter of Lord Castlereagh, in which Mr. Sydenham was directed to reduce his expenses to the lowest scale. He seemed to have taken a former suggestion of his noble friend—to have "two strings to his bow"—for when he was forced to acknowledge that the object of his mission had ceased, as there was no probability of the Prince of Brazil's return to Europe, he contrived to discover that it was essential to the political welfare of England that his salary should be continued; he discovered, in short, that as Sir Charles Stuart had a large allowance, because he was a member of the Regency, so he (the right honourable gentleman) ought to have a large allowance, because he was not a member of the Regency. The rest of this letter of the right honourable gentleman's was unimportant, except as it displayed talents for finance, which, although in this instance elicited for his own advantage, it was to be hoped he would henceforward contribute to the public service, and in support of his friend the Chancellor of the Exchequer, in this season of financial difficulty.

From all these documents it was evident, that the plain and almost avowed purpose of the mission was, to procure a place for the right honourable gentleman. He was therefore sent, with a salary of £14,000 a-year to a capital where there was no court, and to which, even while it had a court, no ambassador had been sent for almost a century. He superseded a deserving servant of the public acting there, as envoy with a salary of £5,000 a year. He said, superseded designedly, for Mr. Sydenham's intention of resigning was not known to Ministers when they made Mr. Canning's appointment, and when he had amassed a sufficient sum, or when a place was provided for him, or when the job became too glaring and called forth the public censure, he left the important business of the Lisbon mission under the sole guidance of a chargé d'affaires; and during the whole of this mission, the only duty performed by him was a speech to the factory. The defenders of this mission had talked of the efforts which the right honourable gentleman had made to complete the abolition of the Slave Trade; and one of his friends, on a former occasion, had said, "that if there was the least chance that the abolition of the Slave Trade would be accelerated by this measure, the opposers of the appointment of the right honourable gentleman should pause before they called on the country to pronounce it a gross and scandalous job." He could prove, however, that since the appointment of the right honourable gentleman, the trade of Portugal in human flesh had increased instead of decreasing; and that not one single favourable declaration was procured from the Portuguese Government by the efforts of the Ambassador.

Under all these considerations, he called on the House to come to a decision on the merits of the case. He had now to put to the test the sincerity of the professions of the House, of economy and vigilance over the extravagant conduct of Ministers. He showed them a case in which the public money had been most culpably and disgracefully squandered;—no sort of necessity had been shown in the papers which the Government had submitted as their justification; on the contrary, every document tended to prove most clearly that in no one instance had they more abused the confidence reposed in them by Parliament than in the present. If, in these times of distress and discontent, it was important for the House to acquire a reputation for strict public virtue, and incorruptibility, they would mark their sense of this proceeding, and show the people that they still retained within themselves the means of satisfying their just claims, and of protecting them against the culpable and profligate extravagance of Ministers. He should move the following Resolutions:

1. "That it appears to this House, that on the 18th of July 1814, Lord Viscount Castlereagh addressed an official despatch to Thomas Sydenham, Esq. then His Majesty's Minister at Lisbon, acquainting him that it was the command of his Royal Highness the Prince Regent, that during his residence at the Court of Portugal, he should confine his personal expenses within his ordinary allowances as Envoy Extraordinary and Ministry Plenipotentiary, viz. £5,200 per annum; that he had directed Mr. Casamajor to lose no time in removing the mission from the house of the Marquis de Pombal, and that he could not anticipate any public grounds for continuing the expenditure of His Majesty's servants at Lisbon on the scale on which it had been conducted during the war in the Peninsula.

2. "That it appears that under the pretence of congratulating the Prince of Brazil, on his return to his native dominions, the Right Honourable George Canning was appointed Ambassador Extraordinary to the court of Lisbon, with the increased emoluments and allowances belonging

to that character, viz. £8,200 as salary, £6,000 as extraordinaries, £1,500 as outfit, and £3,180 as plate money, amounting in the whole to the sum of eighteen thousand eight hundred and eighty pounds.

3. "That such an appointment, on such a scale of expense, appears to this House inconsistent with the recorded declaration in Lord Castlereagh's despatch to Mr. Sydenham, of the 18th of July 1814; was uncalled for by any change in the circumstances of the mission subsequent to Mr. Sydenham's appointment; and has been attended with an unnecessary and unjustifiable waste of the public money."

After the speech of Admiral Sir John Beresford, there was a considerable pause in the House,—Sir Francis Burdett alone having spoken in support of Mr. Lambton's Motion. At length, no other Member offering himself, and the Question being about to be put from the chair,

Mr. Canning rose, and spoke nearly as follows:—

Sir,—Upon a question which, however disguised in form, I cannot but feel in common with every Member who hears me—in common with the honourable mover of the Resolutions, and in common with the honourable baronet, who has fairly stated the real object in view,—to be an attack directed against me individually, I trust I shall not be considered as having shown any blameable reluctance in pausing before I offered myself to the attention of the House. Sir, I could not bring myself to believe, that, in the two speeches of the honourable mover, and the honourable baronet; I had heard the whole of what is to be alleged against me; and yet I must suppose that, if others intended to add their weight to the accusation, I must suppose that, in a case in which every thing that is dear to man, in character, in reputation, and in honour, is at stake, they would have had the fairness to give to the accused an advantage which is not withholden from the meanest criminal,—that of hearing the whole indictment to which he is to plead.

If, after a year of menace, and after three months of preparation, from amidst all the array which I see opposed to me, these* are my only accusers; if the speeches which I have heard, contain the whole of the charges which are to be urged against me; charges, which those who bring them forward, state to be directed to no other object than the public weal,—but which I know, and which they know, to be intended to disqualify me for ever from serving the public with credit to myself or with advantage to the state; if this be all,—it falls, indeed, far short of the expectations excited by such mighty menace and by such deliberate preparation? But, Sir, if this is *not* all,—if there are gentlemen, who hold themselves in readiness to aggravate the matter preferred against me,—whose speeches, prepared for the occasion and now throbbing in their breasts, are reserved till I shall be disabled from

* Mr. Lambton and Sir Francis Burdett.

answering them,—from such I appeal to the candour of the House and of the world; declaring, and desiring it to be understood, both within and without the walls of this House, that if I do not refute what they may hereafter advance against me, it will be only because I am precluded by the forms of the House from speaking a second time (cries of No, no). Oh, Sir, I am not to be told that the motion consists of a string of Resolutions—that each Resolution is a separate question—and that upon each separate question I *may* speak:—but neither are my accusers to be told that this is technical nonsense:—that the effective debate must take place upon the first Resolution,—and that the question upon that Resolution once put to the vote, I should be heard upon those which follow, to very little purpose indeed.

I agree with the honourable baronet, that I have often deplored and deprecated; and, in spite of the honourable baronet's warning, I shall continue (not for myself but for the public good) to deprecate and to deplore—the practice of calumniating public men on either side of this House, by imputing to them motives of action, the insinuation of which would not be tolerated in the intercourse of private life. If, indeed, I shall be found to have forfeited all claim to the confidence of the House, the honourable baronet needs not fear that I shall again offend him by such unpleasant animadversions. But if on the other hand,

I shall be fortunate enough to make plain to others, that which I myself confidently feel—my perfect clearness from any of the imputations attempted to be thrown upon me—the honourable baronet may depend upon hearing from me hereafter the same language which I have used heretofore on this, and on other subjects still more disagreeable to the honourable baronet and his followers.

Sir, the charge which the honourable gentleman's Resolutions involve, is this,—That the Government, being perfectly aware that the Prince Regent of Portugal had no intention of returning to Europe, pretended a belief in such intention, for the express purpose of corruptly offering that mission which I corruptly accepted. It is true, that a distinction is most disingenuously affected to be drawn between the Government and me, of which it is hardly necessary to say, that I disdain to take advantage. It is pretended, that a charge is brought forward only against the Government for making the offer, but that I might have accepted that offer, if not altogether without blame, at least without absolute criminality. Sir, I disclaim this insidious distinction. I will allow no such exception in my favour. As my noble friend has claimed that my case shall be considered as that of the Government; so do I declare on my part, that the case of the Government is mine.

The *first* head of charge, therefore, against the Government and myself is, that there was no belief on the part of the Government, or on mine, that the Prince Regent of Portugal intended to return to Europe : the *second* is, that the Mission sent to receive and congratulate the Prince Regent on his return was on a scale of unnecessary, unexampled, profligate prodigality. To both these issues, distinctly, I mean to plead. All that I require of those who are to judge me is, that they will keep these two issues separate in their minds; that they will not confound them, as has been industriously done in the speeches of the honourable gentleman and the honourable baronet. If a fraud were purposed—if the Government did not believe in the return of the Royal Family of Portugal—there is crime enough for an impeachment, if you will, without entering into the question of expense. In that case the expense of one farthing was too much. But if, on the contrary, the Government was sincere in its belief of the occasion for the appointment when they made it,—and I, when I accepted it,—then the question of expense is indeed a fair subject of parliamentary jealousy (I am far from denying that it is so); but the amount of that expense must be estimated, with reference to its object, and not upon the unfair and fallacious assumption that there was no occasion for any expense at all.

As to the first point, if I were pleading for myself alone, all that it would be necessary for me to do, would be to refer to one only of the papers before the House:—the extract of Lord Strangford's despatch to Lord Castlereagh, dated Rio de Janeiro, June 21st, 1814. It is in these words:—

"The glorious events which have given peace and independence to Europe, have revived in the mind of the Prince of Brazil those eager desires to revisit his native country, which had been for a time suppressed.

"His Royal Highness has done me the honour to state his anxious hope that Great Britain will facilitate the completion of his wishes upon this subject; and that he may return to Portugal under the same protection as that under which he left it."

The despatch, of which this is an extract, was, in fact, the only one upon the subject that I happened to see before I went to Portugal.

Before I proceed further, I must here vindicate my noble friend the Secretary of State for the Foreign Department, from the allegation of the honourable gentleman, that my noble friend studiously delayed, or wilfully confounded, the papers moved for by the honourable gentleman or his friends. The honourable gentleman accuses my noble friend of having produced a despatch, addressed to *me* by Lord Bathurst (No. 2, of the papers first presented to Parliament), instead of the despatch of my noble friend to Mr. Sydenham of the 18th of July—well knowing that this latter was the paper really moved for. Now, Sir, I cannot pretend to say in what terms the motion of the honourable gentleman was conceived: I was not in the House (so far as I know) when he made it. The first knowledge that I had of it was from a note of my noble friend, inclosing a copy of the despatch addressed to me by Lord Bathurst; informing me that this despatch was to be laid before the House of Commons; and desiring to know, whether there were any papers which I might wish to be produced in order to meet the charge, whatever it might be, which appeared, by the call for this despatch, to be meditated against me. This was a courtesy which my noble friend, or any Minister, would have equally shown to any other individual menaced with a parliamentary attack; and I only mention it, as affording a strong proof of the sincerity of my noble friend's belief that the paper first produced was that which had been moved for by the honourable gentleman. Lord Strangford's despatch being (as I have said) the only document that I happened ever to have seen, relating to the Prince Regent of Portugal's return, it was the only one that occurred to me as at all necessary to illustrate that matter. It was the only one therefore, of which, with that view, I suggested the production; and, upon looking it over —as I was extremely desirous to bring forward nothing but what was absolutely necessary—I thought the two or three sentences, which are given in the *first* set of papers presented to the House, amply sufficient. I knew, indeed, that the Prince Regent of Portugal's intention of returning to Europe had been questioned; but it was not until after the production of these papers that I had any suspicion that it was denied. The honourable gentleman now professes that his intention was to move, not for any despatch to me, but for a despatch to Mr. Sydenham. It is to be regretted, in that case, that the honourable gentleman did not mention Mr. Sydenham's name in his motion, which would have obviated any possibility of misapprehension. I am not without my suspicions, indeed, that if in return to the honourable gentleman's ambiguous motion my noble friend had laid upon the table the despatch to Mr. Sydenham, he would then have been accused of keeping back the despatch to me. In truth, Sir, if the honourable gentlemen wanted complete information, their obvious course was to move for *all* despatches relating to the subject in question, within a certain specified period. But if their object was to feel their way, paper by paper, in order that they might proceed or not, according as the information obtained by their successive motions should or should not correspond with the prejudices which they had endeavoured to raise; why, then, Sir, perhaps they had not gone far in this course of discovery before they repented of having engaged in it.

But to return to the despatch of Lord Strangford.—The extract from that despatch which I have just read, appeared to me quite sufficient to establish the Prince Regent of Portugal's intention.—I confess, indeed, that my belief in that event rested on authority short even of this extract. It rested on the authority of a private letter from Lord Liverpool, received by me on the 28th August, at a considerable distance from London; which,—though it is not pleasant to quote in public discussion the contents of private letters, I will now (having my noble friend's permission), read to the House. It is dated, London, August 26th, 1814.

"Letters have been this day received from Lord Strangford, by which it appears, that the Prince of Brazil has intimated his desire to return to Portugal (in consequence of the recent events in Europe), and the gratification which he would feel at the arrival of a British squadron at Rio de Janeiro, for the purpose of conveying the royal family to Lisbon.

"Under these circumstances, Melville has given orders for preparing a proper squadron for this service, and it will sail as soon as the necessary arrangements can be completed."

This letter, Sir, I received on the 28th of August, at Manchester, in my way from London to a distant part of the country, from whence I had no thoughts of returning till the middle of September. My right honourable friend, now sitting near me (Mr. Huskisson,) was with me when I received it. Now, the hypothesis of my accusers is, that the whole notion of the Prince Regent's return was a feint and a fraud on the part of the Government, if not on mine. But, I ask of any candid man, if he can believe, I ask of any man living, if he will avow the belief, that supposing a fraud to have been intended, it is likely that such a letter as this from Lord Liverpool, written in the unguarded style of private friendship, and addressed (as any gentleman who would take the trouble to look at it would see that it is) with the usual formulary of the most familiar correspondence, should have been one of the documents *got up* for such a purpose? Is it likely, that of two men, known to each other by nearly thirty years of intimacy, one should practise such a delusion upon the other? Or, is it likely that two such men should carry hypocrisy so far as to provide beforehand for the support of a public fraud, by the contrivance of such a private communication?

This letter from Lord Liverpool was founded upon that despatch from Lord Strangford of which I have already read the extract, and which appears at full length in the papers *last* laid upon the table. The extract was moved for at my desire, the extract only, when I conceived that *my* justification alone was in question: the whole despatch was afterwards moved for, also at my suggestion, when I found that the Government were suspected of having deceived *me* into a belief, for which they had no foundation. I will now take the liberty of reading the whole despatch.

"*Rio de Janeiro, June* 21, 1814.

[*Received August 26th*, 1814.]

"My Lord,

"The glorious events which have given peace and independence to Europe, have revived in the mind of the Prince of Brazil those eager desires to revisit his native country, which had been for a time suppressed.

"His Royal Highness has lately done me the honour to state his anxious hope, that Great Britain will facilitate the completion of his wishes upon this subject, and that he may return to Portugal under the same protection as that under which he left it. And His Royal Highness has, during the last week, intimated to me, four or five times, as well publicly as privately, that, in case Great Britain should send a squadron of ships of war to this place, for the purpose of escorting His Royal Highness to Europe, it would be particularly and personally gratifying to His Royal Highness that ———— should be selected for this service.

"I have the honour to be, &c.

"Strangford.

" *To Viscount Castlereagh, &c. &c. &c.*"

(The name of the officer is omitted from motives of delicacy. Sir John Beresford had been already appointed and announced to the Court of Rio de Janeiro, before this despatch was received.)

Submit this document to any man in the habit of canvassing evidence, and ask him, whether there is any thing in it that could create a suspicion of the sincerity of the wish which it announces?—whether the Government could reasonably doubt the authenticity of the intelligence conveyed in it, any more than I doubted the fidelity of the abstract of that intelligence transmitted to me by Lord Liverpool? A man might say, that he intended to go a journey, and the fact of his entertaining that intention might, perhaps, not be considered as altogether established by the mere intimation of it: but, when he ordered his carriage to the door, and named the servants by whom he wished to be conducted, then, surely, one would consider him to be really in earnest.

This despatch, however, I did not see till after my return to London in September. I was quite satisfied of the fact, as stated to me by Lord Liverpool. Nothing is more easy than, when an event has, or has not, actually taken place, to find out that you ought to have foreseen how likely, or to have discovered how unlikely, it was to happen. But who balances probabilities in this way, in the ordinary transactions of life? Who is the wise and happy man that receives every friendly communication with distrust; that calls for proofs of the most credible expectancies, and deems every occurrence problematical till it has actually occurred? The Prince Regent of Portugal announced to the British Cabinet his intention of returning; he requested that a squadron might be sent to escort him to Europe; he named the officer by whom he wished that squadron to be commanded: yet Ministers were to suspect that he entertained no intention of the kind! For myself, I protest, that no shadow of doubt ever crossed my mind, as to the reality of this intention. Perhaps it may have been rash to believe: if so, I must acknowledge my error. But when, in addition to such positive testimony, I considered how desirable it was, with a view to the interests of the Portuguese Monarchy, of this country, and of the world; how essential to the complete restoration and tranquillity of that order of things which the French Revolution had disjointed and broken up, that Portugal, now sunk into a province, should resume her station among the States of Europe;—when I felt that no efforts of the British Government ought to have been spared, and had reason to be assured that none had been spared, to induce that return, I confess I know not on what I could have founded the smallest doubt that the return of the Court of Portugal was really determined upon, and that this determination was upon the eve of execution.

It may be true, that there were, as has been asserted, at the precise period to which I am alluding, conflicting reports on this subject; that merchants in Lisbon had received letters from their friends in Brazil, contradicting the opinion that the Prince Regent would return; that there were rumours of opposition to the measure in the councils of Rio de Janeiro; and that persons, supposed to have access to correct intelligence, avowed the conviction that the Court would remain in South America. If there were such reports, I knew nothing of them. But I fairly own that had they come distinctly to my knowledge, had I even been consulted as to the weight to be allowed to them, I should have considered the British Minister's testimony as outweighing them all. I will tell the House why the testimony of Lord Strangford would have had so powerful a weight with me on this subject. In 1807, at the time when the Court of Portugal emigrated to the Brazils, I had the honour to fill the office now filled by my noble friend—(Lord Castlereagh.) When the first intelligence of the intended emigration reached this country, there was then, also, an abundance of conflicting and contradictory reports; and I believe I may say that for several days I alone, in London, alone perhaps among my colleagues, was persuaded of the existence of that intention. At that time, I knew nothing of Lord Strangford, except from his official correspondence: but that correspondence had inspired me with a full reliance upon the authenticity of his sources of information, and upon his knowledge of the Prince Regent's mind; and Lord Strangford all along affirmed, that the Prince Regent intended to emigrate. The general persuasion at Lisbon was that the Court would not emigrate; even up to the very day, when, as Lord Strangford had predicted, the Prince actually embarked in the Tagus, and set sail for Brazil.

My belief therefore in the present instance was founded, first, on positive information,—secondly, on the obvious desirableness of the return of the Prince Regent to Europe, and on the certainty that this country must have used all means of counsel and persuasion to ensure that event. I was persuaded both of the reality of the intention, and of the probability of its instant execution. Nothing, absolutely nothing, had come to my knowledge that could excite a reasonable distrust. But even had such distrust been excited in my mind by any rumour, or any testimony less than official, it would have been dispelled by the assurances of Lord Strangford. Such was my belief, my credulity, if you will—but a credulity of which I have assigned the grounds,—a credulity which was assuredly not so fatuitous as to be fairly construed into crime.

I must, however, beg not to have it understood that my belief in the return of the Prince Regent at once determined my acceptance of the mission; though it might have done so, for aught that I can see, without blame. Undoubtedly no earthly consideration would have induced me to accept it without an assurance as to that return: but it required a combination of other circumstances, with which I need not trouble the House, to induce me to go in an official character to Lisbon; and in fact my acceptance was not determined till after my return to town, late in September.

The Government had stronger grounds for their belief than I had. They had before them the communications contained, or referred to, in the papers last submitted to the House:—letters, namely, from Lord Strangford, of so early a date as February, and the autograph letter of the Prince Regent of Portugal to the Prince Regent of Great Britain, dated the 2nd of April. Of these I knew nothing till the other day, when the honourable gentleman's inquiries and denunciations led to an examination of the correspondence in the Foreign Office. This autograph letter disproves the notion of the honourable gentleman, that there was an interval between the month of February and the month of August in the communications respecting the Prince Regent's intended return. This letter fills up the supposed chasm in the correspondence. The reason why a copy of this document has not been laid before the House, is, that as many gentlemen who hear me must know, it is contrary to the etiquette observed towards Sovereign Princes so to make their letters public. The practice is for the Secretary of State to refer to the substance of such letters in an official despatch accompanying them, or acknowledging their receipt: and such a record of the letter in question is to be found in the despatch from the Secretary of State to Lord Strangford, of the 25th of July. In that despatch, this autograph letter is noticed as stating that the Prince Regent of Portugal only waited for intelligence of the final success of the allies, in order to determine his return to Europe.

But all this evidence, all this testimony, is, it seems, to be considered as fallacious, if not absolutely false, because there is a solemn, indubitable, irrefragable witness at variance with it—a paragraph in a newspaper of the 29th of July, which announced my actual appointment as Ambassador to Portugal! An appointment of the 29th of July could not be in consequence of information received on the 26th of August.—Clearly. But events might be contemplated as probable before the 29th of July, which intelligence of the 26th of August might confirm: and a speculation might be founded upon those probabilities, contingent upon their fulfilment or non-fulfilment. I do not affirm that some such speculation, founded on some such possible contingency, but absolutely dependent for its realization on the happening or not happening of that contingency, might not be afloat before the 29th of July.

The despatch, of the 25th of July (of which, however, any more than of the autograph letter alluded to in it, I had not any distinct knowledge till it was brought into notice the other day in consequence of the honourable gentleman's inquiries)—the date, I say, of this despatch renders it not improbable that it may have been about that time that a mission to Portugal began to be contemplated as probable. But that I was at that time, or near that time appointed, that I then accepted such appointment, if offered to me, or that it could then have been offered to me, if I had been willing to accept it, I utterly deny. I deny here, Sir, in your presence, and in the presence of my country, that which has been assumed as established because I did not deny it when asserted in a newspaper. Sir, I value as much as any man the liberty of the press; I acknowledge its utility, I bow to its power; in common with all public men, I listen to its suggestions, and receive its chastisements, with all due humility and thankfulness: but I will not plead at its bar! I will continue to treat with scorn the attacks of anonymous malice. I disdain to make any answer to such charges, whilst there is a House of Commons before which I can vindicate my character. This is the place where it is my right as well my duty to plead, before a competent tribunal, and in the face of known and accountable accusers. And in behalf of all that is sacred and decent in private life, as well as in behalf of the honour of public men, I protest against the inference, that he is to be held guilty of a charge, who resolutely declines to answer it at the bar of the daily press.

But the newspaper had, it seems, announced not only that I was appointed Ambassador to Lisbon; but that my right honourable friend near me (Mr. Huskisson,) was appointed Surveyor of the Woods and Forests, and my right honourable friend (Mr. W. W. Pole), at the end of the bench, Master of the Mint; both which nominations were immediately verified. It is very true that the latter office was shortly afterwards filled by my right honourable friend (Mr. W. W. Pole), who has discharged the duties of it with so much honour to himself, and advantage to the public: but I disclaim in the most peremptory terms any merit or influence of mine in that appointment. My right honourable friend (Mr. Huskisson) near me, was, it is also true, appointed to the office of Surveyor of Woods, and undoubtedly not without my intervention. On the 30th of July I think it was that I moved the new writ for my right honourable friend. I moved that writ for the express purpose of showing that I approved, and was party to, the accession of my right honourable friend, and of other friends of mine, to the Administration. And had I myself accepted office at that time, I should have been equally ready, nay, anxious to avow it.

At different periods of my political life, I have held, I have resigned, I have refused, and I have accepted office. And there is no occasion on which I have taken either of these courses, on which I am not perfectly prepared to vindicate (I will not say always the prudence, but I will say confidently) the purity and honourableness of my conduct.

I know, Sir, how difficult it is to speak plainly on subjects of this nature, without transgressing the decorum, if not the strict order of our debates. But is it brought as an accusation against me, that, having no difference of opinion with the Administration, I did not neglect an opportunity which presented itself of furnishing an accession of strength to that Administration, which I wished to strengthen and uphold? Why ought I to have declined this? And by whom am I accused for not declining it? By those who consider the principle of party as a virtue—as a badge of distinction, and a pledge of purity, when predicated of themselves; but who are intolerant of any party, presuming to connect itself together, except under their banners. And, what is the bond of party? what are the boasted ties that connect the honourable gentlemen on the other side of the House with each other? Fidelity in private friendship, as well as consistency in public principle. Their theory of party is a theory which they would confine exclusively to their own practice. One may become a satellite in their system, and welcome; but any eccentric planet, moving in another system, they view with jealous, yet with scornful eyes, and denounce its course as baleful and destructive. To this exclusive doctrine I have never subscribed. To these pretensions I have never listened with submission. I have never deemed it reasonable that any confederacy of great names should monopolize to themselves the whole patronage and authority of the state: should constitute themselves, as it were, into a corporation, a bank for circulating the favours of the Crown and the suffrages of the people, and distributing them only to their own adherents. I cannot consent that the administration of the Government of this free and enlightened country shall be considered as rightfully belonging to any peculiar circle of public men, however powerful, or of families however preponderant; and though I cannot stand lower in the estimation of the honourable baronet than I do in my own, as to my own pretensions, I will (to use the language of a statesman,* so eminent that I cannot presume to quote his words without an apology), I will, as long as I have the faculty to think and act for myself, "look those proud combinations in the face." I plead guilty, then, to the charge, if it be one, of having treated with an Administration, with the principles of which I perfectly agreed. I plead guilty to the charge, if it be one, of having on this, aye, and on

* Mr. Burke.

other occasions, postponed my own interest to that of my friends. If, indeed, the charge could be turned the other way; if, occupied exclusively with any personal objects of my own, it could be said that I had neglected the claims, the interests, or the feelings of any individual connected with me in political life, I should, indeed, hear that charge with sensations very different from those which I now experience: then, indeed, should I hide my head with shame.

When I moved the writ of my right honourable friend, on the 30th of July, I declare, upon my honour, that I thought it very doubtful whether I should myself have any official connection whatever with the Government. I do not mean to say, that the question had not been mooted, as to my undertaking the mission to Portugal, if it should turn out that such a mission was to be sent. But many circumstances might have prevented the result that did afterwards happen. I was not pledged, I was very far from having made up my own mind, to accept the mission if it should be offered to me; nor had the Government, as yet, any assurance that they should have it to offer. I had previously made arrangements of my own. My plans were to go where I did go, but from different motives and with a different object. What that object and those motives were, I am not called upon, nor do I think it necessary to state in this place. It is sufficient for me to say that

I was master of my own actions, and that I chose to go. My intention was known to my private friends, and had been communicated to my constituents two months before the close of the session.

The first official tender of the mission was made to me by my noble friend, the Secretary for Foreign Affairs, I think about the end of the first week of August:—I cannot be positive as to the day; but I recollect perfectly that I had but two interviews with my noble friend upon the subject, within a few days of each other,—and that at the date of one of those interviews, Mr. Sydenham had arrived in England. He arrived on or about the 8th of August. My noble friend was then on the eve of his departure for Vienna. His tender to me was altogether contingent and conditional. The way in which the matter was left, was this; that if the certainty of the Prince Regent of Portugal's immediate return should be established, I should hear from him (or, in his absence, from Lord Liverpool) again. I did hear again, in the manner that I have stated: but, in proof that I had not, in the mean time, acted on the presumption that I should go out in an official character, I can appeal to some of the members of the Board of Admiralty who sit near me, that I was, so late as in the month of September, a supplicant at the Admiralty, as a private person, for a ship to convey me and my family to Lisbon ; and when I arrived in Portugal, I found a house provided for me, as a private person, through the kindness of a friend,—a house in the neighbourhood of Lisbon, which, in my official character, I could not occupy.

But all this, it may be said, was but contrivance,—an artificial chain of circumstances forged and linked together, with a view to the present discussion. Has such an imputation the colour of probability? What I have now stated both as to facts and motives is the truth. If any man shall contradict this statement, I can only say that he will affirm that which is not true. Where a matter rests—and from its nature must rest solely—on the consciousness of an individual, there is no other answer (that I know of) to be given to an arbitrary contradiction. I speak this, I hope, without offence. But, on this part of my case, I know of no other possible answer.

I did believe then in the intention of the Prince Regent to return. The Government believed in it. Their belief would have been ground enough for mine. But I have shown that they had good grounds for their belief. Further, it appears, from what has been stated by the gallant admiral behind me, (Sir John Beresford,) in anticipation of a question which I might perhaps have taken the liberty to put to him, that not only had the royal family really entertained that intention, but that the disposition to carry it into execution survived the report of its abandonment; that he was repeatedly requested by the Prince Regent of Portugal to defer his departure from Rio de Janeiro from time to time, in hopes that the next arrivals from Europe might bring intelligence decisive of the voyage; and that it was not until the beginning of April that those hopes were finally relinquished, and the gallant admiral permitted to take his leave.

Contrary and contradictory rumours did, no doubt, continue to prevail on this subject, in London, as they certainly did in Lisbon. Even when I received at Lisbon, in the beginning of April 1815, the first intimation from England on which I founded my resignation, I was in possession of most positive assurances the other way; and on the very day on which I sent off my resignation, I had heard through what I might have considered as authentic channels, that the Prince would certainly embark. The day was specified on which the embarkation was to take place; and we were to look for the first news of that event in the arrival of the squadron off the bar. But did I act on this information? Did I endeavour to shake any credit which the Government at home might be disposed to give to their accounts from Rio de Janeiro? Did I contrast the rumours of Lisbon with the rumours of London, for the purpose of clinging to my office? No. It appears, from the papers on the table, that upon the 29th of March the information of the Prince Regent's abandonment of his design was received here in an official shape. Probably this official information must have been preceded some days by private intelligence. The intimation which reached me on the 9th of April certainly was not official; I did not wait, however, for its official confirmation: on the 10th of April, I wrote and sent off by an express packet the following despatch to the Foreign Office:

"By the mails which came in yesterday, I learn, (though not officially,) that the accounts received in England from Rio de Janeiro since Admiral Sir John Beresford's arrival there, create a doubt of the Prince Regent of Portugal's present intention to return to his European dominions.

"Nothing has been received here from the Brazils, which indicates any such change in His Royal Highness's intention. But should any impediments have been interposed to delay the execution of it, until the intelligence of the late astonishing and afflicting revolution in the state of Europe shall reach Rio de Janeiro, it is possible that the receipt of that intelligence may determine His Royal Highness to remain there for the present.

"In that case, or in the event of your lordship's receiving such positive accounts, as satisfy your lordship's mind that such a determination has been taken by the Prince Regent of Portugal, I have to request your lordship, to lay at the feet of His Royal Highness the Prince Regent my humble resignation of the commission with which he was graciously pleased to honour me, in contemplation of the Prince Regent of Portugal's return."

So much for the first head of the charge against me, and against the Government. I have shown, I hope to the satisfaction of the House, that we did believe in the return of the Court of Portugal to Europe;—that we had good grounds for that belief;—and that, upon that belief exclusively, any mission to Lisbon was founded.

It remains to be considered, whether upon that ground, *such* a mission was necessary or justifiable. And this question again divides itself into two heads; first, whether necessary at all; secondly, (if admitted to be necessary,) whether conducted on a scale of disproportionate expense—disproportionate either to the unavoidable expenditure of the mission, or to its political importance.

In the first of these questions—Was an embassy to Lisbon necessary, in the event of the Prince Regent's return?—is involved another more personal question, from which I must not shrink:—namely—Was there any unfitness in the offer of that mission to *me*, or in *my* acceptance of it?—I feel all the difficulty of arguing this point in a manner at once satisfactory to the House and not unjust to myself. It is distasteful and revolting to one's feelings to be obliged to speak of one's-self, and of one's own fitness for any situation, or any undertaking. But it will be remembered, that I am upon my trial—that I am defending myself against a criminal charge; and if in such a defence, something like egotism should be unavoidable, I hope the House will have the goodness to excuse it.

Sir, to place this question in its true point of view, I must once more go back to the year 1807. I have said that when in that year the royal family of Portugal adopted the resolution of emigrating to the Brazils, I had the honour to hold the Seals of the Foreign Office. I had thus an opportunity of becoming acquainted with the wishes of the Prince Regent of Portugal in favour of Lord Strangford, who had been employed to advise and to urge that splendid and magnanimous emigration. It was my duty to report these wishes, and to recommend the services of Lord Strangford to the consideration of my royal master. The result was, that his lordship was appointed Envoy Extraordinary and Minister Plenipotentiary; was invested with a red ribbon; and might also have received an advance in the peerage—which (for reasons nothing to the purpose of this night's discussion) he declined. There was, however, another point respecting which the Court of Portugal was extremely solicitous,—a reciprocation of missions of the highest rank: and this point, from the period of which I am speaking to the last moment at which I held the Seals of Office, the Portuguese Minister never lost an opportunity of pressing upon my attention. It has been said, by shrewd observers of domestic politics, that when once a coronet gets into a man's head there is no driving it out again : and I believe it may be as justly said, that when once a Court takes up the notion of reciprocation of embassies, it is no easy matter to get the better of it. Such a notion reproduces itself on every occasion. A Secretary of State is sure to be assailed with repeated solicitation till the favourite measure is accomplished.

To this application I at that time did not listen. And I believe I reconciled the Court of Portugal to the refusal of it, by showing that it could not then be granted in the person of Lord Strangford ; whose diplomatic standing would not admit of such an advancement—having been already so recently raised from the station of Chargé-d'Affaires. I promised, however, that on the occurrence of any signal event which might constitute a proper occasion for an embassy, (and the two possible events in contemplation were either the final establishment of the Portuguese Court at the Brazils—should the cause of Europe be lost, or, what was then a distant, though never with me a hopeless prospect—its restoration to Europe on a successful termination of the war,) I would recommend to my Sovereign—should I be then in office—a compliance with the wishes of the Court of Portugal.

Long after I quitted office, and more than once, or twice, or three times, I was appealed to for the truth of the assertion, that such a promise had been given; not that any engagement of mine could be binding on my successors. At last, I believe in 1811, without waiting for these long coming events, the Portuguese Minister here assumed the character of Ambassador. The reciprocation was declined. Much discussion, it seems, followed during the three succeeding years upon the refusal to name an Ambassador at the Court of Brazil: and I perfectly remember, that in one of the conversations which I had with my noble friend the Secretary for Foreign Affairs, he reminded me of the circumstances which I have here recapitulated, and observed, "We shall, besides, thus have the long disputed point of a reciprocation of embassies settled, and your pledge to the Court of Portugal redeemed in your own person."

If it is supposed by honourable gentlemen, that the aggregate allowances of the mission were necessarily increased by giving the name and rank of Ambassador, instead of that of Envoy Extraordinary, to my appointment, I assure them they are mistaken. The question of expense I reserve for separate consideration; but as it here mixes itself with the question of the rank of the mission, I am compelled shortly to advert to it, a little before its time. There are (or were before the regulation of 1815,) two different scales of ambassadorial allowances; the higher scale with a salary of £11,000 a year, and the other, on what is called the *old* salary of £8,200. The difference between these two salaries is nearly the same as the difference between the lower of them and that of an Envoy Extraordinary and Minister Plenipotentiary,—which is £5,200. Now, Sir, a man who coveted an embassy for the sake of emolument would hardly fail, once Ambassador, to choose the higher scale of salary. I chose the lower. But I do not claim any merit from this preference. For as neither £5,200, (the salary of Envoy Extraordinary,) nor £8,200, (the salary of Ambassador on the old scale,) nor even the higher salary of £11,000 reduced by deductions at home and abroad, was expected to cover all the expenses of the mission, without an addition of extraordinaries (as I shall presently show) it became indifferent in *that* point of view, what should be the nominal rank of the mission.

But it was not indifferent in *other* respects. I flatter myself, that I shall not be suspected of the idle and stupid vanity of caring under what name I did the public business. I believe, however, that it will be generally acknowledged, that having once,—with however little pretension to so high a station—filled that office which presides over the diplomacy of the country, I could not consistently assume any other than the highest diplomatic rank—that which alone represents the Sovereign—in any mission on which I should happen to be employed. Much less could I have done so with propriety on a mission to the Court of Portugal, with which I had, as Secretary of State, engaged for those exertions, and (sanguinely, perhaps, but, as it has turned out, safely) anticipated those results, by which that Court was now enabled, if it so thought fit, to accomplish its return to Europe.

But neither was the question of what might be individually becoming, the whole of this question. The character of Ambassador, though it may make little difference *here*, where every negociation passes through responsible Ministers, is by no means a matter of indifference in many foreign courts. The mere question of precedency, trifling as it may seem in itself, is not a thing of no moment, in diplomatic transactions. The facility of access to the person of the Sovereign, without the intervention of a Minister, perhaps hostile to our interests—and the right of pre-audience of that Sovereign himself—are advantages of no inconsiderable moment in courts where the will of the Sovereign is mainly the policy of the State.

But what good did I expect to achieve through these advantages? What was there for me to do? What did I expect to be able to do? First, it was not for me to judge of my own qualifications; it was for the Government. I might entrench myself behind this answer. But in the spirit in which I am stating my argument, taking the defence of the Government upon myself (as my noble friend has taken mine upon the Government) I will not do so. I must again remind the House, that I speak of myself, only because I am upon my trial. With the allowance belonging to that consideration, I may be permitted to say, I think that there *was* good to be done; and I think that *I* had as fair means, and as probable a chance, as any other man, of doing it.

I pass by many obvious difficulties and embarrassments in the present state of the relations of the Court of Portugal with other Governments in Europe, which might have been avoided had that Court returned. But there is one subject which seems to be comparatively forgotten at this moment, but which, in 1814 (the year of my appointment) was the theme of loud remonstrance and incessant reproach against the Government—as though they had been indifferent or lukewarm in their exertions upon it,—I mean the Slave Trade. I *did* hope to be able to effect something on this great and interesting subject. I cannot conceive a more favourable opportunity for this purpose than would have been afforded by the return of the Prince Regent to the kingdom of his ancestors: a kingdom saved, through the blessing of Providence upon the arms and counsels of this country. Of those counsels I had, from my official situation, been the humble instrument and organ: nor was it perhaps altogether an unreasonable presumption, to hope that the share which I had accidentally had in them might have conciliated, even to so humble an individual as myself, something of kindness from the Sovereign whose crown and whose dominions had been thus preserved and restored to him. I say, therefore, Sir, I cannot conceive circumstances which would have afforded a better chance of making some impression on the mind of a prince naturally good —naturally religious—upon a matter in which his personal character was the best, perhaps the one, hope of success.

I can assure the honourable gentlemen, that of the instructions which I carried out with me, three-fourths were directed to this object. And, besides the instructions of my noble friend, the Secretary of State, I had with me ample and most useful suggestions from an honourable friend of mine (Mr. Wilberforce), whom I do not now see in his place, which should not have lain idle in my desk. I hoped nothing, indeed, from the "oratory" which the honourable baronet is pleased (I suppose ironically) to attribute to me; but much from a good cause in zealous hands. I did believe—I do still believe, that had I had the opportunity of personal intercourse with the Prince, I might have effected some good in this matter; and if it had pleased God that I should succeed in it, I should neither have thought the expences of my mission ill employed, nor have felt any disparagement to myself in having undertaken it.

So much for the objects in contemplation at the commencement of the mission. But these objects were not attained.—True. And it is supposed, that not to have attained them was to me matter of great disappointment. In one sense, undoubtedly it was so. I should have thought the settlement of the question of the Slave Trade with one of the Peninsular Powers, an object of importance not easily to be over-rated. In another sense, I do assure the honourable baronet and the honourable gentleman, that I had not experienced one half of the satisfaction in accepting my office which I felt when I was permitted to resign it.

When, after writing the letter of April the 10th, tendering my resignation, I yielded to the request of my noble friend, and consented to remain at my post so long as my services might be thought necessary, I must beg the House to observe that the whole question of the mission had assumed an entirely new form. The war had broken out; and if there had not then been a Minister of high diplomatic rank at Lisbon, it would have been absolutely necessary to appoint one. I failed, it is true, in the main object of my negociations during the war,—the obtaining the aid of a corps of Portuguese troops to act with the Allies in Flanders. But why did I fail? Precisely because that state of things existed in Portugal—because that form of local government remained there—which it was the interest and the wish of this country to see altered. I failed because the Sovereign himself was not at Lisbon; an additional proof, if any had been wanting, of the advisableness of that return which we had endeavoured to invite by every proper inducement; an additional proof of the inconvenience of leaving one of the kingdoms of Europe with which Great Britain is most intimately allied, under a delegated Government; a Government incapable, from the very nature of their trust, and from the immensity of distance which separates them from their Sovereign, of acting in all cases with the promptness and energy necessary for the glory of the absent Sovereign, and for the welfare of his people.

Sir, I venture to hope that the House will feel that I have satisfactorily disposed of the first part of the question as to the embassy, and justified the nomination of a mission of that character, on the supposition (which I had before justified) of the Prince Regent of Portugal's return. I now proceed to the second part of that question, the expense of the mission.

If there was no delusion in the cause assigned for the embassy—if I have shown that it was necessary or highly expedient in the case supposed to exist—it still remains to be inquired whether or not it was conducted on too costly a scale. I must observe, however, again, that if the belief in the return of the Prince and the expediency of an embassy to welcome him are not made out, one farthing of expenditure was too much; and if, therefore, in the opinion of one honest and impartial man who has heard me, what I have stated appears to be founded in fraud or artifice, the question of pecuniary expense is at an end. On the other hand, if I have been so far successful, I am prepared to challenge a like decision on the issue now to be joined; and to demonstrate that the cost of this mission was not only not prodigal in proportion to its rank and character, but that it was economical, in comparison with any standard with which it can in fairness be compared.

The honourable baronet has quoted a *dictum* of Sir Robert Walpole's, that "every man has his price." I do not think this maxim true of men:—I do not think it true that even every *thing* has its price. Things must be estimated not merely by their intrinsic qualities, but by their relative fitness and value. There is no rule for judging absolutely what ought to be the cost of *an* embassy. There is no forming such an estimate *à priori*. Facts and experience are the only grounds on which you can safely or justly proceed.

I beg gentlemen then to look at the printed accounts of missions in the years 1812, 1813, and 1814, and I ask who could tell, on going to Lisbon in the autumn of the latter year, what his expenses were likely to be? Who is there, that having before him the expenditure of Sir Charles Stuart for the years 1812-13, and 1813-14, would have ventured upon such a mission, without coming to some understanding as to the extent of his expenditure, and as to the principles of its limitation?

I shall perhaps surprise the honourable baronet when I confess that an application on the subject of extraordinaries was made by me to the Government. But in what sense was this application made? Was it for latitude and indulgence? Was it that I might be put upon the same footing and allowed the same range as my predecessor? No; Sir; it was for strictness, for definition, for restraint. In the beginning of October I wrote a letter to my noble friend, Lord Liverpool, (my noble friend, Lord Castlereagh, near me, was then abroad), an extract of which, with their permission, I will now read to the House. The House will see that it was of as private and familiar a style, and as little destined for public citation as that from Lord Liverpool to me, which I read to the House a short time ago.

"I have been looking over Stuart's extraordinaries, and they really frighten me. It may be very well for him or any man not connected with politics, to draw thus at discretion, but it would not do for *me*. For God's sake, limit me to what you think right—I can form no judgment of the matter: only limit me, so that I may have no responsibility."

This letter shows at least the *quo animo*—the disposition with which I entered upon the subject. Is this the language of rapacity? Is this a petition for large emolument and unbounded discretion? Or does it not rather indicate a cautious dislike of discretionary power, arising from a dread of responsibility, and an anticipation of injustice—the former of which I am not ashamed of confessing I did feel; the latter, I have at this moment, God knows, no reason to disavow.

Sir, in entering upon this most disagreeable discussion—disagreeable, because I must mention the names of honourable men in a way which may be liable to misconstruction—disagreeable, because I must speak (though but to repel them with scorn) of imputations with which I never thought my own name liable to be stained, I beg leave to preface what I have to say by observing, that the name of Sir Charles Stuart, or of any other person whom I may have occasion to mention in my defence, is brought forward by me most reluctantly. I have no choice, the necessity is forced upon me. The name of Sir Charles Stuart I mention with the respect due to his talents and character. I consider him as one who has rendered eminent services to his country, and from whom his country may confidently look for such services hereafter. I believe him to be as free from pecuniary taint, as I know myself to be. Large as his expenditure at Lisbon may appear, I am persuaded that it was at once justified and limited by the necessity of the case. It is to be borne in mind also, that of the aggregate sums which appear to have been expended by him, no small proportion was simply and absolutely loss upon the exchange, and upon the conversion of English into Portuguese money. After these declarations, I proceed to state the expenditure of the Lisbon mission, as it stood in Sir Charles Stuart's time, and the amount of his regular and extraordinary allowance.

For the year, from the 5th of April, 1812, to the 5th of April, 1813, Sir Charles Stuart's extraordinaries appear to have been £26,807
Salary 5,200

Total £32,007

For the next year, from the 5th of April, 1813, to the 5th of April, 1814, the extraordinaries are stated at...£26,006
Salary 5,200

Total £31,206

This was the conclusion of Sir Charles Stuart's

mission. These statements are all before the House. They are to be found in pages 30 and 31 of the Report of the Committee on the Civil List, in June, 1815;—which Report I wish that the honourable gentlemen opposite would have the goodness to take into their hands, as I shall have many occasions to refer to it.

Then comes a period which is particularly selected as a contrast to my expenditure;—namely, the half year, beginning the 5th of April, 1814, (the termination of Sir Charles Stuart's mission,) and ending the 10th of October, 1814, (the commencement of mine). Here my accusers take their grand position. This is the narrow isthmus between two rushing seas of expense, on which they plant their standard of economy!—I do not complain of them for doing so. I do not blame the honourable gentleman who brought forward this question, for moving for papers to illustrate this position. But what I do think I have some right to complain of is, that having obtained these documents, they have somehow or other totally forgotten to notice their results. When it suited the honourable mover's purpose, he asked for the information; and when he got it, and found that it was not precisely what he wanted, it suited his purpose to abstain from any observation upon it. In this respect, he will excuse me if, instead of following his example, I endeavour to supply his omissions.

At Sir Charles Stuart's departure from Lisbon, Mr. Casamajor, the Secretary of Legation, was appointed Chargé-d'Affaires, receiving of course the regular salary belonging to these two appointments. As Mr. Casamajor's salary during this half year was nearly the same as his salary of Secretary of Embassy with me, and made but a trifling part of the expenses of either mission, I shall not take it into calculation. Not so, however, as to his *extraordinary* allowances; which during this economical half-year appear, by the Civil-List Report, p. 32, as well as by Mr. Sydenham's testimony, to have amounted to upwards of £2,500.

I am not exactly informed at what period between April and July Mr. Sydenham was named Envoy Extraordinary and Minister Plenipotentiary to the Local Government of Portugal. The first official despatch to him that I have seen is dated in July: but his nomination must have preceded that despatch by some weeks. He had from the 5th of April the same salary as had been enjoyed by Sir Charles Stuart. I speak here of the regular salary of £5,200 a year,—not of extraordinary allowances. Mr. Sydenham arrived at Lisbon the end of the first week of July. He remained there until the 27th or 28th of that month, when he embarked for England, being obliged to quit his station suddenly on account of his health. These three

weeks (or thereabouts) were the whole of Mr. Sydenham's residence at Lisbon; and for these he received (I am not blaming him, but I state the fact) two quarters' salary, at the rate of £5,200 a year—that is to say £2,600
He received also, for outfit, ... 1,500
He received for his journey to Lisbon 1,100
And lastly he received (at a subsequent period) for losses occasioned by his sudden relinquishment of the mission 2,000

In all £7,200

Add to this sum, Mr. Casamajor's extraordinaries for the same period 2,500

The result of cost to the public, for the half-year intervening between Sir C. Stuart's mission and mine, is therefore £9,700

This was the reformed period which is to put all past and future Ministers to shame! This was the rigid scale of economy which I ought to have taken for my guide, and for departing from which I am arraigned before this House and the country! Yet hear how Mr. Sydenham describes Mr. Casamajor's way of life. "I find," (says Mr. Sydenham, in his letter to Mr. Hamilton of the 8th July, written immediately upon his arrival at Lisbon),

"I find that Mr. Casamajor has been living in a very quiet retired way, with no suite to feed and lodge; and by the examination of his books I perceive that he does not live on less than £100 a week."

Here was no establishment, no representation, no call for display of any kind; and yet the ordinary expenses of Mr. Casamajor's household were £100 a week, or at the rate of £5,200 a year!

It is true, at least I have heard and believe, that during the three weeks that Mr. Sydenham passed at Lisbon he lived in Mr. Casamajor's house. But, as to charge upon the public, Mr. Sydenham was then in the enjoyment of a yearly salary of £5,200, which comes to exactly another £100 a week. So that independently of the *extraordinary* allowances of Mr. Sydenham, for outfit, journey, and losses, the aggregate of the regular salary received by him, joined to the extraordinaries allowed to Mr. Casamajor for weekly expenditure; for *victus* and *convictus*, during the economical half year, was at the rate of upwards of £10,000 a year.

There is not upon earth a more honourable mind than Mr. Casamajor's; and I had myself the opportunity of verifying the statement respecting his expenditure, by the inspection of his books, at his own particular desire. But I must take the liberty of reminding the House, that from the moment at which I arrived at Lisbon, Mr. Casamajor, then becoming Secretary of Embassy, became part of my family; and as such, lived at my table. From that time, therefore *his* expenses (salary excepted) were involved in mine. Why, Sir, if I were to calculate by simple addition, or by the rule of three, I might say, that, according to what I have shown you, on Mr. Sydenham's testimony as well as my own—*two* Casamajors ought to have eaten up my whole allowances, ordinary and extraordinary. And, by the way, I *had* two Casamajors—for in addition to the gentleman of whom I have been speaking, and of whom I speak with every feeling of kindness and of respect, another gentleman, Mr. Croft, who was recommended to me by my noble friend as Secretary for the Portuguese Language, (and who had been with Sir C. Stuart in the same capacity) lived with me as one of my family, during the whole period of my mission. I, of course, do not mean seriously to state that the increase of my expences was in exact proportion to the number of persons whom I had to maintain. But I *do* mean seriously to show the different footing upon which Mr. Sydenham and Mr. Casamajor *separately*, or even Mr. Sydenham and Mr. Casamajor *jointly*—stood, in respect to the claims upon *their* expenditure, from that in which I stood,—with all the accessary burdens, and all the unavoidable representation, of an embassy. With neither of the two gentlemen, whom I had the good fortune to have attached to me—Mr.

Casamajor or Mr. Croft—had I any personal acquaintance before my mission began. I learnt, during our official and domestic intercourse, to value and esteem them both. I am sorry to be forced to mention their names in connection with these miserable details; but I am driven to it by the unsparing coarseness of the attacks which have been made upon me, and by the foolish, fallacious, and dishonest contrast of my expenditure with that of Mr. Sydenham:—Mr. Sydenham's, who, during his three weeks' residence at Lisbon, was an inmate in the house of Mr. Casamajor, —and mine, who, during the whole period of my mission, had the suite of an embassy to maintain!

And now, Sir, come we to the famous letter of letters, upon which it seems that the whole of the case against me is made to turn—the letter from the Secretary of State to Mr. Sydenham, directing him to confine his expenditure within his regular allowances. Before this letter is made conclusive against *me*, I might perhaps contend that it should be shown that I was in some degree, if not party to it, cognizant of it. Upon my honour, I never saw it till after the honourable gentleman's first notice of his motion. I cannot say that I had never heard of it. I had heard, or perhaps seen in a newspaper, that some such letter had been written to Mr. Sydenham by my noble friend: and I well remember that the same authority stated the rate of £5,000 a year as that which covered *all* Mr. Sydenham's allowances. I have already shown the accuracy of *that* statement.

But I waive this plea: I acknowledge the authority of the letter; and, *if* the circumstances of Mr. Sydenham's situation and mine were the same, and *if* the meaning of this letter was what has been attributed to it; and *if* that meaning was enforced against Mr. Sydenham, or was not remonstrated against by him; I will admit that, notwithstanding my ignorance of the law, I was bound by it, and am guilty of not conforming to it.

And, first, what was Mr. Sydenham's situation? That of Envoy to the Local Government; mine, that of Ambassador to the Sovereign. (With the propriety of the appointment we have in this part of the argument nothing to do). Secondly, What was the meaning of the letter? My noble friend, the writer of it, has told you, that it did not mean the absolute exclusion of extraordinaries, which he held to be almost impossible; but it did mean to prescribe the discontinuance of that rate of expenditure which had brought, during the war, such heavy charge upon the public. The letter itself says,

"I cannot anticipate any public grounds for continuing the expenditure of His Majesty's servants at Lisbon, *on the scale on which it has been conducted during the continuance of the War in the Peninsula.*"

To be sure he could not. Who dreamt of an expenditure of upwards of £30,000 a year in time of peace? Lastly, the instructions which were given, were they executed? Did Mr. Sydenham think it practicable to conform to them? Did he receive them without a remonstrance, and act up to them with strictness and fidelity? With fidelity, in the moral sense of the word, I have no doubt he would have acted up to them if he had remained at Lisbon; but have we no positive proof that he regarded the literal execution of them as impossible?

And here, Sir, again I feel myself called upon to guard against being supposed to mean any thing unkind in the reference which I am compelled to make to Mr. Sydenham. That gentleman is no more! He has closed a distinguished and honourable life, during which he endeared himself to his friends, and has left behind him an unspotted character. I implore of those who hear me, that if a word should escape me in the heat of argument, which can be thought to bear any colour of disrespect to Mr. Sydenham's memory, they will believe it to be wholly unintentional. I am the last man living who would wantonly throw a slur upon his reputation, or give a wound to the feelings of those who mourn his loss. I would most gladly have avoided any allusion to him: but his name has been made the vehicle for a foul calumny against my character;

and the House will feel that not to me who repel an attack, but to those who have misused Mr. Sydenham's name for the purposes of attack upon me, is to be imputed the guilt of profaning (if it be profaned) the sanctity of the tomb.

The fact is, that while the mandate to Mr. Sydenham, directing him to confine his expenses within certain limits, was traversing the ocean in one direction, a remonstrance, by anticipation, against such a limitation was on its passage to the Foreign Office. Mr. Sydenham, I suppose, might have heard rumours of such intended restriction; he knew, from what he saw of Lisbon himself (in the amount of Mr. Casamajor's weekly bills,) and from what he had heard of it from others, that a literal compliance with that restriction was impracticable; and, on the 8th of July, the very day (I believe) after his arrival at Lisbon, he thus addressed himself to Mr. Hamilton, the Under Secretary of State (for the information of my noble friend), in the letter from which I have already quoted an extract:—

"While the Duke of Wellington was at Madrid, he spoke to me on the subject of my allowances at Lisbon, and he gave me the comfortable assurance of my being ruined, unless Government allowed me something more than the usual salary, diminished by the usual deductions in England, and the loss of exchange. He promised to mention the subject to Lord Castlereagh; and I have written to him to remind him of his promise. I find that Mr.

Casamajor has been living in a very quiet, retired way, with no suite to feed and lodge, and by the examination of his books, I perceive that he does not live on less than £100 a week."

So far is printed. Further on, in the same letter, the extract of which now lies before me, he states that he "shall live with the greatest possible economy; but that what he cannot pay out of his allowances he shall trust to the Government to pay for him."

Mr. Sydenham, as I have before observed, resided about three weeks in Lisbon, namely, from about the 7th or 8th to the 27th or 28th of July. I have already stated the allowances, regular and extraordinary, which he received during that period or on account of it—viz. £2,600 salary; £1,500 outfit; £1,100 for the journey from Paris and Madrid to Lisbon. All these sums are in the printed accounts of the Civil List Report; and therefore gentlemen might have known them without moving for papers: but I was not aware, and I suppose they were not aware, till in an evil hour they brought it out by their own motion for papers,—of the sum of £2,000 for losses, which makes up the aggregate of Mr. Sydenham's receipts on account of his half-year's mission, to £7,200.

If it is said, that as this sum of £7,200 includes outfit, and allowances for journey and for losses, it is not fairly to be stated as Mr. Sydenham's expenditure for *half a year*, I readily admit that it is not so: but then I must observe, that, on the same ground the aggregate of *my* allowances cannot be fairly stated as the expenditure of *a year*. The cost of outfit and plate in *my* case would not have been repeated another year, any more than that of outfit, and allowances for journey and for losses would, in Mr. Sydenham's case, have been repeated in another *half* year. But it *is* quite fair—it is indeed absolutely necessary, since the contrast between Mr. Sydenham's half year and my year, has been so much insisted on—to state, as I have done, Mr. Sydenham's *salary*, joined to Mr. Casamajor's *extraordinaries*, for the *same half year*, as constituting the expenditure of *the mission* for that period. And it *is* fair to state *the whole* of Mr. Sydenham's receipts joined to Mr. Casamajor's *extraordinaries*, as the aggregate expense of that half year with which the aggregate of my receipts for a whole year is to be compared.

Whatever comments, therefore, gentlemen may think proper to make on my conduct in other respects, they will at least, I think, abandon the contrast between Mr. Sydenham's mission and mine, as to the rate of their respective cost to the public. This point, on which they relied so confidently, completely fails them. They may, if they will, continue to arraign my political sins; but if comparison with the period of Mr. Sydenham's mission be a decisive test of economy, they must on that comparison absolve me from pecuniary transgression.

But, Sir, it is not on pecuniary matters only that they have guessed wrong as to me and Mr. Sydenham. They flattered themselves that they had another case against me on his account; a case of hardship—as if this valuable public servant had been displaced purposely to make way for me. It has been asserted that I superseded Mr. Sydenham. Sir, I did *not* supersede Mr. Sydenham. If the fact were so, I know not that it would constitute any charge against me. It would, I believe, be the first time that the undoubted right of the Crown to appoint and to change its foreign Ministers has been made matter of charge, or even of question, in Parliament. But the fact is not so. Mr. Sydenham's mission was irretrievably at an end before mine began. He quitted Lisbon not only unrecalled, but without leave. He did this from necessity, on account of the impaired state of his health. He arrived in England (as I have already had occasion to say) on or about the 8th of August. From that day to the 10th of October he received in England his appointments as Minister at Lisbon. Are the economists angry that he did not continue so to receive them longer? He was neither then, nor at any subsequent period before his death (as I shall presently show, by a document founded on his own representations) in a state of health to admit of his resuming the Lisbon mission—or accepting any other. If he had happily been so, my noble friend will bear testimony not only to the fact, but to my knowledge of the fact, that another and more important employment was in contemplation for him. So much for that charge.

I have in my hand a copy of the letter from the Foreign Office to the Treasury, which authorized the payment to Mr. Sydenham of that sum of £2,000 for losses, which forms the last item in his account. I almost wonder, by the bye, that I have not been told, in distinct terms, that this £2,000 was given to Mr. Sydenham to reconcile him to my supersession of him. The House, if they will allow me to take the liberty of reading this letter to them, will see how that matter stands. I am ready to move for its being laid on the table, if they think it necessary. It is luckily the last document of the kind with which I shall have occasion to try their patience. It is as follows:

" *Foreign Office, Oct. 25th*, 1815.

" My Lords,

" Thomas Sydenham, Esq. late His Majesty's Envoy Extraordinary and Minister Plenipotentiary to the Court of Lisbon, has represented to me the very great expense he was at in making preparations to undertake that mission, with a view to a permanent residence at Lisbon, and the great loss he sustained by the sudden disposal of his effects, &c. on his *being obliged to relinquish that mission, on account of the dangerous state of his health*, after a residence of only a few months, whereby he has been a loser of considerably more than £2,000 and is thereby involved in difficulties beyond the reach of his private fortune to satisfy."

(There is a slight error of inadvertency here as to the period of Mr. Sydenham's actual residence at Lisbon—which was, as I have shown, weeks only and not months. I now come to a passage to which I particularly wish to call the attention of the House.)—

"Having considered this application, it has appeared to me, under the peculiar circumstances of the case *(Mr. Sydenham's state of health still preventing his being employed in the diplomatic service of His Majesty)*, to be just and reasonable that Mr. Sydenham should receive a compensation on account of these losses.—I am, therefore, to desire your lordships will be pleased to take the commands of His Royal Highness the Prince Regent, with regard to the issue of the sum of two thousand pounds, *nett*, to Mr. Sydenham, or his assigns, as a compensation for the losses above-stated."

Is this also a sham letter and a concerted fraud? Perhaps the *date* will help us to a solution of this question. It is dated the 25th October, 1815,—that is to say, six months after I had tendered the resignation of my mission, and three months after my resignation had been accepted—a period, therefore, when, if Mr. Sydenham's health had been sufficiently restored to enable him to resume his station at Lisbon, there had been for three months no impediment whatever, and for six months no impediment on *my* part, to his resuming it. It was manifestly the hopelessness of his return to public life that weighed with the Foreign Office in writing this letter, to which I am happy to have had an opportunity of referring, both for the proof which it affords of good-natured and considerate disposition, and the just testimony which it bears to the merits and character of Mr. Sydenham. I had not the honour and the happiness of a personal acquaintance with Mr. Sydenham. I knew him only by reputation; by the report of common friends, whose report would of itself have been sufficient to ensure my belief of his good qualities,—and by the exhibition of his talents in that memorable investigation which was carried on in a Committee of this House upon the renewal of the East-India Company's Charter. In the course of that examination the gentlemen connected with India displayed a degree of ability and information, which perhaps could not have been matched, certainly not excelled, in any other service, or in any other country. Among these very able men Mr. Sydenham stood eminently distinguished,—evincing a capacity for great affairs and a fitness for important employments, such as are rarely to be found even in more practised statesmen. If, therefore, I have been driven to say any thing of this gentleman (I hope I have not, I am sure I have not intended it) which may have appeared in any degree disrespectful or disparaging,—if I have been obliged to soil the name of a high-minded and liberal man with money,—the blame (I repeat it) is not with me,—but with those who forced Mr. Sydenham's name into this discussion.

I now, Sir, come to the details of the expenditure of my own mission, the account of which is among the papers upon the table. The honourable gentleman who made the motion, has had the goodness to compliment me on the minuteness and accuracy of my calculations. I understand the nature of the honourable gentleman's compliment; and I see that he has been taught thoroughly to understand the nature of the advantage which he has over me on this day. Undoubtedly any charge connected with money places the accused in a dilemma of painful difficulty,—a difficulty the more painful in proportion to the consciousness of his innocence, and to the warmth of his indignation. If he contents himself—as is the first natural impulse of every honourable mind—with general and lofty denial, he exposes himself to be triumphed over as having evaded investigation;—and figures are then invoked as the only test of truth. If on the other hand he condescends to detailed arithmetical calculation, he becomes liable to such compliments as those of the honourable gentleman; and must feel (as I do now) a certain inevitable degradation in the very process by which he is to be justified. It is certainly not without such pain that I made up my mind to this latter alternative. Those who know me in private life are, I am afraid, too well aware how little I am versed in questions either of arithmetic or of economy, not to have been as much surprised, as the honourable gentleman professes himself to be gratified, at the proficiency in figures which is displayed in the papers before the House; particularly in that laboured despatch of mine of the 30th May, 1815. In truth, I availed myself, for the purpose of those statements and calculations, of the aid of persons much more conversant with such matters than I can pretend to be. I beg the honourable gentleman also to understand that I do not profess, in these accounts, to state my *whole* expenditure at Lisbon, but only my expenditure of *public* money,

Sir, the expenditure of Sir Charles Stuart's mission for the two years, 1812-13, and 1813-14, and that of the interval between the conclusion of Sir Charles Stuart's mission and my appointment, can hardly be denied to justify the nominal amount of the allowances assigned to me. But that *nominal* amount and the *real effective* value were very different indeed. For my actual *expenditure* (as distinguished from nominal *receipt*, or rather nominal *issue),* a fair but strict standard of comparison is furnished by the Report of the Civil-List Committee of June, 1815. If it shall appear that my whole *actual* expenditure as *Ambassador,* tallied within a very trifle with the amount fixed by that Committee and sanctioned by the House for a *Minister* at Lisbon *of the second order,* I think it will not be imputed that I abused the discretion confided to me.

Assuredly I did not, on going out to Lisbon, anticipate the trial of this day; but I did, as has been seen, dread and deprecate any unlimited pecuniary discretion. It has been shown how anxious I was to have the limits of my expenditure defined: and within those limits, whatever they might be, I resolved to restrict myself.

My *nominal* allowances were, as I have said, and as appears from the papers upon the table—

Salary	£8,200
Extraordinaries, not to exceed	6,000
Total	£14,200

Of this amount of extraordinaries I drew only for three-fourths, or £4,500. I received (like every other Minister of whatever rank), the sum of £1,500 for outfit. If that sum be taken as replacing the £1,500 extraordinaries which I declined to draw, the result of salary, extraordinaries, and outfit for that *one* year *(outfit* could only be a charge on the *first* year,) is, as above, £14,200. I had plate, like other Ambassadors and Envoys Extraordinary, &c., but upon the scale of an Envoy.

Having no rule or experience to guide me, all that I could determine was to consider the established recognized amount of the *salary* as the limit of my public expenditure, and to draw for no more *extraordinaries* than should make up the *nominal salary* of £8,200 to that *effective* amount. Had therefore that salary been paid free from deductions at home, and without loss on the exchange and on the conversion into Portuguese money, I should not have drawn for one shilling of extraordinaries for my expenses at Lisbon. But the case was very different. This *nominal* salary was liable to deductions amounting to no less than about sixteen per cent. in England, which reduced it from £8,200 to about £6,900; and this latter sum again to a loss of something more than twelve per cent. in its transit and conversion, reducing it from £6,900 to somewhere between £6,100 and £6,000.

This statement applies to the first three quarters of the year, ending the 5th of July, 1815. In July I received the Report of the Civil List Committee, to which I have so often had occasion to refer. From that time, therefore, I had—what I had always wished—a positive written public rule, not laid down indeed for my mission, but which I might safely take for my guide. By the Civil List Report, the Minister to Portugal was considered prospectively on the footing not of an Ambassador, but of an Envoy Extraordinary and Minister Plenipotentiary. To that Minister of the second order, the Report assigned a salary of £8,000 a year. It further recommended that all sums for foreign missions should be paid free of all deductions except the property tax; thus relieving the issues of salary from all the established legal defalcations at home, amounting to about six per cent. (in addition to the property tax), and from all losses by exchange or otherwise, in the transmission abroad. At the same time, the allowance for outfit—which had been hitherto in all cases, and for all ranks, only £1,500 —a sum which is stated by the Report not to be sufficient to cover above one-third or one-fourth of the real expense, was raised to £4,000, and an annual allowance of £500 was given for house rent. The several arrangements are to be found in pp. 47 and 48 of the Civil List Report, to which I beg the gentlemen who do me the honour to watch what I am saying, to refer. Deducting £800 the property tax, from the *salary* of £8,000, these issues to the new *Envoy* would amount to £11,700 nett for the *first* year; and to £7,700 nett for every subsequent year. And this, exclusive of plate, for which the Report makes a special provision.

When I received the copy of this Report, I instantly determined that, so long as the mission continued in my hands, I would limit myself strictly to the amount specified in it. For the *last* quarter, therefore (from July the 5th to October 10th, 1815), I conformed to the new scale of ordinary allowances, and received only £1,800 *nett*, without any extraordinaries whatever. The exchange was now, in consequence of the termination of the war, become so favourable as in a great measure to counteract the loss upon the paper money, which continued to be about seven per cent. The result of this counteraction was, that the loss upon £1,800 by the exchange and paper money jointly, which three months before would have been about £220 and now only about £70.

Of the £6,000 extraordinaries which I had liberty to draw, I drew only for so much as was sufficient—

First, to replace the deductions on £6,150 being three quarters of *nominal* salary at the *old* rate of £8,200 *(gross)*, and on £1,800 one quarter at the *new* rate of £7,200 *(nett)*.

Secondly, to make up the old allowance for outfit, viz. £1,500 to the sum of £4,000 specifically allowed by the Committee, and not one farthing more, so help me God.

So scrupulously did I adhere to these limits, (which seemed to me to have been formed on a clear principle, and which had the sanction of the

House of Commons), that finding that my agent had drawn for the last quarter a sum of £1,500 as *extraordinaries* (at the rate of the £6,000 originally allowed to me), I directed him to return that sum to the Treasury: and I declare, on my conscience, that when I gave this direction, I had no more expectation that the transaction would ever be known to any one except to my agent, to my right honourable friend near me, Mr. Huskisson, whom I requested to see my direction executed, to my noble friend, Lord Castlereagh, (whose permission was necessary); and to the Treasury, (to which the return was made), I had no more expectation that I should ever have to state this transaction privately or publicly in vindication of my character, than I had apprehension that on such grounds my character would ever be assailed.

It is undoubtedly still open to the honourable gentlemen who are the framers and supporters of the impeachment against me, to recur to the charge that the mission to Lisbon was unnecessary; to find fault, if they please, with my personal conduct in accepting it (of which a word by-and-by), and to censure the mode in which I may have discharged the duties of it. But as to pecuniary imputation, I stand upon a rock—I stand upon the authority of a Committee of this House, appointed long after my embassy was established and endowed, and not merely approving by retrospect the amount of its actual endowment, but recommending prospectively the same endowment for a mission of a lower character. Before that Report was known to me, with the power to go to a certain extent of expense, I restrained myself within that extent, to limits narrowed by my own sense of what was right. As soon as I had the authority of that Report to guide me, I adhered to it voluntarily and strictly, living as an Ambassador, within the allowances assigned for an Envoy. To other allegations of misconduct, political or prudential, I may be obnoxious; but surely no fair adversary, after this exposition, will impute to my embassy either a wasteful prodigality on the part of the Government, or a corrupt rapacity on mine.

I am afraid I have already wearied the House with figures, but there is another calculation, of which the result is so striking, that I cannot help requesting of the House to allow me to state it to them. Its elements are few, and the process short and simple. I particularly request attention to it from the right honourable gentleman (Mr. Tierney), who sits opposite to me, whose skill in these matters peculiarly qualifies him to detect any error in the statement.

The Report of the Committee on the Civil List fixes the salary of the Lisbon *Envoy* at £8,000 to be reduced by the deduction of the property tax to £7,200. This sum of £7,200 was to be received *nett* at Lisbon, free from all other deductions at home, and from loss by exchange and conversion abroad. Sir, I desired a person far better skilled in calculations than I am, to make out for me how much must have been received *nett* from the Treasury *here*, to produce £7,200 *nett*, in *Lisbon*, during the years 1814-15? The following is the statement of my arithmetician.

The first addition to be made is that of the amount necessary to cover the average loss of something more than 12 per cent. by exchange and paper money: this would be about £ 980
which being added to 7,200

Gives £8,180

as the sum necessary to have been received *nett* in England, in order to produce £7,200 *nett* in Lisbon.

But, again; how much would it have been necessary for the Treasury to issue *gross* to produce (on the footing on which my salary was issued) £8,180 *nett* in England? The deductions at the Exchequer, I have shown, amounted to about 16 per cent., the property-tax included. The sum necessary to cover these deductions, would be about £1,556
Which, added to 8,180

Shews, that the *gross* issue at the Treasury must have been about	£9,736
Add to this sum the allowance for outfit	4,000
Add the allowance for house-rent (to which, by the way, might be added 12 per cent. for loss on exchange, &c.)	500
And the *gross nominal* issues at the Treasury to meet the recommendation of the Committee, for the first year of the new Envoy, must have been	£14,236

Does not the very *sound* of this sum carry conviction,—and I could almost hope compunction, to the bosoms of my accusers? Does it not excite in the minds of all impartial men, an indignant recollection of the arts and the clamours, by which, during two years and a half, I have been stigmatized to the country as an instance of unexampled waste,—as an insatiable pillager of the Exchequer?

Sir, of the pecuniary charge I trust that I may here take my leave. After my own vindication, however (which must on every account be nearest to my heart), I confess, I am most anxious to put the well-intentioned part of the nation on their guard against those exaggerations, for mischievous purposes, by which public men are run down. If the result of this night shall warn them not to be too easily misled into the belief of monstrous and improbable corruptions, I cannot say that I shall not still regret the calumnies with which I have been overwhelmed ; but I shall be in some degree rewarded and consoled for them.

I have thus disposed of the two main heads of accusation. I have shown that there was a sincere and well-grounded belief in the return of the Prince Regent of Portugal to Europe : and I have shown that the cost of the embassy appointed to receive him on his return was not only not extravagant, but that according to every test by which expenditure can be tried, whether of contrast with what had gone before, or of comparison with what has been deliberately established for the future, it was limited by a reasonable and scrupulous economy.

Some minor charges remain to be refuted.

I am accused of having held the mission after all hope of executing the duty which I undertook to fulfil was abandoned. But, before I enter on this point, I am reminded that I am accused also of having assumed the mission too soon. It is said that I assumed it in October, although the Prince of Brazil could not be expected in Europe for six months from that date. Now if there were any ground for supposing that the return was altogether a false pretence, the acceptance of the Embassy sooner or later would be of no consequence ; the acceptance of it at all was a crime:

But if the Prince Regent of Portugal was to come to Europe, there was fair probability that Sir John Beresford might have landed him at Lisbon in February. Sir John Beresford sailed from Portsmouth on the fifth of October. True, he was driven back to Plymouth after having been some days at sea. But, as to the length of the passage, he *did* reach the Brazils in seven weeks from the date of his last sailing (that too with a convoy under his protection); and it was not only no improbable expectation, but it was the belief of Sir John Beresford himself, stated repeatedly to the Prince Regent of Portugal, that from five to six weeks would be sufficient for the voyage from Rio de Janeiro. It is true, that the hypothesis was, that the Prince Regent would be ready to embark, and would have made all the preparations necessary for his departure, between the period of his writing for a squadron and its arrival. Such in fact was our expectation; and upon that supposition (as I have said before) the arrival at Lisbon of the Prince Regent himself would have been the first intelligence that would have been received there of his departure from Rio de Janeiro. I sailed in the beginning of November. I landed at Lisbon (I think) on the first of the following month. I had no more doubt of the impatience of the Portuguese royal family to return to Europe than I have that I am now addressing this House. I consequently reckoned upon their arrival in Lisbon almost as soon after my own as I could conveniently be prepared to receive them. In the month of February, I well remember, we used to be looking out at Lisbon, at every favourable turn of the wind, for the arrival of Sir John Beresford with his royal passengers, in the Tagus. The only period, therefore, during which I can be accused of receiving a salary without executing a public duty, is that between the date of my appointment and my sailing for Lisbon, a period of about three weeks. Surely this then is a charge of minute and petty captiousness. It is said that nature abhors a *vacuum;* and I believe it may be equally said that an Exchequer Quarter abhors a fraction. My salary was reckoned from the 10th of October, the quarter-day which preceded by about ten days my taking leave at Carlton House;—and which preceded my actual departure (as I have said) by about three weeks. Of the scores or hundreds of missions which have gone out from this country for the last century, I very much doubt whether *one* could be found whose allowances had begun to run from so short a period before its departure. If this, Sir, be not a sufficient defence on such a matter, I can only give myself up to the mercy of the House, with a frank expression of my regret that I was gazetted three weeks too soon.

As to retaining my office too long, I have already answered to this point incidentally; but I must briefly answer to it again here in its proper order. The first loose intimations of a doubt of the return of the Prince Regent to his European dominions, arrived in England in the month of March. They reached me at Lisbon on the 9th of April. On the 10th of April I wrote to the Foreign Office, tendering my resignation. I was desired to continue in the exercise of my functions; and from that moment the mission entirely changed its character. I was no longer the pageant Ambassador to a non-forthcoming Sovereign. The war had broken out, with the ominous re-appearance of Buonaparte: and who was there in this country, or in Europe, that ventured to predict its speedy, its miraculous termination? Who could presume to say what might be its course; or what the extent of effort required to give effect to its operations? Henceforth, therefore, I filled (whether worthily or not, is another question), a situation of business at a not insignificant post, and at a most eventful crisis. If *I* had not been on the spot, another must have been appointed—a Minister *of the second order*, if you please—but even if so, with all the allowances and expenses incident to a Minister of the second order at Lisbon—which I have already shown to be, according to the recommendation of the Civil List Report, substantially the same as mine. Henceforth, therefore, I did not add one farthing to the unavoidable expenses of the country. It may be alleged, that a more able individual might have been found to discharge the duties of the mission; and that I did wrong in continuing to do what others might have done better; but there is not a shadow of pretence for affirming that my continuance at Lisbon laid any burden upon the public, or that any saving could have been effected by the acceptance of my resignation on the 10th of April.

It is obvious that in the refusal to accept my resignation, I was wholly passive; but neither does my noble friend require any justification for having recommended to the Prince Regent to decline accepting it. My noble friend is sufficiently justified by the case itself, and by his subsequent conduct. For no sooner was the battle of Waterloo fought, and the war thus happily ended, (almost as soon as begun,) than my noble friend signified to me His Royal Highness's acceptance of the resignation which had been before declined. It is true, that it was not until three months after this notification that I was finally relieved from the mission. Amidst the important negociations in which my noble friend was then engaged, he appears to have forgotten that he had not appointed any one to receive the business and correspondence of the Lisbon mission, out of my hands. Portugal and myself had (no wonder) sunk into insignificance and oblivion; and up to the beginning of August, no successor to me was appointed. Did I think this a lucky chance?

Did I go on quietly to enjoy the advantage of this oblivion? No. After about a month had elapsed without hearing any thing from the Foreign Office, I wrote to my noble friend, to remind him of my existence: and, apprehending him to be—as he in fact was—absent from England, I wrote by the same packet a private letter to Lord Bathurst, begging leave, in case any difficulty should have occurred in the nomination of a successor, to recommend Mr. Croft (whom I have already mentioned as having been first introduced to me by my noble friend,) as a person perfectly competent to act as Chargé d'Affaires; and offering, at the same time, the aid of my unofficial advice, so long as I should remain (which I intended to do through the winter) in Portugal. I desire to know if this conduct can be characterized as a clinging to my office? or whether my pertinacity in adhering to it was more than exactly on a par with my eagerness in seeking it?

Perhaps, Sir, I might now sit down, perfectly satisfied with having cleared the integrity of my conduct; and, perhaps, with a feeling rather of gratitude than of hostility towards those who, by manfully giving a distinct and substantive shape to their allegations, have afforded me an opportunity of refuting them. But I cannot pass by the taunts of the honourable baronet, and the grave admonitions of the honourable mover of the question, without assuring them, that so long as I possess in my own breast the consciousness of integrity, such assailments, whether taunting or monitory, will excite in it no emotion warmer than contempt. I must above all things assure the honourable baronet, that no attempt to impeach my character and to degrade me (as he flattered himself this proceeding might do) in that estimation with this House which constitutes all that is valuable, and all that is efficient in a public man—no such attempt, I say, will cause me to lower my voice one key, or to abate one jot of my exertions, in opposing and exposing those doctrines of which the honourable baronet is the representative and the champion. Let not the honourable baronet flatter himself with any such result from this attack upon my reputation. Let him not flatter himself with the hope of such a result from his asperity to-night, or from his menaces for the future. If I am satisfied to have done right, for the peace of my own conscience—I am also glad to have made that right apparent, mainly because I know how necessary are the good opinion and the favouring attention of this House, to enable me to exert myself successfully for the defeat of those projects which the honourable baronet has at heart, and which, I verily believe, would bring this country to ruin. The honourable baronet has spoken out: and the only sentiment with which I am inspired by the bitterness of his declared enmity, and by the burst of his anticipated triumph, is that of a pride—I hope an honest and pardonable pride—at the proof which he has thus unintentionally afforded of the reasons to which I am indebted for his hostility. It is because I am held in hatred and in fear by those who share the honourable baronet's opinions, that by them I have been sought to be destroyed. I have been sought to be destroyed, because I have declared myself—(with what effect it becomes not me to say, but with all my heart and soul)—against schemes, which, if unchecked, would bring destruction upon those hallowed institutions by which the mixed and free Government of this great kingdom is upholden, and from which the practical blessings of our constitution are derived.

Sir, I thus dismiss all that part of the charges which, if substantiated, would have established against me the guilt of criminality or of culpable misconduct. But I wish to leave nothing unnoticed, whether of charge or of insinuation; whether conveying the imputation of positive guilt, or only implying discredit and disparagement.

It is made matter of accusation and reproach against me that I have accepted office with my noble friend (Lord Castlereagh) who sits beside me,—between whom and myself it is assumed that our former differences had placed an impassable barrier. First, from what quarter comes this reproach and accusation? From a bench, on which I do not see any two neighbours who have not differed from each other, and that within short memory too, much more essentially than myself and my noble friend. But it is insinuated that the differences between my noble friend and myself were of a sort which precluded reconciliation! Since when have such matters become topics of parliamentary discussion? Since when has it been the practice of this House to take cognizance of the disagreements of individuals, and to indulge in such animadversions on the most delicate topics of personal conduct as in private society no gentleman would venture to hazard? Since when, I say, has this practice commenced? and how far is it to be carried? I know of no precedent for it. I know of no authority. It is not for my own sake, but for the sake of this House, that I protest against it; for, if this practice be permitted, our discussions must inevitably sink into grosser personalities than have disgraced the meetings of Palace Yard and of Spa Fields.

The honourable baronet is entirely mistaken as to what he supposes me to have addressed to my constituents at Liverpool in 1812. Nothing that I then said was intended to convey, or did convey, the notion that I was precluded by any feeling, or (in my own judgment) by any principle, from acting in office with my noble friend. I had declared the directly contrary opinion some months before, in a correspondence respecting the formation of an Administration, which the discussions of those times brought before the public, and which is now upon record. What is *not* publicly recorded is, that some time after those discussions had closed, but six or eight weeks before my Election at Liverpool, other negociations, which had for their object my return to office, had taken place; amongst the proposed arrangements of which, my noble friend, with a manliness and generosity which I hope I felt as they deserved, had voluntarily tendered to my acceptance the seals of the office which he now holds. Other reasons induced me to decline that tender; I might be right or wrong in my view of those reasons. One among them was, that I was at that time embarrassed with respect to a most important question (the discussion of which is now fixed for no distant day) by pledges which I could best hope to redeem with unquestioned fidelity and honour, by remaining out of office till I had redeemed them. But what would be thought of me, what should I deserve to be thought of by any liberal mind, if, after such a transaction as I have described, I could ever pause for a moment, to consider in what order with respect to each other my noble friend and I should march towards our common objects in the service of the country? In that transaction, any feelings which had previously separated my noble friend and myself were buried for ever. The very memory of them was effaced from our minds: nor can I compliment the good taste of those who would call them up from oblivion; surely not with the vain hope of exasperating differences anew, but with the purpose of making a reconcilement now of five years' standing, a subject of suspicion, taunt and obloquy.

What I have said, Sir, is, I hope, a sufficient comment upon the notable discovery that I accepted public employment not *with*, but *under*, my noble friend. This paltry distinction, I can assure those who are so vain of it, occasions me not the slightest uneasiness. When Lord Pembroke went out to Vienna, and the Marquis Wellesley to Spain, during (or *under*, if you will) *my* administration of the Foreign Department, had *I* the ridiculous vanity to fancy that these distinguished noblemen acted *under* me, in any sense of degrading subordination? Or is it imagined that when the Duke of Wellington undertook his mission to Paris, my noble friend, conceived that *he* was therefore entitled to claim a pre-eminence over the deliverer of Europe? They know little, Sir, of the spirit of our Constitution, they are very ill acquainted with the duties that it imposes, and the privileges that it confers, who are not aware, that in whatever station a man may be called upon to serve his Sovereign and his country, there is among statesmen, co-operating honestly for the public good, a real substantive equality which no mere official arrangement can either create or destroy; they, who are yet to learn, that in a free country like ours, it is for the man to dignify the office, not for the office to dignify the man.

Sir, I have now done. I have humbly to apologize to the House for having trespassed upon them so long, and to thank them for their indulgent attention. The manner in which I have been heard by the House, has been such as satisfies me that they justly and kindly considered how much I had at stake on this day. If I have succeeded, (as my conscience tells me that I must have done,) in refuting the charges brought against me, I have not spoken in vain; and you, Sir, will not regret having listened to me. If I have not succeeded; if the House shall be of opinion that any stain remains upon my character, then indeed, Sir, have I troubled you too long; but I have troubled you for the last time.

SIR T. ACKLAND said, that he was confident the candour of the honourable baronet (Sir F. Burdett) would not permit him to hesitate in pronouncing the full acquittal of a person accused, who had proved himself to be innocent.

After a speech so eloquent, which had thrilled through every heart in the House, he should have been proud to have been so accused, in order to have so defended himself.

The House divided :—

For Mr. Lambton's Motion.........	96
Against it	270
Majority	174

END OF VOL. III.

SHACKELL AND BAYLIS, JOHNSON'S-COURT.

Emily's Adventures
in Wonderland

Ryan & Julia

WS - #0011 - 250723 - C0 - 229/152/32 - PB - 9781314498561 - Gloss Lamination